# NETWORK
# DESIGN
# ESSENTIALS

# NETWORK DESIGN ESSENTIALS

**ED TITTEL**
**MARGARET ROBBINS**

**AP PROFESSIONAL**

Boston   San Diego   New York
London   Sydney   Tokyo   Toronto

*24.95 RB*

AP PROFESSIONAL
955 Massachusetts Avenue, Cambridge, MA 02139

An Imprint of ACADEMIC PRESS, INC.
A Division of HARCOURT BRACE & COMPANY

*United Kingdom Edition published by*
ACADEMIC PRESS LIMITED
24–28 Oval Road, London NW1 7DX

**Library of Congress Cataloging-in-Publication Data**

Tittel, Ed.
    Network design essentials / Ed Tittel, Margaret Robbins.
      p.   cm.
    Includes bibliographical references and index.
    ISBN 0-12-691395-1
    1. Computer networks--Design and construction. I. Robbins,
Margaret. II. Title.
  TK5105.5.T58   1994
  004.6'5--dc20
                                        94-25468
                                        CIP

Printed in the United States of America
94 95 96 97 98 IP 9 8 7 6 5 4 3 2 1

# CONTENTS

# II  Making Networks Happen

## III  Rules of Thumb

# FOREWORD

## INTRODUCING THE *ESSENTIALS* SERIES

Welcome to networking! You may be new to the topic, or have some experience with computer networks; either way, we want to help you learn more. Maybe you've looked for a reference on running a network and found that while there is a lot of information out there, not much of it is aimed at assisting with the day-to-day operation of your network. There are a great many books available that can explain the mathematical theories behind networking or discuss the engineering principles behind the hardware over which networks run. But unless you're building network hardware or writing network software, those books won't do much good for you—the network administrator who needs a reference book to help in setting up a network and keeping it running.

The *Essentials* series aims to fill the gap between theory and practice for networking. It offers solid, practical, networking information, without jargon or unnecessary detail. It explains networking topics in clear, concise language, and plainly defines terms that may be unfamiliar. The series is divided into the topics that are most likely to be of use to network administrators, from setting up a network, to finding problems with it, to more specialized topics such as mobile computing and electronic messaging. Each book takes a gentle, lighthearted approach to the material that focuses on the basic principles an administrator needs to know to master the topic, with plenty of tips and proven techniques gleaned from the authors' wealth of practical experience in putting theory into practice.

The first two books of the series will be of interest to anyone operating a local area network. The first, *Network Design Essentials*, covers everything the reader needs to know to put a smoothly running network in place, including the maintenance tasks that will keep it running. The second book, *E-Mail Essentials*, will be useful to anyone who uses message-based applications over a network.

The remaining books in the series are intended to expand on networking topics that should apply to most, but not all, network administrators. *Network Troubleshooting Essentials* will discuss in practical detail how to identify, diagnose, and solve problems on a local area network. The recent explosive growth of that huge network of networks, the Internet, will make *Internet Access Essentials* a must-read for anyone wanting to tap into that treasure trove of information. And if your computing needs extend to large, far-flung networks, you'll definitely want to refer to both *Internetworking Essentials* and *Wide Area Networking Essentials*.

The authors want to hear from you about these books. Please write to us, care of the publisher, or contact us through the electronic mail addresses we provided earlier in the About the Authors section. We'd like to hear more about what you liked and didn't like about these books, and on your ideas for other topics or more details that you need for your networking life. Thanks for buying this book. We hope you find it worth the money and the time it takes to read!

# ACKNOWLEDGMENTS

Together, we have lots of people to thank for helping us with this book. First and foremost, we'd like to thank Dave Pallai, the editorial director at AP PROFESSIONAL who had the gumption to take on this project. We sincerely hope that this series lives up to his expectations, and repays him for the time, effort, and attention he's lavished on us. To Karen Pratt, the editorial supervisor: thanks for getting us set up and working so smoothly and quickly! To Reuben Kantor, Mike Lindgren, and Pascha Gerlinger: thanks for working out all of the details with us, for being there when we needed you, and for making this project so easy to finish! If there's anybody else at AP PROFESSIONAL we haven't mentioned, we want to thank them for their help and to apologize for omitting their names.

Finally, we'd like to thank our production person, graphic artist, and print professional extraordinaire: Susan Price, proprietoress of Susan Price and Associates, and the fastest keyboardist on the planet. We couldn't have done this project without you, Susan, especially the typesetting. We also appreciate your sterling sense of humor, especially when the deadlines loom large. Let's do this again real soon!

## ED TITTEL

I'd like to start out these acknowledgements with a vote of gratitude to my family: thanks to Suzy, Austin, and Chelsea for putting up with the many nights and weekends spent staring at the tube when we could have been having fun together! Thanks also to Carole McClendon, my agent, and to all the other people at

Waterside Productions, who've taken me from the back room and put me into the public eye—you're the greatest! I'd also like to thank the many people who helped me with questions, information, and ideas, not least of whom is my co-writer, Margaret, who helped keep me on track and focused on the job. Other folks in this category include my once and future co-writers, Deni Connor and Earl Follis, and my networking buddies: Jim Huggans, Ron Lee, Ed Liebing, Larry Teitelbaum, and Tom Jones, all of whom helped me with this book without knowing it.

## MARGARET ROBBINS

On the professional side, I'd like to thank Cheryl Currid for helping me get started in this field. A big thanks to Ed, for his quick sense of humor and amazing resourcefulness; he's a pleasure to work with. I also owe thanks to all the friends who helped me during this project and others, and I hope they know I couldn't have done it without them. In particular I'd like to acknowledge Kathy Mitchell and Roy Christmann for many unfailing years of encouragement, support, and patience; and of course, my family, without whom I wouldn't be here at all!

# ABOUT THE AUTHORS

## MARGARET ROBBINS

Ms. Robbins is co-author of two other books: *Networking With Windows for Workgroups* and *Novell's Guide to NetWare 3.12 Networks*, both with Cheryl Currid. When not writing, she works as a software developer, and has spent over a decade programming software involving various aspects of networking and telecommunications. Most recently, she spent four years at VTEL Corporation helping develop easy and fun user interfaces for their line of video conferencing products. You can reach her on CompuServe at 75730,1451, or via Internet at mrobbins@bga.com.

## ED TITTEL

Mr. Tittel is the author of numerous articles for the computer trade press and of five books on computer-related topics, including *NetWare for Dummies* (IDG Press, 1993) and a series of PC shareware books, co-written with Bob LeVitus. He's recently concentrated on computer networking, for which he is best known, and has written extensively on that subject for the likes of *MacWeek, MacUser, ComputerWorld, Byte, WindowsUser,* and other publications. Ed moonlights during the day as Director of Corporate Marketing at Novell, Inc., where he's responsible for technical content of trade shows and Novell-sponsored conferences, which is why he knows something about networking. You can reach Ed on CompuServe at 76376,606 or on the Internet at etittel@novell.com.

# INTRODUCTION

## WELCOME TO THE NETWORK DESIGN ESSENTIALS

Welcome to the *Essentials* series from AP PROFESSIONAL. *Network Design Essentials* is the first book in the series and is dedicated to telling you everything you need to know about setting up your own local area network—from designing the network to living with a network from day to day. Like the rest of the *Essentials* series, this book concentrates on the real-life information a network administrator needs to install the network and to keep it running smoothly and efficiently.

## ABOUT THIS BOOK

This first book in the series will take you through the process of setting up a network, from the initial planning and design of the network, to the actual installation and construction involved in getting the network running, through the crucial but oft-overlooked phases of maintenance, expansion, and even disaster recovery. This book covers everything you'll need to know about installing a network, from creating the original design to putting that design into action, and also has tips about what to do in special circumstances, including problem situations.

# How to Use This Book

We've designed this book so that you don't have to read it from cover to cover. If you like, you can just pick it up at any point and start reading, or you can begin wherever you find a topic of interest. The cross-references, along with the index and table of contents, will help you build your own thread through this material in whatever way makes sense for your particular situation. Of course, if you want to read it straight through from front to back, that works too! It's a tool, though, not the "Great American Novel." We want you to find it valuable enough to carry it with you as you work, and hope it ends up dog-eared and stained from constant use.

# About the Reader

Is this book for you? We assume that you, our gentle reader, have some familiarity with personal computers—you probably know a little of the jargon and most likely have one on your desk. You're probably not a complete beginner, but just in case, we define most terms so that you can get around without trouble. You know a little bit about networks and what they can do for you, and you want to know more.

Here's what we think might be driving you to read this book: perhaps you have a network in your workplace already and have been asked to administer it. Or perhaps you don't have one yet, but have been charged with installing one (or have volunteered to install one). Whatever your reason for wanting to learn, *Network Design Essentials* will supply you with everything you need to know to get the job done.

# How This Book Is Organized

This book is divided into four sections. The first section contains orientation information. Scan this introduction, along with the table of contents, to get your bearings about what's in the book and where to go to find what you need.

## Part 1, Introducing Networks

This part of the book covers all the background you'll need to set up your network. We discuss what a network is, what it does, and how it works. We go over the fundamentals you'll want to apply when you sit down to design a network, as well as some key concepts to make the whole process easier (such as mapping). Also, we'll look at some strategies for getting the most for your networking money.

## Part 2, Making Networks Happen

In this part we get into the real nuts and bolts of network installation. Here we describe how to run the wiring and get the network running. We include crucial strategies for keeping it running, both in terms of routine maintenance and (perish the thought) problem-solving.

## Part 3, Rules of Thumb

This is your reference section. Here, everything in the previous parts is distilled into easy-to-read checklists and charts. If you're looking for a specific point or a quick tip, check here first. If you need more background on why you should do what we say, please refer to the relevant explanations in Parts 1 or 2.

## Part 4, Case Studies

Here we give you some real-life examples. In this part we look at three different networks, one small, one of medium size, and one quite large, to examine their installations in terms of the principles covered in the first three sections of the book. We discuss what worked for them and what didn't and how these organizations are trying to fix their problems. These examples may help illuminate some pitfalls in your own operation, or suggest potential trouble spots for you to avoid. In addition, they may point you at some design elements and strategies you might otherwise not have considered. Either way, it represents what we hope is a valuable opportunity to learn from the experience of others!

## Reference Materials

Next you'll find the Network Design Resource Guide. Here we list all the products and services mentioned in the book, with all the vendors' names, addresses, and phone numbers so you can contact them. We also give you sources for publications, if you're inclined to pursue the networking industry's news and information.

Finally, if you run across any unfamiliar terms, or need to cross-reference something, we've provided a thorough glossary and index at the back of the book to assist your search. Happy hunting!

## READING THE ROAD MAP

Remember, there are no rules about how to read this book. Start at the front and go straight through to the back if you like; you'll absorb everything you need to know about network design that way. Or, if you have a specific topic you'd like to investigate, start anywhere that interests you. Use the cross-references, along with the index, glossary, and table of contents, to jump to other sections of the book and move through the book in whatever way makes the most sense for your needs. Each chapter is designed to be complete by itself, so dive right in. Whatever you do, enjoy it!

# INTRODUCING NETWORKS

## OVERVIEW

Welcome to networking! This first section contains everything you need to get started designing your network. When you finish this section, you will understand how networks work and what pieces you need to put one together, what a network is good for, and how to lay out your network and prepare for its installation and growth. You'll also know how to get the most equipment and service out of your network budget, without sacrificing quality or reliability.

The nine chapters in this section fall into three categories. The first three chapters cover the basic concepts of networking, the next three discuss some techniques that will make your network installation easier and more fun, and the final three chapters in the section give you tips on maximizing your networking budget.

## BASIC NETWORKING CONCEPTS

The first three chapters cover the basics. In Chapter 1, Networking 101, we'll give some background history and define some essential terms that you'll be seeing throughout the book. This chapter will also give you a broad overview of how networks work. Chapter

2, The Pieces and Parts of Networking, describes in more detail how a network operates, and will introduce you to the various components that make up networks. Some of
these components appear in every network while others depend on the type of network
services you want, so this information will help you select the right network for your
needs. Then in Chapter 3, What Can Networking Do for You?, we look at what services
a network can provide and the advantages it can bring throughout an organization.

## Tools and Tricks

In the next three chapters we get down to actually designing the network. First, Chapter
4, Networking Design Fundamentals, introduces the basic concepts of network design,
from whatever you have now to whatever you might need in the future. Chapter 4 also
offers some tips on working with the other folks in your organization who might be
involved in the network installation. In Chapter 5, Mapping Out Your Network, we discuss the tracking and record-keeping that will be necessary to keep your network running
and growing smoothly. And on the topic of growth, Chapter 6, Building for the Future,
explains how to make sure your network works for your applications and your users now
and for a long time to come.

## Spending Your Money Wisely

No question about it, setting up a network will cost money. But it doesn't have to break
your budget, and in the final three chapters of this section, we go over some techniques
to help you make sure that you're spending your money wisely. In Chapter 7, Managing
Your Installation, you'll learn how to create a budget for your network, and some planning
tricks that can save you money. Chances are that you won't want to do all the installation
work yourself, though, so Chapter 8, Managing Contractors and Consultants, describes
what to expect from contractors, what to give them, and how to utilize them most effectively. Finally, turn to Chapter 9, Smart Network Buying Techniques, to find out how to
keep costs down as your network expands. That chapter offers lots of hints for getting
equipment as inexpensively as possible, and also warns you of some potential pitfalls.

# NETWORKING 101

**1**

## BASIC DEFINITIONS

At first glance, learning about networking is daunting. It might seem that you need to learn an overwhelming number of new terms and concepts just to begin to define what you want a network to do, much less set it up and make something useful out of it! Don't worry. Networking is really not very complicated. It's true that it does have a lot of its own terms and acronyms, but if you break networking up into its basic components and familiarize yourself with the major terms for each component, you will go a long way toward becoming network-savvy. You'll pick up the rest of what you need as you go along.

So in this chapter we'll present a simple and organized way to look at networking. In order to do that, let's look at some basic terms. You've probably heard most of them before, but some have slightly different meanings in the context of networking.

### *Personal Computer (PC)*

This name originally referred to a computer that only one person could use at a time. That restriction no longer holds, thanks in part to networking, but the name has stuck and we'll use it in this book. Note that a PC can be a Macintosh, an IBM-PC or clone, or some other small computer. Generally it sits on or near your desk. Your PC is the computer you use to go about your usual computing activities, be they publishing, accounting, graphic design, or whatever.

## Workstation

This is just another word for your PC. When you call a PC a workstation, you are emphasizing that it is a computer you use primarily for your usual computing work. This term distinguishes that machine from a *server*, described below.

You might also hear workstations called *desktop systems* or simply *desktops*.

## Client

Here is another term to describe your PC, but this one emphasizes that your PC is requesting a service from a network service provider (see *server* below).

## Server and Dedicated Server

A server is a PC, too, but with a different function from a workstation PC. Servers provide services, such as access to printers or large disk drives. Workstations make requests for these services, and the server performs them. Servers are also sometimes called *hosts*.

It's possible for a PC to be both a workstation and a server. For instance, you might have a printer connected to your PC. You could set up your PC so that other users on the network could print files on your printer, while you are working on your PC. In this case, the PC is both a file server and your workstation.

A server that does not also act as a workstation is called a *dedicated server*.

## Cabling and Wiring

These terms are used interchangeably. They simply refer to the physical medium that connects the computers in a network.

## Local and Remote

You'll see the terms *local* and *remote* fairly often in discussions of networking tasks. They indicate whether a service executes right there on your desktop system, or some distance away over the network. For instance, if you have a printer attached to your workstation and print a file using that printer, you have printed the file *locally*. If you print the file by sending it to a network printer, however, you are printing *remotely.* Most things that you can do locally you can also do remotely, including running programs and accessing files.

## Local Area Networks (LANs)

This is one type of network, and the one we will focus on in this book. This is a group of PCs that are connected together to share information resources, typically within a single building. The number of computers on a LAN could be as few as two or could number into the thousands. A bit of trivia: most LANs today connect fewer than 20 PCs.

## Wide Area Networks (WANs)

When a LAN extends outside a building, it becomes a WAN. Think of a WAN as a collection of LANs, communicating with each other by telephone, satellite, or some other non-LAN type of connection. A WAN can extend between two adjacent buildings, across a city, or across the world.

# WHEN THE (COMPUTING) WORLD WAS YOUNG

In the early days of computing, computers were enormous things, easily taking up entire rooms or often even entire buildings. These huge machines were called *mainframes.* Everyone who used one of these machines did so through a "dumb" terminal, so-called because it just sent messages to the mainframe and displayed the results—if the mainframe was not running, these terminals were useless. The administration for these huge machines had to be centralized, which meant that only a few people in any installation made the decisions about what software they would run, who could access data, and when they could access it. Also, since only a few companies made these computers, the choices of software and services were fairly limited. They did have some advantages, though: All users saw the changes to data at the same time, and everyone had access to the printers and other attached devices.

With the advent of personal computers, users began leaving the mainframe world in droves, lured by the flexibility of the smaller computers, and also by the wider array of software available. They also found that it was much cheaper to buy a couple of PCs for an office than an entire mainframe, so organizations that could never have considered using computers in the days of mainframes suddenly found that adding computing capability was quite affordable. A problem emerged, though: they still needed to share resources. They found themselves passing data around on diskettes, or buying a printer for every PC in the office. While these small printers were a lot cheaper than the big high-speed line printers of the mainframe world, the total cost of one for everybody was pretty significant, especially when they noticed that each printer was used a rather small percentage of the time. These were the motivations for networking of PCs.

You are setting up your network for the same reasons: to share expensive or scarce resources. Sharing printers is the most common reason for first setting up a network, but we're using networks today to share a lot of other peripherals as well. Your network might provide access to large disk drives, fax machines, modems, CD-ROM drives, and many other devices.

# The Big Three: Connections, Communications, and Services

It's useful to think of networking as a conversation. If you want to have a conversation with another person, you need three things to do it: a medium, a language, and something to say. The medium is anything that enables you to hear each other. It might be a telephone wire, a satellite, or, if you're in the same room, the air that transmits the sound of your voice. Secondly, you need a common language with the person. It's fine if you can hear each other, but if you speak English and they understand only Arabic, you're still not communicating. And finally, for a truly satisfying conversation you need something to say, ideally something that has some relevance to the other person.

Network conversations have a lot in common with human ones, to a certain point. Again, you need a medium, a language, and a topic. In networking terminology we refer to these components as *connections*, *communications*, and *services*. Let's look at each in turn.

Connections are the hardware items that make networking possible. This category includes the wires used to carry the messages, and the network interface cards that go into your computer to interpret the electronic blips that come across the wires. Without this stuff, your PC stays lonely and isolated.

Communications are provided by software. This term refers to the portion of the networking software that gives two computers a common language in which to communicate.

Services are the whole point of networking—they are what computers can do for each other. Cooperation between the two systems is necessary here, too. If one system has software to ask the other to print a file but the second one does not have printing software, they're still not really communicating, even though they may be wired together and speaking the same language.

# How Do Networks *Really* Work?

The preceding model gives you a picture of the components of networks, and it describes why each component is necessary and how each component relates to the others. Now let's get a little more specific, and take a look at what happens when you ask the network to print a file.

First of all, you probably don't explicitly ask the network to print a file. This is the beauty of networking. It's often transparent—you don't need to know it's there. If things are set up correctly, it's possible that asking to print a file on a network printer is exactly like asking to print a file on a printer attached to your own PC. How does this work?

The answer is in the networking software installed on your PC. In order for your PC to talk to the network, it must run some sort of software that examines each of your commands and decides whether to handle the command on your local system or to send it to the network. The software that performs this important task is called a *redirector*.

## Redirectors

Let's continue with our file printing example, first considering the case where you have no networking software loaded. If you have a printer attached to your workstation and issue a command to print a file, the printed file comes out on your local printer (assuming, of course, that the printer is set up correctly!). The result is the same whether you print the file from a word processing program, a spreadsheet, a command line, or a print manager program. Your local PC's system software, called the *operating system,* detects your printing command and executes the software that sends printing commands to the printer.

When you install your networking software, however, you add in a piece of software that grabs commands before they get to your PC operating system. This networking software looks at each command to see whether it should be handled by your local machine or by a network service. If the request is a network command, the networking software sends the command over the wire to the appropriate place on the network. Otherwise it passes the command on to the operating system, which handles it in the usual way. The software piece that performs this checking and routing is called a *redirector*.

## Of Stacks and Protocols ...

As you can see, quite a bit is happening every time you issue a network command, and you can look at the activities from several different perspectives. Electronic blips go across the wires, network interface cards interpret patterns of those blips in particular ways, software that talks to those cards interprets those patterns in particular ways, redirectors send out their own patterns which other components must interpret, and so on.

Network theorists like to look at each of these different activities as a different functional layer in the total network, and they divide these functions into seven different layers. Each layer has its own precise rules of operation that it must follow. All of the layers must work together for the network as a whole to function properly.

The seven-layered model of networking appears quite often in technical or theoretical discussions of networks, but you can understand networking without understanding the details of each of the seven layers. For our purposes, we will keep in mind that networks have layers of functions that fit together in predictable ways.

Because these layers have to work together, they must each have a set of rules that they follow for formatting, sending, and receiving data. Several companies have come up their own sets of network data rules, and these sets typically describe between one and four layers of the seven layers of networking. For this reason, each of these sets of rules is often called a *protocol stack*, or, more commonly, a *protocol* (which means, simply, a "set of rules").

Several different protocols are in widespread use today, and you have probably heard of at least a couple of them. Among the most common are SNA, IPX/SPX, and TCP/IP. Each of these has its own set of advantages and disadvantages; we'll talk more about these trade-offs in Chapter 2.

## What Do Computers Say to Each Other?

A conversation between computers on a network usually involves a request. One computer asks the other to send a file, for instance. Or perhaps one of them needs the other to print a file. Sometimes one system just asks the other for status information—the computer equivalent of "How have you been doing?" We can think of each of these conversations as service requests, and though the number of possible different requests is huge, the structure of each request is pretty much the same.

Computers are much more literal and less flexible than humans, so as you might expect their conversations are much more rigid. They can't assume much at all from the last interaction. Therefore, a network conversation begins with each computer announcing who it is and to whom it wants to talk. Once they have each other's attention they can determine whether it's possible to talk; this phase establishes access and sets up the connection. Next the initiator asks for a service or provides one that was requested previously—this is the bulk of the exchange. Finally they close down the connection in an orderly fashion, leaving the network free for other such transactions.

## COMPLETING THE CIRCUIT: REQUESTS AND REPLIES, QUESTIONS AND ANSWERS

Let's look at these conversations in more detail. Once the redirection software on your local computer has determined that a particular command should be handled by the network, things happen in a fairly predictable way. A typical networking conversation has three phases: setting up the connection, sending the information, and disconnecting.

### A Note about Addressing

Every computer on a network must have a name by which it is known to the other systems on the network, and this name must be different from the names of all the other computers on the same network. These names are more often called *network addresses*, or simply *addresses*. Setting up these addresses is part of the process of installing the network. Typically the addresses are strings of numbers, or numbers and letters, but sometimes you can use actual recognizable words. Once the network is properly set up, however, you will probably never need to know the address of any computer on the network, because the network software will take care of all that for you.

### Establishing the Connection

In order to set up the connection, then, the requesting computer must know its own address and the address of the computer to which it is sending the message. It sends a message to the target computer requesting a connection. In the ideal (and usual) situation, the receiver is free and available and returns a message accepting the connection. If the receiver is unavailable for some reason, the requesting computer will get an error message back. The requester might then try again later, or might send a message to the user indicating that the request failed. For now, let's assume the two computers successfully establish a connection.

### Holding the Conversation

The exact format of this portion of the conversation varies widely, depending on the type of request. This is where a client computer might request access to a particular data file, or send information to a print server about a file that the client needs the print server to print. The conversation could go in the opposite direction, too: a server might be requesting status information from the client. The receiver, in either case, responds with the requested information (or possibly an error message if it cannot perform the service).

### Ending the Conversation

Once the requester has the information it wants, the two computers must disconnect so that other computers can connect to the server, and so that the client can make other requests.

## SUMMARY

This chapter introduces the basics of how networks work. It gives you the background you will need in later chapters when you analyze your networking needs, select a protocol, design your network layout, and prepare your network to serve you efficiently now and well into the future.

# THE PIECES AND PARTS OF NETWORKING

**2**

## ANOTHER VIEW OF HOW NETWORKS WORK

To better understand networks, let's go back to the three essential components of networking that we discussed in Chapter 1: connections (the medium), communications (the protocol), and services. This time, we'll look at these pieces from the point of view of the messages that the network sends. First, though, we'll answer the most basic questions of all: How do those messages get out of your PC to the network, and how does your PC respond to incoming messages?

## GETTING TO THE WIRE: DRIVERS AND INTERFACES

Recall the *redirector* from Chapter 1, a piece of software that runs on your PC and examines all of your commands to see whether to send them to the network or not. When it detects a command that is network-bound, the redirector sends the message to the network driver, which in turn sends the message to the network interface card. Finally, the network interface card sends the message out over the wire. Each of these items merits a little more investigation.

For incoming messages, the redirector alerts whatever applications are "listening" for network messages that one has arrived, and delivers that message to the appropriate recipient when it's completely received and assembled.

## The Network Driver

The *network driver* is another piece of software that, like the redirector, you must install on your PC before that PC can talk to the network. This software acts as the translator between the redirector, which speaks in terms of your network's protocol, and the network interface card, which is a hardware device and thus speaks the language of hardware: electronic signals over the wire, or pulses of light over fiber-optic cable.

For incoming messages, the driver converts the low-level messages delivered from the network interface into the specific protocol required by your computer's networking software and applications.

## The Network Interface Card (NIC)

The *network interface card*, usually called a *NIC*, is the final item you need to attach your PC to the network. If a network interface isn't already built into your computer, the NIC is a piece of hardware that fits into your PC or attaches to a serial or parallel port on your PC. The type of NIC you need depends on what kind of wiring your network uses: You can't use a NIC designed for twisted pair wiring if your network cables are all fiber optic, for instance. For this reason, you need to consider both the costs of wiring and the costs of the NICs when deciding what type of wiring to use in your network.

The NIC takes messages from the driver and transmits the message by sending signals out over the wire to the rest of the network. For incoming messages, the process works in reverse: The NIC takes incoming signals and converts them into equivalent messages.

# THE MEDIUM SENDS THE MESSAGE

Clearly, you need some connection between your computers to have a network. It might be radio transmissions, in the case of wireless networks, but most often networking is done through some type of cabling. These cables are the medium that transmits the messages in the conversations between networked computers. Along with NICs, cables compose the connections component of networking. The cables carry the signals from the NIC in your computer to the NIC in the computer you're talking to, and also carry that computer's response to your request back to your PC. Without these cables, no messages get through. For clarity's sake, cables, wires, or radio transmissions—whatever signal-carrying technology a network may use—are called *networking media*.

Networks are typically connected with coaxial cable (commonly called coax), twisted pair wiring, fiber-optic cable, or, increasingly, some combination of all three. We'll discuss each of these in more detail in Chapter 10; for now, you just need to know the names.

## THE PROTOCOL CARRIES THE MESSAGE

The network interface cards send messages out over the wire in precise patterns. The layout of these patterns depends on which protocol you are using, and every different protocol divides data into packets in a different way. This is how a protocol distinguishes one message from another, or, in the case of a large message, one part of a message from another part.

The "letters in envelopes" analogy might be useful here. You want to send a message to another computer, so you put it in an envelope, write the address on the outside, and send it off. The contents of the envelope are the data of the message, and the envelope, address, and contents together are called a *data packet*, or just *packet*. Each different protocol has different requirements about size, that is, how much data can fit in a packet, and about addressing. So you can't send a message designed for one protocol to a computer that only talks in some different protocol.

Because some network information transfers are large and others small, part of what happens when envelopes get created is that information gets chopped up into smaller pieces to be shipped across the networking media. That way, nobody can hog the network with an enormous file transfer; shorter packets also reduce the possibility of errors occurring along the way from sender to receiver as well.

## THE SERVICE DEFINES THE MESSAGE

Continuing with the letter analogy, what's in the envelope? The answer depends on the service that the message is requesting. If you want to print a file on the network printer, for instance, the messages that your redirector, driver, and NIC send to the print server include information about how to print the file and the file itself. Put another way, what messages you send depend on what services you desire. Of course, these services must also be available; you can send a message to a print server to print a file, but if no print server is attached to your network, the message is useless, even though the message might get across the network without trouble.

Some examples of typical network services include the following:

- file services, which let users store and retrieve files from network servers
- print services, which let users print to shared printers anywhere on the network from within their applications
- messaging services, which let users send and receive electronic messages over the network, either for electronic mail or applications that send and receive other information (like electronic forms, workflow, and the like)
- database services, which let users query networked databases for shared information, like employee directories, parts or inventory information, or other large collections of shared data

Whenever messages move across a network, they're typically requesting some kind of service to be delivered, or they're acting on requests for service from a user or an application.

## MAKING CONNECTIONS WORK

By now it's clear that the basic requirement for a working network is working connections, whether they be radio transmissions or wires. If your wires are damaged or if they are picking up electrical interference, messages might get through only part of the time, or might be garbled when they do get through. For this reason, be sure to place your wiring where the cables won't get stepped on, run over, or accidentally disconnected. For some network types, if someone disconnects just one wire from the network, the entire network stops functioning.

Cables can also break, and these types of problems can be hard to find, because if the break is inside the wire's shielding, the broken wire looks just the same as a working one. Fortunately, some companies make network analysis tools that can pinpoint the exact location of a break in the network, if necessary. Start with prevention, though, by making sure that none of your cables run under chair wheels or across the floor. Guard against electrical interference, too, by making sure not to run cables near large motors or other sources of electrical noise (more on these matters in Part II).

## TIP-TOP TOPOLOGIES: RING, BUS, AND STAR

The word *topology* refers to the pattern in which you lay your wiring; it's how you physically connect your computers to each other. The three basic network topologies are ring, bus, and star, though in practice network layouts often combine topologies.

## The Bus Topology

Sometimes known as "daisy chaining," this method of wiring connects each computer to the one next to it. A major drawback of the bus layout is that if a single wire gets disconnected anywhere along the bus, the entire chain of computers can no longer talk to the network. Also, the wiring for this topology is messy, because you have to have one wire going into each machine and another going out to the next machine, or you have to insert a physical tap into a cable to attach a computer to the network (in extreme cases, this even requires cutting the network cable to insert a device that lets your computer hook up to the network). Some network equipment manufacturers have solved this by combining the two wires in a single wire; you need their special NIC to make this work. Figure 2.1 illustrates two bus topologies, a straight bus (uses taps) and a daisy-chain (requires two connections for each computer, or a two-way network connector).

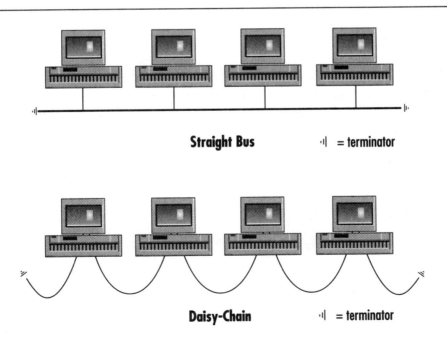

**Figure 2.1**  *Bus topologies: straight bus and daisy chain.*

## The Star Topology

In this layout, every computer connects directly to a server or to a network hub, which is why this topology is also called a hub topology. Since the PCs are not connected to each other directly, removing one computer from the network does not affect the others. For this reason, star topologies have the advantage of greater robustness than bus layouts, but they also use more wire, and they require additional equipment—namely the hub, or a special hub card for the server. See Figure 2.2 for a diagram of a star topology.

## The Ring Topology

This topology, shown in Figure 2.3, is seldom used to lay out wires. Don't confuse it with ring network types such as Token Ring and ARCnet, which send messages in a ring, though their layout could be either bus or star. In its purest form, a ring is really a daisy chain with the first computer in the chain attached to the last. Therefore, it suffers from vulnerability to cable breaks or disconnects. For those technologies

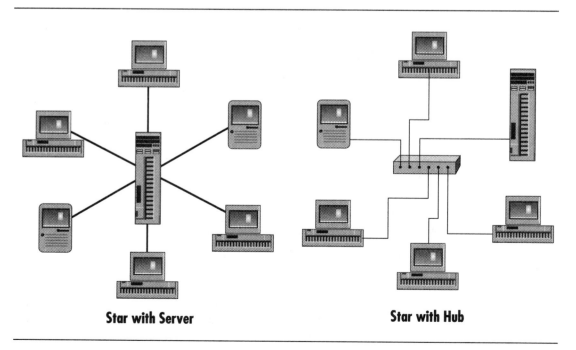

**Star with Server**                          **Star with Hub**

**Figure 2.2**  *Star topology.*

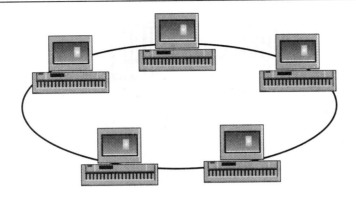

**Figure 2.2** *Ring topology.*

that use actual rings, they most often double up on cabling to provide a fallback in the case of a single cable failure.

# Basics of Network Types: ARCnet, Ethernet, Token Ring, and More

The type of networking technology you select for your network will affect the performance, flexibility, and expansion of your network well into the future. In this section we'll go over the different technologies and their pros and cons, so you can make the best choice for your environment.

## ARCnet

*ARCnet* usually runs on networks that are laid out in a star topology. It works by a token method: a token gets passed around from computer to computer. If a computer has something to send, it can only do it when it gets the token. At that point it broadcasts its message to the entire network, so everyone sees the message, but only the computer to which it is sending the message will respond. After the computer has finished sending its message, it passes the token on to the next computer.

ARCnet's advantages are that it is inexpensive and common. You'll easily be able to find NICs and people who can assist you with an ARCnet network. The NICs are generally somewhat cheaper than those for Ethernet, and it's much cheaper than a Token Ring network. The cables can run farther than Ethernet's, and ARCnet can use any of the three basic wiring types.

The major drawback of ARCnet, and the reason we don't recommend it, is that it's the slowest of all the common network types, especially if you have a lot of traffic on the network. Furthermore, no breakthroughs in speed are likely, so it is unsuitable for emerging high-intensity network applications that you may want to run.

## Ethernet

*Ethernet* works by a carrier sense, multiple access, collision detect scheme, abbreviated CSMA/CD. *Carrier sense* means that every system on the network is always "listening" to the wire, and so can tell when another computer is sending a message. No one is allowed to send if someone else is already doing so. *Multiple access* means that it's possible that more than one PC can find the wire quiet and begin sending data at the same time. This results in what's called a *collision*. The *collision detect* part of the scheme indicates that the NICs for Ethernet notice when a collision occurs, which causes both of the colliding senders to stop, wait, and try sending again later. You can lay out an Ethernet network in either a bus or star configuration.

The advantages of the Ethernet approach are that it's very well understood, there are many thousands of Ethernet networks out there, and you'll be able to get support and NICs in wide selections. In addition, the NICs are fairly cheap, and Ethernet is flexible, letting you use any of the three cable types, or combinations of the three.

On the down side, Ethernet is no speed demon. It's a good deal faster than ARCnet, but it does not always perform well for the data-intensive activities growing more common on modern networks. Faster versions are in the works, but they are not currently readily available in a standard format. Another disadvantage is the limit to the length of the wires is not very long. You can add extra hardware to get around this problem, but you can't ignore it.

## Token Ring

A *Token Ring* network usually uses a star topology. A Token Ring is another technology that uses a token mechanism, so that a computer that wants to send data must wait for the token. Once the data is sent, the sender does not relinquish the token until its message gets to the intended receiver. Then the token goes on to the next computer in the ring. Everyone gets the same chance at sending data, and a Token

Ring network cannot get overwhelmed by traffic (as can an Ethernet network, for instance). It can run on any of the three wiring types.

Advantages are that Token Ring at its fastest is considerably faster than Ethernet and the network stays solid, without losing packets, even under heavy usage.

The disadvantages, unfortunately, are in the costs. The hubs, NICs, and cables are quite a bit more expensive than those for Ethernet, and Token Ring is more complicated to install and maintain.

## FDDI

*FDDI*, which stands for *fiber distributed data interface*, is the up-and-coming network technology. It runs by a token-passing method on a ring topology. The difference is that it uses two rings and sends two tokens, one in one direction on one of the rings, and the other in the opposite direction on the other ring. FDDI is usually used as a high-speed link between networks rather than as the base of a network, but that is changing. It runs primarily over fiber-optic cable, but comes in a variant for coaxial cable called CDDI (copper distributed data interface), which runs at the same speed as FDDI and can be interconnected with it by using special hubs.

FDDI offers many advantages. It runs some 40 times faster than ARCnet, 10 times faster than Ethernet's top-rated speed, and nearly 6 to 12 times faster than Token Ring (Token Ring comes in both faster and slower varieties). This means that it can offer excellent response for heavy data applications such as voice and video. If you are likely to need to expand to these types of applications in the future, take a long look at FDDI now. Also, FDDI cables can be much longer than Ethernet, and it can support a great many devices on a single run of cable.

Unfortunately, FDDI is expensive. The fiber-optic cable is expensive and not forgiving—if you bend it too sharply, the glass inside the cable will break. Network interface cards are also considerably more expensive than those for other network types. Finally, installation is tricky and is definitely not a do-it-yourself job. If these considerations are secondary to capacity, move to the head of the class and go with FDDI (and CDDI) right away; most of us just can't afford it right now.

## Others

These are not all of the network technologies available—especially for high-speed varieties—but they are the most common. We strongly recommend sticking with one of the types we've discussed here: If you do, your life will be a lot easier when you go to select software, or when you need technical support. If you don't, make sure you have compelling reasons to go off the beaten track, and make sure you have a firm commitment to develop in-house expertise for your choice. Otherwise, you could be heading for trouble later on!

## Selecting the Right Networking Software for Your Needs

Another critical decision for your network is the type of networking software it will use. The major contenders in the world of IBM-clone PCs are Novell, with their NetWare and NetWare Lite, Microsoft with its LAN Manager and NT Advanced Server products, and LANtastic from Artisoft. There are many others, but these are the most widely used. In this section we'll go over the questions you need to ask yourself, and your vendor, before you buy networking software.

First question: How many users will you need? NetWare Lite and LANtastic, for instance, allow around 20 or 25 users, while NetWare 4.0 supports 1,000 users per server. When buying networking software, be sure to allow room for expansion!

Some networks provide a means of ensuring that you will never lose data due to a hardware problem. One technique is to support two server disk drives and write every piece of data to both drives at once. That way, even if one disk fails, the other has an exact copy of all the data. This is called *disk mirroring,* and not all networks allow it.

LAN Manager, and the more advanced versions of NetWare, requires a dedicated server. If this is not possible on your budget, be sure your final choice allows a workstation to act as a server.

The amount of memory that the network drivers and redirectors require on each workstation can be significant, although memory management software might be able to reduce the impact. Know these numbers before you buy.

Think about what kind of printing you want to do, and what other devices besides printers you want to share. Will your networking software let you do it?

Consider whether you need access to Macintoshes, UNIX systems, or IBM mainframes. Not all types of networking software allow you to connect to different kinds of computer, or to different types of network technologies.

## Making Good Choices

Now you know about these options, how do you decide which one to use? It's the same anytime you're going to spend a significant amount of money—shop around. Here are some things you need to consider:

- The network technology will affect the speed and expandability of your network. Consider the pros and cons previously outlined before choosing.
- Your choice of wiring will be based to some extent on how much money you have to spend, but keep in mind what applications you need to run as well. Don't, for instance, wire your building with twisted pair wiring if you will need to send full-motion video over the lines within the next year or two.
- As described previously, your networking software can determine what types of things you can share, and what other types of networks you can link to. Do you need access, for instance, to systems that are not PCs, such as IBM mainframes? Be sure your networking software supports this before you buy.
- Finally, try to picture what will happen if something goes wrong (something will). Can someone nearby help you if you have problems, or will you have to wait for replacement equipment that may take days to arrive? What warranties and service contracts can you get with the equipment?

Use the discussions of the tradeoffs in this chapter to determine your own networking needs, and shop carefully before you buy, because these choices will affect many aspects of your work environment for a long time to come. If you plan and shop with awareness of all the issues, you will create a network that will be a pleasure to use.

## SUMMARY

This chapter introduces networking topologies, technologies, and software. It gives you the background you will need in later chapters when you decide what kind of networking cable and interfaces to buy, and the kinds of software you'll use on your network.

# WHAT CAN NETWORKING DO FOR YOU?

## 3

## DO YOU NEED A NETWORK?

Now you have a picture of how networks work and of the components that make up a network. You have some ideas about the benefits you hope to gain when you install your network, or maybe you already have one and want to learn how to get more out of it. Before you invest a lot of time, expense, and effort into installing or expanding your network, it's a good idea to have a clear image of what you expect to get out of all that work.

It's possible that you don't need a full-blown network at all. If you only want to share printers (the most common reason people install networks), the number of affected PCs is small, and you don't expect your needs to grow beyond that in the reasonable future, put this book down and go buy a printer-sharing buffer or even a switch box for your printer. Installation and feeding of these devices is beyond the scope of this book, but a good PC shop will be able to set you up quickly and inexpensively.

If, on the other hand, you want to share devices besides printers, to link to other networks, to connect more than half a dozen users together, and to grow into the future, read on.

## THE VIEW FROM THE DESKTOP: ACCESS AND SHARING

One of networking's most obvious benefits to users is the ability to access more resources, and more different resources, than they probably could if they were not networked.

Once you attach specialized devices to the network, users have much easier access to these devices than before. These items might include high-performance printers or plotters, CD-ROM drives, modems, fax machines, and more. It's unlikely that any one user would have all of these gadgets attached to his or her own machine, but the network makes them look as if the devices were all right there.

Networks, when equipped with proper software, allow users to make changes to a particular data file simultaneously. Without networking, they would have to copy the changed file to a diskette and carry it around to the PC of each person who needed it. This is a tedious, time-consuming, and dangerous process—dangerous because of the possibility that someone will overwrite the changes that someone else made. The right kinds of networking software will prevent this and will make the data a lot easier to share.

## THE VIEW FROM THE SERVER: SHARED RESOURCES

When you share things, you need fewer of them. You can buy most software with site licenses, which can be a big money saver. You might, for instance, buy a spreadsheet program with a license for 10 users. This means that only ten people can be using the software at any one time without violating the software license. Install that software on the network so that everyone can get to it (along with an access product such as SiteLock, which prevents more than the allowed number of users from using the product at the same time, keeping you honest on the license). Voilà! You have saved disk space on the users' workstations because they don't have to keep that software on their local hard drives. You have also saved money, because you'd probably have to install it on more than 10 systems to provide it to everyone who ever uses it. But since only a few use it at once, it makes sense to only pay for what you actually use. The potential cost is in increased network traffic, though. If the application is one that transmits a lot of data across the network, it might be better to install it on each user's workstation separately.

Similarly, you'll need fewer peripheral devices, such as printers, than you would without networking. Instead of one printer for every PC, you could, for example, get one basic dot-matrix printer for simple printing and perhaps a high-quality color laser printer for more sophisticated applications.

By sharing, you are consolidating your resources, enabling you to spend less money, or to spend money on a wider variety of tools and resources.

# THE VIEW FROM THE HEAD OFFICE: BETTER COMMUNICATIONS MEAN IMPROVED PRODUCTIVITY

From a manager's perspective, anything that improves productivity without undue expense is a benefit, and in that view the benefits of networking can be enormous. Networks improve productivity in a number of ways, by providing e-mail, shared data files, and shared scheduling, just to name a few.

Electronic mail (*e-mail*) can greatly increase productivity in an organization all by itself, by allowing better coordination between workgroups and improved information distribution. When you send a memo over e-mail, everyone gets the same information at the same time—it's a quick and reliable method of spreading news.

Shared data files are a boon of networks, because they allow everyone working with a file to see a change as soon as it happens. Users don't have to wait until someone brings them a diskette with the change, or, worse, worry that someone will make a change that they might not know about.

A popular form of a shared data file is a *template file*, or a blank form. Everyone who needs to use the form can make a copy locally and fill in the blanks. This ensures that everyone is always using the same version of the form. Some examples might be purchase requests, maintenance orders, and even performance evaluations, all of which can be built in electronic form and shared over the network.

Scheduling meetings and meeting rooms using a network is a relatively new application for networking technology, and a highly useful one. All users can have access to the same schedules and can coordinate electronically—no more running around trying to find out who can attend a meeting when, or where; no more phone tag trying to pin down all your invitees to a specific time and date!

# INDUSTRY TRENDS AND PHENOMENA

When evaluating what a network can offer you, keep in mind where the networking industry appears to be headed in the next few years. More and more people are using networks, and more businesses are installing them. At the same time, as the numbers of networks and network users are increasing, costs are coming down, and these two trends are feeding on each other. Because so many more people are now "network-aware," users are demanding the ability to do more tasks and more different types of tasks over their networks, and network vendors are obliging them. This is resulting in an explosion of the kinds of things that people can do with networks, even as the number of networks (and the number of users on those networks) is also growing dramatically.

These new uses for networks include packaging and sending many different kinds of data, including sound, full-motion video, and still images. Because some applications are being built around multiple types of information, ranging from text and graphics all the way to full-motion video and sound, this is called *multimedia*. People are even running interactive systems, by using their LANs for video conferencing and other types of complex communications.

These new types of information are voluminous: It's not unusual for a complex color graphics file to be 10 megabytes or larger, and sound and video are also notorious space hogs. Because of the data volumes they demand, these emerging types of applications require much faster networks with much higher bandwidth than were available even a couple of years ago, just to keep up with the increased level of traffic. Looking ahead, the appetite for network capacity and connections appears to be limitless.

Overall, networks are getting bigger, cheaper, and faster. At the same time, applications are getting bigger, more complex, and hungrier for larger amounts of data than ever before. Be sure to plan your network to take advantage of as many of these advancements as you might possibly need, but be sure to budget for as much capability and bandwidth as you can afford. Otherwise your network might run out of gas before your users run out of requirements!

## The Emergence of Distributed Computing

Suppose you have one machine on your network that always runs some very high-powered computer-aided design (CAD) software, and another that generally runs a simple word processing program and sits idle much of the time. Wouldn't it be nice if the CAD system could "borrow" some processing power from the less active system?

In the same vein, wouldn't it be great if you decided that you needed a color brochure for your current desktop publishing project and could just ask the network to help you find the nearest color printer, handle your print job for you, and tell you when it was finished? Or, if you needed to send a package to a co-worker, that you could ask the network for his or her mailing address, and maybe even get a preprinted label to stick on your package?

All of these scenarios fall into the category of distributed computing. The term refers to the general concept that it is possible to use the network to access many types of resources, not just printers and plotters but also directories, databases, and processors. It's a shift in how we see networks: Whereas the conventional view sees networks as a collection of independent machines that just happens to include your PC, distributed computing views your PC as a front end that interacts with the network as if it were one great big computing environment. This latter use of a network requires a network that is fast and robust, because you'd expect to be able to access all these resources through the network at least as fast as you could access things on your stand-alone PC.

The emerging industry trend is that the network begins to look and act as if it were a single, coherent computing system, as it gets easier and easier for individual machines—and users—to share not just information and peripherals, but also the processing power of the computers that compose a network. There's a great deal of work underway in the computing industry today to make distributed computing happen, and it should result in networks that are easier to use and understand than many of the ones we all work with right now.

## What's in It for You Today?

Although many exciting new applications for networking are on the horizon, the bottom line in making your decisions must be what you can do right now. As you can see, the benefits of linking up are immense: You can share equipment and software to reduce costs and can share data to improve group productivity and enhance communication between people in your organization.

Evaluate your specific needs carefully as you plan your network. Think about how many people will use it and what types of things they do with their computers throughout the day. You may be able to make many of those tasks more efficient and even pleasant by implementing them on the network. In the next chapter, we look at some basic principles to consider while designing your network, to start turning these expected benefits into reality.

## Summary

In this chapter you've learned what networks are good for and what benefits they can provide. These hidden treasures include improved communications, shared resources and equipment, and the ability to work together more effectively. The future promises even more powerful networking benefits, as the promises of distributed computing are delivered. In the meantime, there is significant value to be gleaned from what networks can do for you today.

# NETWORK DESIGN FUNDAMENTALS

**4**

## START WITH A MAP OF THE WORLD AS YOU KNOW IT

Once you have a map of your network you will use it constantly. This map will show the floor plan of the building or buildings in which your network resides, and all the features of the building that might affect your network. These include the building's ductwork, the locations of potential sources of interference (such as electrical motors), and so on. Finally, it shows the network itself: all the workstations, servers, cables, hubs, and other equipment that make up your network. In Chapter 5 we go into more detail on how to make this map and collect all the necessary information. Making such a map should be the first step toward designing your network.

If you already have a network installed, map it out now—you'll use this information both to better understand your existing network and to expand the network later on. If you don't have any kind of a network right now, your map will show the building's layout and its other characteristics, alerting you to features that could affect your network. Over time, your map will grow with your network so that you'll immediately be able to see every detail comprising or affecting the network.

## WHAT'S YOUR PLAN FOR
## GETTING NETWORKED?

Now that you have the fundamental tool in hand, the second step in network design is to figure out your plan of attack. How are you going to get from maps and drawings to a working network?

The key concept here is not the specific content of your plan, but the need to have a plan at all. If you dive in one Monday morning by deciding that this is the week that you set up a network, you will immediately find yourself drowning in details. It might even take you longer to do it that way than it would if you had a clear plan, but it will certainly be more painful.

Our advice: start small. Don't try to implement an entire network at once. The installation will go much more smoothly if you start off with a small network, as a test base to shake all the bugs out. Once a few PCs are running nicely you can go ahead and expand the network to the rest of the folks who need to use it, armed with the knowledge you've gained from getting the first few systems working.

In a fairly small installation (a final user base of 10 or so), you can probably get a reasonably representative test network running on two or three PCs. If you're going into a larger group with your network, say 20 or 30 users, try it out first in a lab or some isolated environment on about half a dozen PCs. Be sure you have machines that represent all the platforms that need to be networked, be they IBM clones, Macintoshes, or whatever.

Once you have the network running on the test systems, extend it to the rest of the users in an orderly way. Again, don't do it all at once. Add a few users, maybe five at a time, then sit back and make sure things are still working for everyone before adding the next batch. Keep this up, a little bit at a whack, until you're where you need to be. While this may take longer, it will alert you to potential problems along the way, and it will save you from developing a reputation as a miracle worker, able to implement whole networks in a single bound (not having this reputation will come in handy later on, take our word for it).

## STAYING CLOSE TO THE (RE)SOURCES

Staying close to your sources makes good sense in networking just as it does in business. In the case of networking, these are output sources—the fax machines, printers, and other equipment that people use to get information out of their networked computers; and input sources—the servers, modems, and other connections that supply information and services to those same networked computers.

As you plan your network, a guiding principle should be to minimize the distances between the equipment and the people who use it. At the same time, you will probably want to keep related pieces equipment close together. Keep the print server near the printer that it serves, for instance, and keep file servers close to the backup tape drive.

Your small test network will help you work out the details of what peripherals need to be near which users and what equipment goes together. Once you learn what pleases the people in your test network, you can spread that knowledge to the rest of the user population. This is one reason why we recommend you proceed in stages: While the number of users may be small at first, that also limits the number of unhappy customers you have to deal with as everyone is learning what works best (and what doesn't work at all).

## WORKGROUPS OR COMPUTING COMMUNITIES?

The next decision you must make covers how you want to organize your users. You will probably want to base this decision primarily on what types of work they do. You can have one big network with everyone in the organization on it, or you can organize along workgroup lines, with small sub-networks for each group of people who work primarily with each other.

In either case, you won't go wrong by starting off small. Get a single workgroup up on the network, and expand that small network to the larger world later. You can do this expansion a couple of ways. You could create another small workgroup network and then link it to the first network, creating several small linked communities. Or you could simply add new users to the first network, increasing its scale.

It's helpful for the final decision to reflect the structure of your organization. If different groups have fairly distinct computing needs and don't interact much, a workgroup organization probably makes the most sense for you. If, on the other hand, people often move between workgroups and have somewhat homogenous computing needs, you might find that a community organization is the way to go. Either way, start off small to minimize your regrets!

## RULES FOR PRACTICAL PRINTER PLACEMENT

Nearly everybody needs a printer at some time or another, so you have the opportunity to win the admiration and respect of all your users (or their scorn and curses) just by how you arrange access to the printers they want to use. The same guidelines supplied here for printers apply to all other public equipment on the network, including plotters, CD-ROM drives, or anything else your users might need to share.

Make sure the peripheral is easy for the users to access. This means not only that you should place it in the building near the offices of those who use it, but that those people should not have to squeeze behind a file cabinet or step over cables to pick up their printouts. Don't place a piece of equipment where it will get bumped or jostled. If it's a line printer that spills tractor-fed paper onto the floor, make sure there's room behind the printer for people to find their listings and tear them off. We have seen some installations where all the printers were mounted onto wheeled carts, making it easy to move the whole thing to get behind it. The carts have the additional advantages that you can store paper, toner, ribbons, and a stapler right underneath the printer and they're easy to move around when necessary.

You'll want to position printers so that they're easy for users to get to them, but don't neglect your own needs as a network administrator. For instance, you'll want to make sure the print server is near the printer, so you can adjust print job priorities and perform routine server maintenance as needed. And there is a security component to equipment placement as well. You'll want to keep an eye on public equipment lest it walk off, or at least place it near someone who's usually around to be your designated watchdog. It's unfortunate to have to mention it, but unmonitored equipment has been known to disappear. Whether it's been "borrowed" by the CAD group down the hall, or has really been pilfered, dealing with returns or replacements adds to a network administrator's burden unnecessarily. This is one of many cases where prevention beats cure, every time!

Finally, you'll need to be sure that the peripheral has clean power—sags or spikes in its AC can be disastrous for some equipment. And while you're at it, please make sure the air conditioning in the room is adequate for the device. Chapter 12 goes into more detail on these mechanical aspects of placement, but it's wise to consider them when planning for placement.

## MANAGING MULTIPLE SERVERS

If you have only one server on your network, the most practical arrangement is probably to leave it out in public, available to everyone, though not everyone will need (or even want) access to it. If, on the other hand, your network is large enough to warrant more than one server, you might want to consider controlling access to them.

## Leaving Servers in the Open Air

Small networks, with only one or two servers, are often found in small businesses, where space is at a premium. If you do leave a server in a public area, there are plenty of options to protect it from accidents or injury. Most network servers' software includes options to lock the keyboard to those who don't have the right password to unlock it; failing such a utility, you could even remove its keyboard entirely to achieve the same goal. A stranger who wants to borrow a keyboard will attract more attention than a stranger sitting at a machine, acting like he or she is supposed to be there!

## Locking Up the Servers: When, Why, How

In larger computing environments, a network administrator will frequently place servers and other network equipment in a locked server room, away from the public. Not only does this prevent theft and other malicious acts, it also ensures that well-meaning but ill-trained users can't make any mistakes that might damage the network.

If you decide you need to lock up your servers, it might be inconvenient for you always to be running in and out of the inner sanctum of the server room, and anyway, doing so compromises security, which defeats your whole purpose. So how do you administer machines when you're not sitting in front of them? Several companies have recognized this problem and created software to solve it. Your options for Novell networks include:

- *Network Management Services* (*NMS*) from Novell. Works over Novell networks. Allows an administrator with appropriate permissions to access servers across the network remotely in order to monitor and control servers across the network.
- *RCONSOLE*, which comes with NetWare, from Novell. Allows across-the-net operation of the server console.
- *ACONSOLE*, also provided with Novell NetWare. Permits operation of the server's console via an asynchronous dial-in connection.

For networks that use TCP/IP, you have a number of options as well. Most devices that you can manage via TCP/IP's Simple Network Management Protocol (SNMP) could also be operated remotely using SNMP-based management tools such as SunNet Manager, from Sun Microsystems, or Hewlett-Packard's OpenView.

## *To Lock or Not to Lock: How to Decide*

When deciding what access to allow to your network equipment, you must also factor in the needs of your users. If you are in a development environment, for example, where software or hardware engineers need to get to the network equipment frequently, locking up the servers will avail no one, least of all yourself. If you're in a more typical office environment, your users should be cheerfully oblivious to where the servers are located, and you can put them where they're most convenient for you.

In any case, network servers are often home to a workgroup's most precious assets—the files and applications that let its members do their jobs—so it's wise to treat them as if they were extremely valuable and precious. If you do that, common sense can also act as a guide to managing access and use.

# BUILDING BETTER BACKBONES

A backbone is a special link between individual networks, and is primarily used to let them communicate with each other. Often, networks are laid out so that sections that are fairly close together use some relatively inexpensive medium (such as twisted pair wiring), and links between sections use a higher performance medium like fiber optics. These links between sections compose the backbone of the network, and they might run between floors of a building, between buildings, or between sections of a building. Because each section of a network is typically built around a single piece of cable (for a bus topology) or a single hub (for a ring or star topology), the technically correct term for a section of a network is a *segment*. Armed with this information, we can now define a backbone as the network segment whose job is to link two or more other network segments together, as depicted in Figure 4-1.

When you lay out a network that uses a backbone, your goal is to minimize traffic over the backbone. If the Accounts Receivable and Accounts Payable departments communicate over the network more than anyone else in your organization, for instance, it's probably not in your best interest to place them in different network segments, because that will automatically increase the amount of overhead for everyone else attached to the backbone. Where you can isolate groups that must communicate regularly with one another, you should consider installing a special link between them (what we might call a private backbone), or you might place a hub or router between those two groups and attach that router to the backbone. That will keep local traffic local, intergroup traffic local to the two groups, and limit the traffic on the backbone only to information that needs to go there, as depicted in Figure 4-2.

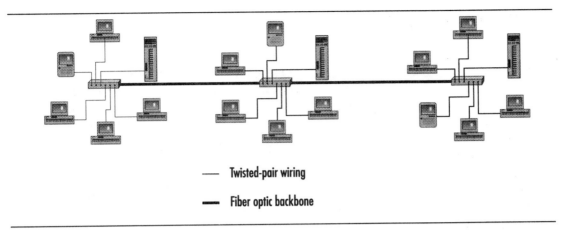

— Twisted-pair wiring

— Fiber optic backbone

**Figure 4.1** *Three twisted-pair networks linked by a fiber optic backbone. Each twisted-pair segment uses the star topology, while the backbone gives the overall network a bus topology.*

A good backbone is a fast one, so fiber is the medium of choice. The overhead of connecting segments of a network is enough of a job for the backbone without also having the drawback of a low-performance medium slowing it down.

Figure 4.3 shows a "star of stars" network configuration, where several networks are laid out using star topology, and the backbone linking them creates a larger star, a common way of linking networks. Where a special high-speed hub is used to link multiple hubs or cable segments together, the backbone might even be a box rather than a cable with multiple connections or hubs (which is why such installations are known as *collapsed backbones*).

## PLANNING FOR PROLIFERATION

The one thing about your network that you can predict with absolute certainty is this: It will get bigger. In fact, the bigger it gets, the bigger still you should expect it to become. As more people join your organization, and as those already there see what you've done with the network and want more of it, you'll be adding users, servers, and peripherals.

You don't want this growth to take you by surprise, so plan for it now, by doing the following:

- Buy hubs that can chain together.
- Select networking software that allows more users than you need now.

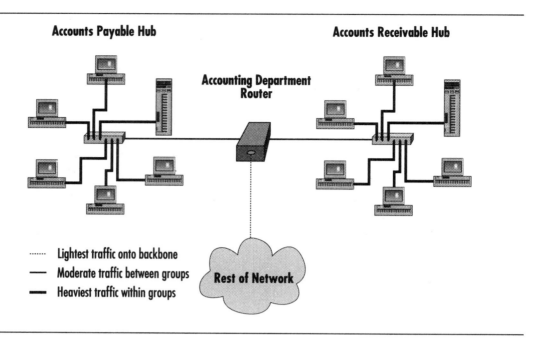

**Figure 4.2** *Two groups with a router between them, all joined by a backbone. Note that the groups are arranged so that the smallest amount of traffic goes over the backbone.*

- When wiring, make choices that will allow you to add more cable, workstations, and network drops per office in the future.
- Run a bit more cable than you need; you can leave the stubs coiled in the ceiling.

Your goal here is to be able to expand the network later without tearing everything out and starting over. Think of your network as a living, growing creature rather than a static one-time solution to a printer-sharing requirement.

# WORKING WITH (OR FOR) INFORMATION SERVICES

You might come to the network administrator role from a number of different starting points. Perhaps you are the one person in the accounting department who showed both the interest and aptitude to set up a network for the department—you

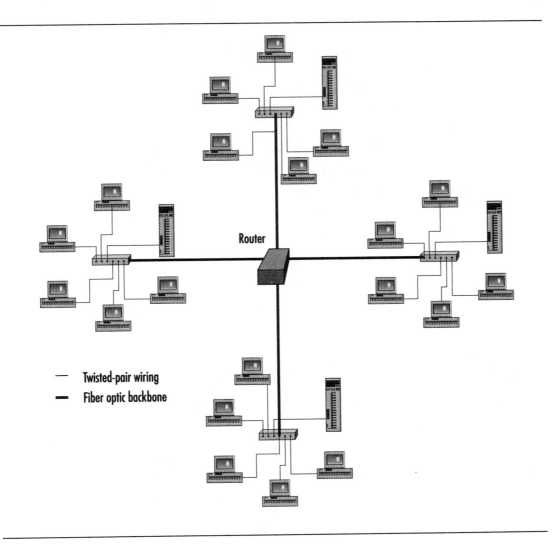

**Figure 4.3**  *A star of stars network layout.*

are a departmental resource. On the other hand, you might be setting up a network for the accounting department, but you work for the Information Services (IS) department of your organization. This section is particularly directed toward those of you who are departmental resources. You need to get to know the folks in the IS department and understand their needs and concerns and their relationship to the new network.

The IS folks in many organizations have typically been the custodians of critical information resources, including corporate databases, Human Resources data, and so on. They have been schooled to guard these resources carefully, because typically such information is both valuable and sensitive. After all, most companies would be in big trouble if their databases were corrupted or made publicly available.

You will at some point in your role as network administrator cross over into what the IS personnel think of as their domain, and this meeting might be productive or not, depending on how you handle it. They might see you and your network as a security risk or maybe even a job threat; try to work with them rather than getting into clashes for control.

Education will be key here. Educate the IS people to your network's abilities and goals, and educate yourself on what the IS resources are, how they are maintained, and what the IS folks are concerned about. This part of your job will involve diplomacy and tact; bring the interest groups together to solve problems jointly, or you will find yourself fighting wasteful, frustrating battles instead.

## SUMMARY

You now have a working knowledge of the basic concepts of designing your network, from preparation to laying everything out to planning for the future. We've also tried to give you a "heads up" to alert you to potential trouble spots so they don't take you by surprise.

In the next chapter we go back to step one, creating a map. This time we get down to the practical details and walk you through all the tasks involved in creating a map, the fundamental network tool around which all your network activities should be based.

# MAPPING OUT YOUR NETWORK

**5**

## WHY MAKE A MAP?

Creating and maintaining a good map of your network will be one of the best investments you'll ever make in your network. You will refer to a good map constantly: to help you add PCs and peripherals, to troubleshoot problems, and to track down equipment. If, on the other hand, you don't have a complete map or if it's not kept up to date you'll have to wander around constantly and pester your users with questions that they just answered for you two weeks ago. This will not inspire their confidence.

Someone, sometime, will probably need to understand your network when you're not there to explain it, so put your map together from that person's point of view. This not only ensures that the map is a better general-purpose network reference, it might also be the difference between being on call all the time and having some weekends to yourself. It's also your company's only insurance against having to do a complete inventory of what's out there should anything ever happen to you!

## START WITH A GOOD SET OF PLANS AND MAKE COPIES

First you need a map of the building (or buildings). If at all possible, use the actual blueprints—these will be by far the most accurate. If that's not possible, you'll have to make a set of to-scale plans yourself. Measure as carefully as you can and draw the layout of the entire building, one floor per page. Use paper big enough to show plenty of detail. At the very least you will need to be able to show where all the cables run within the building.

Whether you get the building blueprints or draw your own map, once you have the picture, get some copies made. Get several, so you can write on them without messing up your master copy. A copier shop or a drafting store will be able to make copies of large pages for a reasonable fee, even if what you're working from is a set of architectural blue-line plans.

## Make Sure the Map Is Accurate

The next step in the mapping process is to mark the map with information about your entire network. This means showing every workstation, server, hub, and peripheral device and where each resides in the building. It also means showing where all the cables in the network run and where and how they connect to each other.

This process would be fairly easy if you could just place an "X" on the map for every PC and a line for every cable. But if you did that, the map would not be of much use. You will want to use your map to find out how a PC is configured, what software is on it, and the length of its network cable. To do all this, you will need a network database that refers to your map, so mark your map with a naming scheme that you can use with your network database. For example, you might mark your two servers on the map with the names "S1" and "S2." It doesn't matter what you call them, as long as you can see them clearly on the map and cross-reference them easily in the database.

## Build a Comprehensive System Inventory

The network map is more than a bird's-eye view of the building with all the wires marked. It's also a complete inventory of everything on the network. Once you have all of this information in one place, you will have a highly valuable tool to assist you in adding new equipment, updating software, and solving problems—everything in a network administrator's job description. This section describes the types of information you'll need to record.

## PCs and Hardware Configurations

You need to capture a great deal of information about every PC in the network, workstation, and server alike. You need to know the computer type (IBM clone, Macintosh, something else?), make, model, and serial number. You also should record the processor type and speed (does it have an 80286 or an 80486 processor? 16 or 66 Megahertz?), the amount of RAM in the system, the size of the hard disk, if any, and the types of diskette drives, if any. Don't forget to note the keyboard type, the monitor brand and model, the display adapter type and configuration, and the serial numbers of all of these items. If additional cards are installed into a particular PC, be sure to mark down the brand, model, configuration, and serial number of each of them.

You also need to record information about the network interface card. Make sure you note the card's interrupt level, I/O address, and any other information that it allows you to configure.

## Software Configurations

The facts you want to record about software for each PC are the operating system the PC uses, what applications are installed on its hard drive, and which network drivers it is using. Be sure also to record the revision level of each of these pieces of software.

It can also be very useful to record copies of the PC's startup configuration files, such as its AUTOEXEC.BAT and CONFIG.SYS[1] files. If you know that a group or all of your PCs are configured in the same way, you need only store these files once for all similar systems. But if you're not sure that they're the same, it would be better to store a separate set of configuration files for each PC.

Don't forget your servers! Collect all this information for each server as well as each workstation.

## Network Equipment

Record the make, model, and serial number of every router, hub, concentrator, or other network-specific item in your network. If the equipment has a size, such as a number of ports, be sure to note that in your inventory. If any piece of equipment runs from software, note the version and date of the program or programs it's currently running.

---

[1]DOS-specific reference.

## Printers and Other Peripherals

Just as you did for the networking equipment, make a note of the make, model, and serial number of each peripheral device, whether it's a printer, modem, or CD-ROM drive. If the device has configuration options (such as a laser printer into which you have installed extra memory), be sure to note those as well. Most printers and other peripherals will have specific software drivers associated with them; it's a good idea to make entries that capture their names, sizes, and dates with the printer (or other device) as well. That way, you can regularly check these ever-changing pieces of software for currency and will know if you need to get a newer version by comparing information about what you've got with what's considered to be the latest and greatest version.

## Cables

Every cable should be labeled at each end. Make a note in your database of the "name" of each cable, its length, and its endpoints. If a cable has intermediate connections, be sure to indicate where they are.

   If you have a mixture of cabling types, such as fiber and twisted pair wiring, be sure your database indicates which types you are using and where you're using them.

## Who's Who

Your database should also include a section of names and numbers of important people. These include the people who installed the network, the people who sold or leased each machine to you, the people with whom you have service contracts, and the manufacturers or support organizations for each different piece of equipment. If you have account numbers with any of these companies, be sure to record those in the database as well, so you don't have to scramble for them before you call these folks.

## WORKING WITH WHAT YOU'VE GOT

It's possible that you won't have to hunt down all of this information from scratch; some of it may already exist in other forms around the company. Your organization's accounting department, for instance, might keep track of capital assets, in which case they would have some of this information already. If you had the network cables installed by an outside contractor, his or her work plans will make a perfect basis for your network map, because they should show the whole building, where are the cables are, what types of cables you have, and where they link to each other. Similarly, if you had another firm install the network itself, it (or its paperwork) will have the data you need about all of the network equipment.

Collecting all of this information is a big job; take advantage of as many sources as you can. Don't expect to be able to build your map in one day, either. It will take longer and will keep changing as your network does, too.

## Staying on Top Means Staying Out of Trouble

Now that you have this map and database, invest a little time in keeping all the information up to date. Nothing is more useless than old information. Suppose you needed to add a new PC to the network; you'd look at the map and see a free cable in just the right place, but after a half an hour crawling around in the ceiling looking for it you might discover that someone else scavenged that cable for another machine. Even more frustrating, at that point, will be the realization that you don't know what else on the map is out of date!

Be sure to update the map every time you change something, and educate everyone else who works on the network about the importance of doing the same. This map maintenance will take a little time, but you'll see a huge payoff every time you use it. Best of all, an up-to-date map means you can look at the map to find things instead of having to go into the building or crawling in a ceiling.

## Dealing with Changes (Are There Louts Loose in Your Ceiling?)

Chances are good that other people will change things on the network without your knowing it, but the frequency of this happening will vary greatly among network installations. Every network administrator has a different solution to this problem, and you'll need to find the level of control that makes the most sense for your user base and workload.

In an environment where users can load their own software onto their PC hard drives and can change their own configuration files, you will have a harder time keeping current information on every PC than you would in a situation where all software is loaded on the network and every PC is configured identically. Nevertheless, you can take some steps to ensure that your information is as up to date as possible.

## Enlist the Help of Management

Request that all software that the company orders gets delivered to you, and you in turn can deliver it to the users. This approach has the added advantage that you can send in the registration cards for new software, thereby making sure that you have technical support when you need it and that you will get notification of upgrades. The same holds for hardware; have technicians check with you before installing new hardware in any machine. Management's support of these policies will make your job a lot easier.

## Enlist the Help of the Users

Remind users that the more information you have about their systems, the better you can help them. If a user makes a change to a configuration file, for instance, which causes his or her PC to stop working, you can come to the rescue by restoring the old configuration file from your database.

## Keeping on Top of Things

It may be necessary for you to strike a balance between staying on top of every detail and putting in a reasonable number of hours per day. In general, the more current the information you have, the better. But if users change the configurations of their PCs regularly, meaning that you have to go to each workstation once a week and collect new information about it, you might find it more cost-effective to update this information as you need it.

Note, though, that this trade-off applies to users' workstations only. When it comes to servers, wiring, hubs, and other network equipment, it's essential that your information is always current. Again, enlist the help of both management and users. If someone needs to move a cable or a printer, or if electrical maintenance requires re-routing some network cables, be sure everyone knows to notify you first. Doing so will make everybody's life much easier.

# How to Use the Map You've Built

Once you put all this effort into building the map, you'll find lots of uses for it.

## Troubleshooting, Anyone?

Troubleshooting is the art of tracking down problems, and your map is a critical tool in the process. Suppose, for example, that a user calls you, unable to access anything on the network. You'll begin checking all the obvious things that might prevent access, including recent changes to the workstation, passwording problems, and so on. But suddenly four other users call you with the same symptoms: It's time to get out your map. Studying it, you notice that all of these users' workstations are connected to the same network hub. That hub becomes your first suspect as the cause of your problem.

## Planning Goes Better with a Map!

Your map will also be extremely useful in planning the expansion of your network. Once you have a complete picture of your network as it currently stands, mark the date on it and make some copies. It's a good idea to give at least one copy to your managers for their records. On the other copies you can try out different expansion scenarios, rearranging resources and adding new ones. Your map indicates all potential trouble spots, such as sources of electrical interference (large motors can wreak havoc with your cables) or places where cables would be too long to be reliable. This means you can solve problems on paper, which is much cheaper than doing it in the ceiling later. Plus, once you've mapped out your plan, you can give a copy to the contractor who will be executing the expansion.

# Summary

This chapter has introduced you to the concept of a network map. This map is more than just a picture of the building; it's the place where you keep all the records about your network. You now know how to create the map, what information you need to produce it, and what it's good for. We hope we've convinced you to create one—you'll be glad you did.

# BUILDING FOR THE FUTURE

## 6

## NOTHING SUCCEEDS LIKE SUCCESS

Congratulations! Now you've installed a new network, and your users are happily using it. The network is doing exactly what everyone wanted, quietly and efficiently, and those using it can now share their printers, plotters, and files more easily than they ever thought possible. The trouble is, word has gotten out about what you've done, and everyone else wants a network now, too.

Recall back in Chapter 4, when we exhorted you to plan for proliferation. Your network will grow, and your life will be much easier if you plan for that rather than letting it take you by surprise. One particular source of growth will be among those users who are not in your department or the area covered by your network. As soon as they see all the things your users can do, they're going to want to join the network, too. If you work for the department that now has the new network, other departments will want to use what you've learned and put together. This could lead to some slightly tricky budgeting and political issues.

Believe us: Demand for your network, the network services, and *your* services will go up exponentially. This can be a relatively smooth increase if you keep it in mind, or quite difficult if you haven't planned on it. In this chapter we'll give you some tips to help you make sure it's as painless as possible.

# LEAVE ROOM FOR GROWTH
# (AND MISTAKES!)

You've probably got the message by now, but we'll say it one more time. When you design your network, plan for it to grow. Expect more users, more servers, faster servers, faster PCs, and more peripherals. Allow extras in the number of cables you run, the number of users your network allows, and the amount of space you expect to use, and you'll be well equipped for the near future.

## Plan on Mistakes

Planning to make mistakes might strike you as a pessimistic approach. But remember, when you make changes and add new functions to the network you will be to some extent learning as you go, and so you will make mistakes—that's how we learn! So the trick is not to deny that mistakes will happen, but to plan on them so you can minimize their impact on your users. If you think it will take you a week to add a new function, for instance, tell everyone it will take two weeks. No one will be upset with you if you're early. Similarly, don't disconnect the old printer until the new one has been up, running, and thoroughly tested for at least a day. Plan on the unexpected happening.

## The Difficulties of Scale

When you have a small number of users on a limited resource, things will probably go along fine; it's when you start overloading that resource (by adding more users, for instance) that you will run into trouble. You begin to have capacity utilization problems, and your old assumptions no longer hold true. Network performance might become extremely slow, even to the point of rendering the network unusable. In some cases, such as when you heavily stress the demand on a distributed application, certain functions might become unreliable or files might get corrupted.

You can count on this: As things get bigger, in size, scale, and scope, the number of possible interactions and new network situations goes up even more, and therefore so does the number of potential problems. Every time you add a new resource to the network, you have added more than one new potential source of conflict. Know this at the outset; if you're close to your limits, allow more time to add the resource than you think you need. This brings us to the next topic: knowing those limits before you hit them.

# Know Your Limits

Your network will always have limitations. Some of them are obvious—you know how many users your network operating system allows, how much disk space you have on the file server, how many workstations you can attach to the network with the available cable. Some of the limitations are less visible—at some point, there will be enough traffic to send your network over the line between being acceptably fast and annoyingly slow.

Keep an eye on these limits to avoid hitting them. A fast-growing network may bump against its limits without realizing it—you might run a few extra cables to some new users without noticing that the new cables are longer than the longest allowable length for your network type. Running up against these limits without knowing it can lead to bizarre, intermittent problems that are difficult to track down and very frustrating to your users. Opt for prevention, so you don't have to spend all your time responding to emergencies, by constantly checking your limits as you add to your network.

# Know When to Add Capacity, and When to Split Systems

When you design your network, you'll want to build in an allowance for growth right from the start. Many people find that a margin of 30–40% unused capacity works pretty well. With that number, you can probably increase the size of your network by 10 or 20 percent without having any noticeable impact on the performance of your network. But after you do this two or three times, you'll be much more likely to run up against some limitation of your network. You can probably ease the situation somewhat by adding to the server with more disk space, more memory, or a faster CPU, but eventually you'll reach a point where you can't do any more of these improvements. When you notice server utilization running close to 80%, it's time to start thinking about splitting groups.

When it's time to split the network and set different groups up with different servers, look for natural divisions along which to make the split. You want to divide groups along the lines in which they work together, and in ways that the different groups won't conflict with each other. It's also helpful if you can make the divisions along the lines of types of network services the different groups use. A natural division in an engineering development organization, for instance, is to place the engineers in one group and the people responsible for company operations in another, because engineers tend to be heavier users of computing resources.

## PLANNING BEATS IMPROVISATION, EVERY TIME

The key concept in planning for growth is in the word "planning." Don't wait until things break to add in something bigger and better. You need to stay on top of things at all times, by keeping informed of how people are using the network, what sorts of problems they're experiencing, and where you might be stressing a network resource. Watch the trends of increases in usage, and notice where your users are now consuming resources where there used to be excess; these trends will show you where your attention will be needed next.

Adding users, adding disk space, adding printers, rewiring the network to make it faster—all of these tasks can be predicted and planned for, and will be much more fun and will work better with planning. If, for instance, you discover that users absolutely cannot squeeze any more data onto your server disk and they revolt on Friday afternoon, you might be tempted to respond by announcing that you will spend Saturday morning installing a larger hard drive on the server. Careful! You will very likely find yourself still working on it on Sunday night, having spent the entire weekend wrestling with things you did not foresee. But if instead you schedule the upgrade in advance, notifying everyone that it is coming and brushing up on everything you need to know to make it happen, the process will go much more smoothly.

## SUMMARY

Your life will be much easier if you plan ahead for the growth that is sure to come to your network. Leave extra room every step of the way for new users, new applications, and new data, and give yourself some space to make mistakes. The key to success is keeping on top of what's going on within your network now and what's coming in the future.

# MANAGING YOUR INSTALLATION

## WHAT'S THE BOTTOM LINE?

Installing a network for your organization is definitely going to cost some money, but it doesn't have to cost a fortune. If you have a good idea what you need, where to get it, and how to install it, you can avoid the major spending pitfalls.

The first step in determining your installation budget is figuring out how much you have to spend. You might need to do a little research first to understand how much things typically cost, but if you have an absolute spending limit on the whole project, find out now and keep it in mind as you shop. Above all, don't spend any money before you know where all the rest is coming from and how it's all going to contribute to the overall working network.

An often overlooked budget item that could make the difference between having a network and not having one is an allowance for unexpected occurrences. Call it whatever you like, but be sure to allow a portion of the total budget for problems that you can't foresee right now. Suppose, for instance, that you're wiring your network and you find a fire wall right across the path of your cable, even though the building plans didn't show one on the map. You'll need to make a hole through the wall and add fireproof partitions on each side of it, which could be quite expensive. If you hadn't allowed some slack for it, this sort of discovery could derail your network.

# KNOW THE TYPICAL COSTS

When setting up your budget, be sure to count not just obvious servers and work-stations, but also expenses such as materials, network hardware, labor, and testing.

- *Materials*. The materials that make up your network are more than just cables. Don't forget to factor in the costs of wall plates, cable connectors, and cable ties. If you're running your cables through conduit, you need to add in the cost of the conduit. If you're making the connectors yourself, be sure to allow for the related costs such as crimping tools, pins, and connector covers.

- *Network hardware*. This includes more than just your PCs. If you're running a fiber network, you may need routers and hubs; if you are combining different kinds of media in your network, you will need equipment to bridge them; if your network is going to need repeaters, be sure to calculate them into the total network costs.

- *Labor*. One of the biggest line items on your installation budget will be the labor costs to get the whole thing installed. You'll need to know how much to allow for the entire job of having someone install the cable, from discussing the installation with them to attaching the very last wall plate to the wall. If you're one of those brave souls planning to install the cable yourself, you'll need to budget time and training costs into your plan.

- *Testing*. Most people forget to budget for the testing and debugging phase of the network installation. To test your network, you will need to rent some type of cable testing equipment to make sure all the cables work correctly. It's much cheaper to find and correct bugs in the network at installation time than to wait until people are trying to connect to your server. See Chapter 8 for more tips on network testing and debugging.

## *Networking at Finish-Out Is Always Cheaper than Retrofitting*

*Finish-out* is the process of adding walls, ceiling tiles, carpet, paint, and maybe even electricity and plumbing, to a building. As you might imagine, it's a lot easier to run the network cables when the contractors (or you) don't need to move ceiling tiles or fish around in the walls. If you add a network to a finished building, you will encounter a whole host of hassles that don't exist during construction: You'll find yourself throwing cables around in the ceiling using fishing lines and weights, crawling around getting insulation in your hair and clothes, disrupting people's workdays, and making a mess. And if it's not you doing all those things, it will be the cabling contractors doing them, and their work will cost you more than it otherwise might.

Another advantage to installing the networking cable during the building construction is that if you have to run cables inside conduit, you can work with the electrical contractors to make sure they install larger conduit that the two types of wiring can share. Furthermore, you can run cables down inside the walls with tidy and attractive wall plates for the connectors; if you add a network to existing office space (called retrofitting), nice wall plates will cost you more, and you may have to settle for dangling the cables from the ceiling.

If you have the luxury of deciding whether to install the network while the building is under construction or after you move in, by all means opt for the former.

## What's on Your Map?

Recall the all-important network map from Chapter 5. It shows all the architectural details of your building: heating, vacuum, and air conditioning (HVAC), electricity, and telephone wiring. Carefully study the routes these systems use. They all involve running cables of some sort, so if you see something curious on the map, such as cables running in a non-direct route, assume that you'll have to follow the same route. The previous installers almost certainly chose those routes for some reason; make sure you're not assuming access where none is possible.

Use your map to estimate cable lengths, as well; buying too little cable can be annoying to your installers, but buying too much can be hard on your budget.

## Expect Disaster, but Hope for a Miracle

Expecting disaster means budgeting for additional unforeseen expenses; most installers allow 20% for these types of things. They often also add a clause to the contract for an emergency override, in case of something really unexpected. We know of one network installation that connected two offices that had several large machine shops between them. The electromagnetic interference (EMI) from the machine shops was so great that the network cables were inoperable on that route; the installers finally had to install a pair of infrared repeaters on the roof of the building to solve the problem. You can certainly hope that you don't run into anything like this, but it's good business sense to have a contingency plan in case it happens.

## STRATEGIC INSTALLATION PLANNING

A number of aspects of network installation have things in common with other tasks affecting the building, and a good strategy is to arrange your network installation to take advantage of as many of these as possible. For instance, try to get in on the building planning at the same time as the electrical contractors and HVAC people if possible. It's cheaper to run with one set of conduit that carries both electrical wires and network cables instead of one conduit for each, so if you can work with the electrical contractors on this, everybody wins.

The other part of your strategy is to minimize disruption to the people working in the building. If you install your network during finish-out this is a moot point, but if you're installing it into people's offices, try to do as much as possible on evenings and weekends. Also, be considerate; if you drop ceiling tile dust on somebody's desk, clean it off. You don't want your network to have a bad name before anyone even uses it.

## MAKE SURE THINGS WORK BEFORE USERS GET RILED

As soon as you announce that everyone is about to get networked, the future users will begin factoring it into their plans. This is a tribute to their faith in your word, so you want to be absolutely sure that you can deliver at the promised time! Allow yourself plenty of extra time for testing and troubleshooting before you advertise the network to the world. We recommend giving yourself some extra time; if you think you'll have the network running at the end of March, tell everyone they'll have it the end of April. You might be surprised at how quickly an extra month can evaporate. If, on the other hand, everything goes perfectly, you'll be in the highly desirable position of making the new services available to users early. No one is likely to complain about that.

## SUMMARY

In this chapter we've gone over two aspects of planning your installation: costs and logistics. We discussed the things that your budget must reflect, including materials, equipment, labor, and your total available funds, and have discussed some techniques for keeping costs down. We also noted some strategies to ensure a smooth transition into networking.

In Chapter 8 we look more closely at how to handle one of the biggest parts of the installation: getting the cable into the building.

# Managing Contractors and Consultants

**8**

## Writing Good Requirements Means Getting Good Bids

The network installation will go much more smoothly if the cabling contractor has all the information needed to give you a fair, accurate estimate of the effort involved in wiring your network. The contractor gets this information from your requirements document, so it should be as clear and concise as possible. To this end, try to find an architect or facilities management person and someone experienced with running cable. They can be a great help to you in writing good specifications. In particular, they will be familiar with building code requirements. Many governments have stringent codes governing cable and its insulation and what types of cable are allowed in walls, conduit, and plenum airspace (that overhead area that is also used for air conditioning ventilation). You have better things to do than to spend a lot of time researching all these laws; try to find someone who already knows them if you possibly can.

Most cabling contractors will go over all of this information with you, and will probably even help you write up the requirements, but we recommend that you find an impartial third party to help you with this phase. We're certainly not suggesting that cabling contractors are out to get you, but you'll feel better knowing you drew up the plans with your own ally.

The requirements document will fold directly into the contract with the cable installers. See Chapter 27 for a checklist of everything that should go into the requirements document and the final contract.

## Selecting Contractors and Consultants

Next you need to shop around for a contractor to install your cable. Ask other people for recommendations; word of mouth can be a great source of information. Check with the folks who sold you the networking equipment; they'll probably be familiar with the biggest contractors in your area.

No matter how you find a contractor or how highly recommended he or she is, be sure to ask for at least three references. The more complex and difficult your wiring medium, the more important it is that you check the contractor's references. Twisted pair wiring is probably about the easiest to install, and fiber the most difficult, with coaxial cable somewhere in between. If you're installing a fiber network, make sure your contractor has successfully installed similar networks before. Unless you're feeling very generous, you probably don't want to pay someone to learn new techniques on your network. Also, when speaking with the references, ask whether there were any problems with the network after the initial installation, and whether they were satisfied with the follow-up support from the contractor.

## How to Arrange a Payment Schedule

It is in your best interest to negotiate payment by the project, not by the hour. This is certainly the norm for cabling contractors, and any reputable contractor should be willing to arrange payment this way. Once you've arrived at a price for the project, the next step is to work out a payment schedule.

Anytime you're paying someone by the project, the following rule holds: The more of your money the contractor has, the less attention you'll get. You will have to pay some of the total up front; 20–50% is typical, and the less you give initially, the more leverage you will have to make sure things are done to your satisfaction.

As the job progresses, pay in 10% increments of the total price. Set small milestones before the work begins and state in the contract what needs to be done to meet each milestone.

The last installment should be larger, perhaps 15–30% of the total, and you shouldn't deliver it until you are completely satisfied with the installation. Don't sign off on completion until the cables have been demonstrated to work, preferably by checking them with network test equipment. Another aspect of completion should be that the work area is clean and neat; a common complaint about cabling contractors is that they leave bits of wire and other trash in ceilings and network closets.

## How to Tell Whether You Are Satisfied with the Work

The only way to tell whether the installation works is to test it, so you need to make testing part of the contract. Stipulate that you will not accept the work until the entire installation has been tested to your satisfaction.

Proper techniques for testing cables vary with the medium. For fiber, you will have to rent a laser device that you attach to one end of the cable; if at least 90% of the light gets through to the other end, that cable is okay. For copper wire you can get devices to check impedance and make sure you have current flow. It's also a good idea to test for electromagnetic interference (EMI) problems if you have copper cable. Check with your local networking supplier to find out where to get these devices.

Thorough checking will reward you in the future. Be sure to check every single cable and wall plug in the network, even if they're unused right now. You don't want to find a batch of problems when you try to add new users to your network later.

## Always Ask for a Guarantee

Following our advice, you carefully checked out the entire installation before you paid the contractor. Even so, it's important to ask for a warranty on the work in case you missed something or a problem develops later. A good contractor will be happy to provide a guarantee.

## Leaving Room for Further Relationships (or Other Contractors)

Part of what you will get from the cabling installers is a new copy of your network map, marked with the actual cable lengths and the locations of all the cables. This map will also show the types and locations of all the connectors. If the network required the installation of repeaters, be sure the map shows where they are (they can be hard to find when you need to get to them).

Don't accept the completion of the network installation until you get this document. It is a critical resource, as we discussed in Chapter 5. It's important not only because you need it to maintain and expand your network, but also because other contractors will need it. Whether you use the same cabling contractor or somebody else when you expand your network, he or she will need to look at a good map to decide what to do next. The map will be useful to other contractors as well, including electricians, telephone repair personnel, and anyone else who might need to dig around in the areas where your network cables sit.

## SUMMARY

Cabling contractors and networking consultants are professionals with a lot to offer you as a new network administrator, but you need to know how to work with them effectively. This chapter discusses the pitfalls you might encounter when working with contractors and gives you some tips to make sure you get the most for your networking money.

# SMART NETWORK BUYING TECHNIQUES

**9**

## PUTTING TOGETHER A PURCHASING PLAN

Before you go shopping for your network equipment, arm yourself with a detailed purchasing plan. This is basically a bill of materials for all of your network equipment, from the server to the cable ties. Putting the purchasing plan together is a great way to look at the "big picture" of your network and get a good perspective on everything your network requires and where all the money is going.

The purchasing plan will serve two purposes. First, it will help you understand the total costs involved in setting up your network, which is something you need for your budgeting anyway. Second, it's an invaluable tool in negotiating for bulk deals with electronics supply houses. We'll look more closely at bulk discounts later in this chapter.

## NEW OR USED?

If you are on a very tight budget, it's especially worth looking into the possibility of buying used equipment. This won't include cables or connectors, but could very well include workstations, NICs, servers, and routers. Check the classified ads in your local PC publications and national PC periodicals for sources of used equipment.

The choice between new and used network equipment is very similar to the choice between new and used cars. New equipment will come with a full warranty, and you know all the parts will be in the box. You'll get whatever service support the manufacturer offers, but you'll also pay considerably more. If you buy used equipment, you don't get the warranty, and you might not even get manuals for the equipment. Effectively you are taking on the warranty work yourself, at a significant savings of start-up costs.

If you're an enthusiastic do-it-yourself type and are willing to spend less money on the equipment, knowing that you'll spend more time on shopping and maintenance, used equipment might be the right choice for you. If you do choose to go this route, shop very carefully and ask lots of questions. Educate yourself as much as possible before you buy, to minimize the risk of ending up with lemons.

If you don't want to make the commitment to finding, maintaining, and servicing the equipment yourself, you'll be better off spending more money for the relief of knowing that if something does go wrong, you have someone else you can call for help.

## STATE OF THE ART OR PLAIN VANILLA?

Another decision that affects the cost of your total network installation is the overall technology type you choose to use. This will depend on your near-term needs as well as your comfort level regarding working with something relatively new. Of course, the cost differences are significant.

Look again at your network needs. Does your network require very fast throughput and high bandwidth, as for video, voice, and data-intensive applications? If so, you're going to need one of the newer technologies that can handle this level of network usage. The drawback is that, because these technologies are so new, you'll have fewer choices of hardware suppliers than you would with an older technology. Competition is not as fierce, and therefore your total price will probably be higher.

If your needs are more modest, however, you're in luck. Because they've been around so long, the older technologies, such as twisted pair wiring running Ethernet, are pretty much commodity purchases. Competition is high and you'll be able to get better prices by shopping around. Plus, you'll have the comfort of knowing that you're using something tried and true; if you run into problems, there are lots of people who are familiar with the equipment and can help you.

# Enough or Too Much?

Certainly you don't want to drastically overdo your initial network purchase, but keep in mind that buying exactly as much as you need right now will not save you money in the long run. Your network will grow (recall Chapter 6), and you'll be much better off later if you plan for that now.

A good rule is to allow about 20–40% of your current capacity for growth. Once again, look at your own network before you settle on a growth figure. Determine how much you expect the network to grow in the next year or two and use that figure instead of our guideline.

We recommend that during your initial installation you install everything you need, not just for your first-phase network but also for the expected growth. No matter what the size of the network, you'll have certain fixed costs at installation, such as the labor of the cabling contractors, and it's more efficient to pay for those things once now than to pay for them again in a year.

# Mail Order versus Local Dealers: Pros and Cons

Another great way to save money on your network equipment is by ordering it through mail-order supply houses. With their lower overhead and higher volume, they can often offer prices significantly below those of your local suppliers. The trade-offs are in the area of support. Telephone support is all you're likely to get from a mail-order shop, so if you need more comprehensive help you'll incur additional costs in getting it. If you're comfortable supporting yourself on your network equipment, go for the savings that the mail-order approach offers.

If you choose to go with a local supplier, on the other hand, you might pay a bit more up front, but you'll be able to get support more easily if you need it. Check on the shop's support policy before you buy, and compare support between local suppliers.

You'll find advertisements for mail-order suppliers in any network magazine. Some of the common, general ones are *LAN Times*, *LAN Magazine*, and *Network Computing*, and you can probably also find periodicals on your particular network type. These magazines will be useful after your network is installed and running, too, so it's a good idea to get familiar with them now.

Even if you ultimately decide to buy local, check out the mail-order outlets before you go into a local shop. The price information gleaned from these investigations gives you a good idea about what you should expect to pay for your equipment. This brings us to the next topic: negotiating a package deal.

## THE FINE ART OF PACKAGE DEALS

The more equipment you are going to buy, the more a dealer will want your business. A vendor will usually be willing to reduce its margin on a sale in favor of greater volume (and the expectation of more sales to you in the future). The more equipment you need to buy, and the more aware you are of prices, the better your bargaining position.

When preparing to work out a package deal, you need to do your homework. Have a complete list of everything you'll need to install your network (you created this list when you prepared your purchasing plan at the beginning of this chapter). You also need to know the going rates for all the equipment on your list; you'll get this information from networking magazines and mail-order shops and by shopping with local suppliers.

Knowing the rock-bottom mail-order discount price on an item is helpful, but you also need to know what other suppliers in your area are charging for the same item. That way, when you're bargaining with your supplier, you can point out that the competition is selling the same widget for 5% less. The supplier will probably be willing to give you the same price in order to secure the rest of your order.

## SERIOUSLY SEEKING SUPPORT

It's not pessimistic to plan on something going wrong—it's just plain good sense. At some point you will need support on your network; it might be the day you start installing or a year down the road, but either way it's better to find support now. Your support might come from the folks who sold you the network equipment, the folks who installed it, or (if you're on a really tight budget and did all that yourself) it might be a local consultant. Especially if you are in that last category, take some time now to find this consultant. Shop around, ask for recommendations, and check references.

Make the name and number of this support person available to other people in your organization, so that if an emergency crops up when you're not there, they still have somewhere to turn. After all, you do want to take a vacation now and then, don't you?

## Summary

With the information in this chapter, you're ready to go out and find the best possible deal on your network equipment. You know which networking options will cost more, and you're aware of hidden costs in apparent bargains.

**B**y now, you should be familiar with the basics of how networks operate and with the components that make a network operate. This is all still fairly theoretical, lacking many of the nitty-gritty details you'll need to know in order to build a real network for your own use, or to keep an existing network running.

Now that you've been introduced to networking technology, and have a feel for what networks can do, you should also have an appreciation for how useful they can be. By now, you should also have a pretty good idea about how networks communicate and about the different kinds of networking technologies, hardware, and software out there in the world.

You should also have an idea about how to lay out a network and how to document what's out there on your network (or at least what's planned to be out there). Armed with this information, you've also learned how to plan for growth, how to budget for installation or growth, and how to spend money and hire talent to help you do what needs to be done with your network.

If this material sounds unfamiliar or strange, we advise you to dig back into the chapters in Part I and try to refamiliarize yourself with whatever is missing. If you're ready to move on to the next phase, that's what we cover here in Part II. This is the section of the book where we tackle the details of putting working networks together, starting with the wiring, through equipment selection and placement, to working through the installation process. In the latter half of this section, we cover the art of living with what you've wrought, as we tackle the ins and outs of maintaining your network. This takes us from the very beginning through upgrades, replacements, and expansion, and also includes methods and techniques to ensure safe, effective everyday operation of your network.

# Wiring Systems

# 10

Throughout the material we've covered so far, we've tried to emphasize the importance of the physical connections that let networking happen. Here, we'll take a long, hard look at the physical media that make networking a reality for most installations.

This chapter is devoted to explaining and exploring your potential choices for cabling a network of your own. It covers the types of media you'll want to consider, their pros and cons, along with their distance and installation limitations. You'll learn that mixing and matching is okay, and that most medium- to large-sized networks make use of multiple media to meet their needs.

Before we launch into our version of Cable Trivia, there's one factoid about networking that could give this chapter a little more appeal: Fully 50 percent of the cost of most networks, including all hardware, networking interfaces, and the like, goes toward the cost of cable and its installation. At less than a dollar a foot (or three dollars per meter), it sounds inexpensive, but when you're dealing with thousands of feet (or meters) and hundreds of hours of labor for installation, small costs have a way of becoming large!

## The Basic Cable Types

Wiring comes in many shapes and sizes and is offered in a bewildering array of coatings, claddings, and types. While it is possible to spend too much on cable, it's far easier not to spend enough. When selecting and dealing with cable planned for network use, you'll be best served if you buy network cable specifically designed for such use. In fact, each of the various networking technologies—Ethernet, Token Ring, and ARCnet—has its own specific cabling requirements, based on the type of signaling hardware it uses and the related electrical characteristics, like impedance, that go along with its needs. Anything less can be an invitation to trouble, or at least a cause for concern.

Cable also comes in many different types, but from a networking perspective, there are three major kinds you'll typically encounter:

- *Twisted-pair*, which consists of two or more wires twisted together, most often covered with an outer layer of insulation. Some types of telephone cable include more than 200 pairs of wires, but this kind is seldom used for networking. Figure 10.1 shows what twisted-pair cable can look like.
- *Coaxial*, which consists of an inner conductor surrounded by an insulator, wrapped with an outer conductor, and covered by an outer insulation layer (and sometimes shielding as well). Figure 10.2 shows what coaxial cable can look like.
- *Fiber-optic*, which consists of one or more light-conducting fibers (typically made of special glass, but some varieties use special plastics), coating by an insulator and an outer layer of cladding. Figure 10.3 shows what fiber-optic cable looks like, for both single- and multiple-fiber versions.

We've introduced these cables in ascending order of cost, but there are many other points of comparison, and lots of other details worth knowing about them. Read on for some of the finer points about each kind.

## Twisted-Pair Wiring

In its simplest form, twisted-pair wiring (or TP, as it's more commonly known) consists of two insulated metallic wires usually copper-wrapped around each other at the rate of so many twists per inch or per centimeter, or per other unit of measurement. In practice, nobody uses that primeval form of TP anymore, although you might find some still in use in older office buildings or homes, where it's commonly used for in-wall telephone wiring.

Today, the minimal twisted-pair cable will include two or three pairs of wires, along with its outer layer of insulation. A minimum of two pairs is required for a network connection, one for incoming, the other for outgoing network signals (three pairs with a single phone connection in the same bundle, which is why three-pair wiring is so popular; additional phone connections require additional pairs).

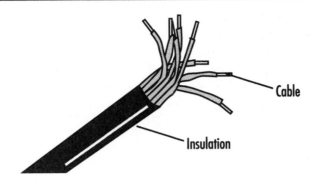

Cable

Insulation

**Figure 10.1** *Twisted-pair wiring.*

There are millions of miles (or kilometers) of twisted-pair wiring already strung in the world, primarily for premises' telephone wiring systems. Unless they're pretty new installations, very little of this existing TP cable is shielded. Unshielded TP (further abbreviated as UTP) is perfectly adequate for standard voice-grade telephone use, but it may not be adequate for networking use. It's important to distinguish shielded twisted-pair (abbreviated STP) from UTP, because it's a much more reliable medium for networking use, even if it is a bit more expensive than UTP.

Because there's so much of it out there in the world, and it's "free" to use existing cable for networks, the temptation will always present itself to build your network using untenanted telephone cable pairs. Under some circumstances, this can indeed be a tremendous money-saver, but under others, it can be a source for tremendous headaches. The reason why STP is preferable to UTP has to do with something called interference, which refers to the sometimes malign effects that running wires near a transformer, electric motor, or other sources of electromagnetic or radio-frequency energy, can have. In plain English, telephone cable installers don't have to worry much about interference, but network installers have to be very careful in avoiding it. Would you want to use cabling installed by people who didn't worry about interference when laying cable for *your* network? We didn't think so!

Dire warnings aside, though, TP in both its shielded and unshielded varieties, is the fastest-growing networking medium in use today. Because we have over a hundred years' experience in manufacturing, installing, and managing telephone wiring systems, the ability to leverage this expertise and the specialized equipment that's been developed for such systems is just too good to pass up. There are wiring systems built around TP for all of the major networking technologies available today, and those that become commercially successful in the future will also find a way to play the TP game as well. For medium- and large-sized networks TP is a very good choice to connect PCs to the overall network, but for small networks, it may be overkill.

Our only caveat on using existing telephone wiring for networking is to hire a professional cable installer to come in and thoroughly test the wires you plan to use, just to make sure they're suitable. You'll want to check cable lengths, signal quality, and look for potential sources of interference from the phone system and from other gizmos out there in your environment.

There's another thing to consider about TP wiring systems as well: They require the use of *wiring hubs* (sometimes called concentrators or wiring centers) to consolidate and maintain the signals that get shipped out over the many individual cable pairs that make up a TP network. While these hubs aren't prohibitively expensive, they're not free either, which is why TP is a better choice for networks of some size (typically, eight or more devices have to be networked to make TP a worthwhile choice) than it is for small-scale networks. On the plus side, TP uses standard telephone-style connectors, and offers support for lots of convenient modular wiring systems, so that hooking a computer up to the network usually involves nothing more complicated than attaching a wire to a wall plate and to a PC's NIC. No one in the networking business will argue that TP systems are attractive, because they're relatively inexpensive, easy to install and manage, and convenient for users and network administrators alike.

## Coaxial Cable

TP wiring acts like the wires we're accustomed to for household appliances, but coaxial is a completely different animal. It works more like a pipe than like a physical link, in that most of the frequencies that get used for coaxial signaling qualify as VHF (Very High Frequency) or UHF (Ultra-High Frequency). That is, the signals that run over the coaxial cable are "broadcast" by the center conductor, and enclosed by the outer conductive braid, so you should visualize the cable as a conduit for high-frequency electrical signals, when looking at Figure 10.2 below.

Your most likely encounter with coaxial cable is probably the cable you use to hook your television set to your cable company's wall jacks, or your TV set to your VCR. The coaxial cable used for network varies with the networking technology involved (and is different from that used for CATV transmission), but they all work pretty much the same way. The everyday name for coaxial cable is coax (pronounced "co-acks"). Following common practice, we'll use that term as well some of the time.

Coaxial cable is more expensive than twisted pair, not just because it costs more to make, but also because it's larger in diameter and therefore more difficult to install as well (the thicker a cable, the less bending it can take without damage).

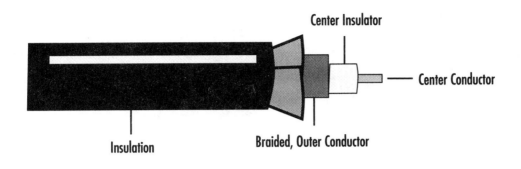

Center Insulator

Center Conductor

Insulation

Braided, Outer Conductor

**Figure 10.2** *Coaxial cable.*

Because of coaxial cable's composition, it also requires special tools to strip the ends, and to attach connectors to those bare ends.

Some kinds of coax cables even require special connectors to attach devices to them, called *taps*, because they provide a "plug-in" connection at some point along a coax cable's length. To add attachments to most types of coax, though, you'll have to cut the cable, attach connectors, and insert a drop cable for device attachment. Your network will be out of service anytime you have to cut the cable, so it's wise to plan this sort of thing for evenings or weekends, to minimize the disruption experienced by your users.

Because of its design, coaxial cable can carry signals for much longer distances than TP, and it's also less subject to interference, abbreviated as EMI for electromagnetic interference and as RFI for radio-frequency interference. However, it's still smart to use shielded coax in environments where interference can occur, simply because it can reduce potential problems. In cases where known sources of interference exist, it's wise to shield cable further by running it inside special metal pipes, called *electrical conduit*. Even though this costs more, it will save headaches in the long run.

## Fiber-Optic Cable

Fiber-optic cable is the current "king of the cables." It offers a transmission medium that is completely immune to EMI and RFI, and also spans the longest distances possible for a single cable segment available today. Given these sterling qualities, why would anybody use anything else? Sadly, the answer is "cost"!

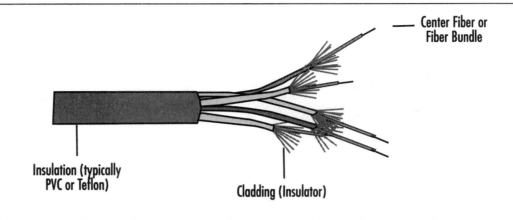

Center Fiber or
Fiber Bundle

Insulation (typically
PVC or Teflon)

Cladding (Insulator)

**Figure 10.3**  *Single- and multi-fiber fiber-optic cable.*

Even today, fiber-optic cable is at least twice as expensive as other kinds. This is not only because of the cost of the cable itself, which is higher than either coax or TP, but also because attaching connectors to fiber-optic cables has not yet been completely automated, and the ends of the conductors themselves must be hand-polished to a mirror finish before the connectors can be attached, as depicted in Figure 10.3. Labor costs for installing fiber-optic networks is where the real cost differential kicks in, partly because of the greater time it takes for installation, and partly because fiber cable installers are scarce and therefore more expensive.

Finally, fiber-optic cable is much more delicate than either TP or coax. Because the fibers are most often glass, exceeding bend radius specifications for the cable you're using will break the conductors and make the cable useless. Its ability to handle pull strain is also lower, making for shorter cable pull lengths and trickier handling when pulling fiber through conduit or threading it through your ceiling for in-building installation. If there's a single watchword for working with fiber-optic cable, it's "handle with care."

Even despite its cost and drawbacks, fiber is the emerging medium for the future, because it gives networks more room to grow in capacity and capability than either of the other two media. It's no accident that most of the regional and long-distance telephone companies are switching over from copper to fiber, and it won't be long before cable TV companies start following suit.

## Wireless Communications

Wireless communications rely on the use of some kind of broadcast technology or another. Because the FCC (and its international equivalents) has pretty much used

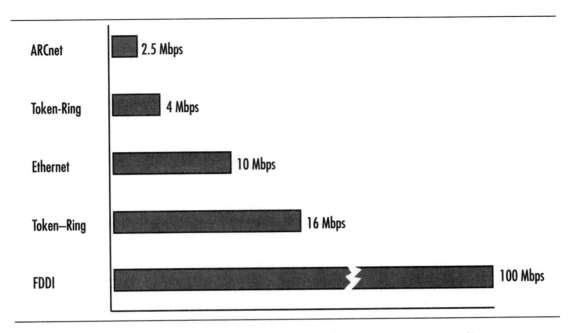

**Figure 10.4** *Bandwidth and distance capabilities of TP, coax, fiber-optic, and wireless media.*

up much of the frequency spectrum, wireless networking tends to rely on multiple-frequency technologies these days. These vary from cellular telephone frequencies, which are growing increasingly popular, to so-called spread-spectrum technologies, which fit networking signals across a broad range of broadcast frequencies.

Today, wireless networking is more of an expensive curiosity than anything else, but it promises to be a major growth area in the next century, as network connections become pervasive and mobile computing becomes the norm. Part of the explanation for this is depicted in Figure 10.4, which contrasts the maximum bandwidths (or signal-carrying capabilities) for the four types of media we've discussed here, along with the distances that each can typically cover. For fiber-optic technologies, its future appeal is in its broad capacity; for wireless technologies, the appeal is in long distances. Both of these are expected to loom large on the wish lists of future generations of networkers.

## PROS, CONS, AND COSTS

When it comes to picking the networking medium that's right for your needs, you'll want to carefully weigh each one's pros, cons, and costs. Table 10.1 covers these items for each of the media we've mentioned.

**Table 10.1.** *Pros, Cons, and Costs for Networking Media.*

| Medium | Pros | Cons | Costs |
|---|---|---|---|
| Twisted-pair | Cheap, easy, convenient; re-use phone wiring; modular standard connectors and tools; add/remove devices at will | Interference; reliability; bandwidth; phone system conflict/overlap | Low |
| Coaxial cable | Medium bandwidth; Special connectors and tools; medium reliability | Less flexible; bulky cables; network down to add/remove; limited devices per segment | Medium |
| Fiber-optic cable | High bandwidth; special connectors and tools; high reliability, security | Labor-intensive connectors; network down to add/remove; delicate cable; tricky installation | High |
| Wireless | Medium bandwidth; convenient, mobile; increased network uses | Third-party carriers involved; costly services; special hardware; highly proprietary; fragmented | High |

For most network installations, your first question should be, "Why shouldn't we use TP wiring of some kind?" Unless you can come up with compelling reasons why not, it's the clear choice. The main reasons companies use coax today is to maintain compatibility with cabling already in place. If you have to pick an alternative to TP, fiber-optic is probably the best choice, because it will give you the most room to grow in the future. Only small networks of less than eight users, or networks that must operate in noisy environments (like a factory floor), will typically have legitimate reasons to use coax for new installations today.

## SAY HELLO TO MR. TELEPHONE!

If you do follow our advice regarding twisted-pair wiring, we'd like to predict there's a telephone in your future. At least, we'd like to predict that you'll have to work with the folks who manage your telephone system and wiring, in order to participate in their bounty and to use their wiring systems. Covering the details of telephone systems is beyond the scope of this book, but we recommend that you find out more about how the telephone wiring system in your building works, especially if you want to investigate the use of telephone wiring that may already be installed.

What you'll need to do to establish a good working relationship is to identify the phone system gurus in your midst. Then, politely ask them for information, and be prepared to be humble when asking for help. Get your telephone experts to walk you around and show you what's out there, and try to learn some of the special terminology typical of phone systems.

As a computer aficionado, you may be surprised to learn that phone systems engineers have been doing some pretty high-tech stuff for about four times as long as computers have been around! If you're prepared to learn some new concepts and master some new technologies, you should be able to figure things out, but be aware that you're working with somebody else's systems and that cooperation and communication will be required in order to build a network around those systems.

## KNOW YOUR LIMITATIONS

Each type of networking technology confers maximum cable length restrictions on the pieces of cable you can use in your network. That is, Ethernet's maximum cable distance for one type of coax may be 180 meters (about 580 feet), whereas ARCnet's equivalent distance for another type of coax may be as great as 6000 meters (about 20,000 feet). Typically, this information will be documented in the materials furnished with your network interfaces, or with the hubs or other networking devices associated with your technology. Likewise, there's usually a limit on the number of devices that can be attached to a particular cable segment (this applies only to coax and fiber-optic; the number of available connections is much more obvious for TP and wireless technologies).

Unfortunately, there are too many kinds of cable and technology combinations for us to document all of these limitations here, but we wanted to warn you that this kind of information is crucial to research before installing a network, or when taking one over for the first time. Unlike speed limits, where penalties are incurred only when you get caught, distance and connection limits are more absolute and will bite you whether you expect them to or not. Because exceeding length and connection limits can manifest themselves in a variety of bizarre and subtle ways, we recommend you opt for prevention rather than cure. Know your limits, and stay inside them!

## MIXING AND MATCHING IS OKAY

Very few networks, other than small ones, actually consist of only one kind of networking medium. Most medium- to large-sized installations try to use their diverse sets of properties to their best advantage, mixing and matching media to better meet their needs.

In fact, most networking hubs for TP come with extra ports for various flavors of coaxial or fiber-optic cable, to permit hubs to be widely separated but still hooked together to form a single network. Even the TP manufacturers, who might be considered to be the most ardent supporters of TP, recognize that TP works best as a distribution medium, to bring the benefits of networking to desktops everywhere. In order to link hubs together, however, media like coax and fiber-optic, which support cable runs that can be orders of magnitude longer than the maximum for twisted-pair, are clearly preferable.

Special circumstances also dictate media choices. In many multi-story buildings, the elevator shaft provides an easy vertical access path for running cable from floor to floor. However, elevators use large, powerful motors to winch themselves up and down their pathways. These motors are dandy sources of interference, and elevator shafts can be hundreds (or thousands) of feet long—both factors argue for some medium other than TP if the shaft is to provide a vertical connection among a building's floors. Fiber is the medium of choice—it's immune to interference and can handle the distance. This is a case where mixing and matching isn't just *possible*; it's absolutely *required*.

Many networks are built around a *backbone*, which is a central length of cable that ties multiple cable segments together. While it's common for the outer segments of such networks to use TP or coax to get to the desktop, it's equally common for the backbone itself to be a high-bandwidth, long-distance fiber-optic cable. This is the method of choice for multiple-building campuses, where fiber-optic also eliminates possible problems from differences in ground potential that can be passed by running a conductor between one building and another.

## SUMMARY

In this chapter you've read about the media that make networking possible. You've seen twisted-pair, coaxial cable, and fiber-optic from the inside out, and should have a better idea of what wireless networking can mean to you. You've also been equipped to understand what these choices can cost you and to watch out for their individual limitations. Last, you've learned that combining multiple types of media is often exactly what's needed to match your network to your needs, or at least to your installation environment.

# FURTHER READING

Each of the major cable manufacturers offers cable catalogs to its dealers and suppliers. Ultimately, the exact type and electrical specifications of the cable you've got in your hands is going to determine what it can and can't do. Therefore, we recommend you contact Belden, Allied, or whichever company may have manufactured your cable, and see about getting a catalog. You're bound to find lots of interesting stuff in these catalogs. A list of the major cable manufacturers is included below, to help you get started on your quest for information.

## Cable Manufacturers

Amphenol (a division of Allied Signal): cables, connectors, tools
1925 A Ohio Street
Lisle, IL 60565
708-819-5640

Belden Wire & Cable, a division of Cooper Industries: networking cable of all kinds
P.O. Box 1980-T
Richmond, IN 47375
800-235-3364; Fax: 317-983-5294

## Other Useful References

Mark A. Miller, *LAN Troubleshooting Handbook*, M&T Publishing, 1989 ($29.95), Redwood City, CA.

This book is full of useful details on networking and includes some of the best coverage of cable details we've encountered anywhere.

# 11

# WRESTLING WITH WIRING

The cables that make networks work are absolutely essential to its proper operation. If you decide to be a total do-it-yourself networker, chances are 100 percent that this means you'll be working with wiring, a.k.a. metallic cables. Why? Because the only other option is fiber-optic cable, and doing fiber-optic for yourself is too difficult (it takes considerable training and practice) and expensive (it takes expensive test equipment and tools) to be worth doing yourself. Of course, we will excuse those who have been trained and have the equipment from this assessment, but that can't be more than .001 percent of the population!

This chapter is devoted to explaining what's involved in doing wiring systems for yourself. We'll cover the tool and techniques you'll need to build your own cables, and some tips guaranteed to make crawling in the ceiling a little more tolerable!

Before we launch into our version of the Cable Follies, here's a warning you should chew on most carefully before walking any further down the do-it-yourself networking road: If you do build your own cables and something should go wrong, you'll have no one to blame but yourself! This might not sound too forbidding but it means that you'll be responsible if anything ever goes wrong. In other words, building your own network cabling means always being on call when the wiring gets weird. . . .

# Pre-Fabricated versus Rolling Your Own

As we said in the last chapter, wiring comes in many shapes and sizes and is offered in a bewildering array of coatings, claddings, and types. If you're thinking about building your own cables, here are a few points to consider when making a build-versus-buy decision:

- **Quantity:** The number of cables you will need is an important factor when deciding whether or not to make your own. The lower the overall number, the harder it's going to be to trade the cost of cable tools and raw materials against the cost of pre-fabricated cables, which are available for all the of the commonly used cable types (twisted-pair with RJ-45 phone connectors, and coax in a variety of styles and sizes for Ethernet, token ring, ARCnet, and other technologies). For small, one-room networks, pre-fab is the only way to go!

- **Aptitude**: If you're pretty much of a handy person and not afraid to get down and dirty with construction projects at home or on the job, building cables requires no special skills or training (but practice is a significant factor in becoming proficient). The less handy you are, the less you should be inclined to try building your own network cable. A good test of aptitude is being able to answer "yes" to the question: "Can you see yourself crawling around in the ceiling slinging wires for your network, covered in dust and grime, over the weekend or late at night?"

- **Time versus budget:** If you've got more time than money, building your own cables is worth doing, providing you can get past the first two factors we've already mentioned. If you've got more money than time, don't even *think* about trying to be a do-it-yourself network cable installer. Free time—or a willingness to sacrifice personal time—is a must for the would-be installer.

- **Cost**: With your network map in hand, you should be able to calculate the lengths of cable you'll need to hook up your network. Don't forget to build in at least 20% overage to cover for undocumented risers, cable trays, corners, and other unforeseen obstacles. Compare the cost of pre-fabricated cables to the cost of materials (cable and connectors) and prorate the cost of your tools over the total number of cables you think you'll need over the next year or so. If the pre-fab cables are cheaper, don't be tempted to build your own anyway. Do the right thing, and use the time you'll save to do other things for your network!

In case we haven't been sufficiently clear, rolling your own is primarily for diehard do-it-yourselfers, or for those whose budgets are so tight that doing it themselves is the only way to get a network up and running—and they'll probably figure out a way to borrow rather than buy the necessary tools and will scrounge as many materials as they possibly can!

## MODULAR CONNECTORS AND WALL PLATES

If you're going to install your own network, it's important to do it right! We therefore strongly recommend that you use standard modular connectors with your wiring, and that you plan on dropping your network cabling to wall plates for hooking up computers and other equipment to the network. What does this mean in English?

Standard modular connectors are the ones that work with your particular network technology. For example, you'll use an RJ-45 connector with most types of shielded and unshielded twisted-pair cable, and a BNC connector with thinwire Ethernet (a.k.a., 10Base2). With most widely used networking technologies, you won't have much choice regarding connectors, but if you do, you'll be best off selecting the most widely used type of connector available. When buying the actual connector parts themselves, we recommend spending the extra money to buy a top-of-the-line connector, such as those supplied by companies like Amphenol or Concord Electronics Corporation.

When it comes to attaching connectors to coaxial cables, we also recommend using the crimp-on type. Even though solder-on and screw-on connectors are also available for most coax types, solder-on is too labor-intensive (not to mention inconvenient when you are crouched in a ceiling somewhere) and screw-on is too unreliable (what screws on, alas, also screws off) to be worthwhile. We'll talk about

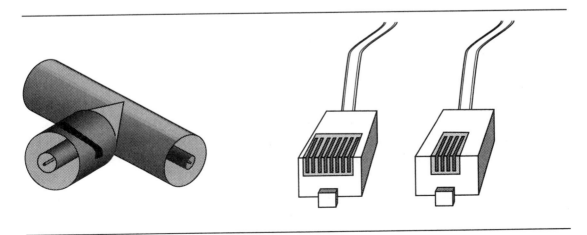

**Figure 11.1** *Some typical modular connectors.*

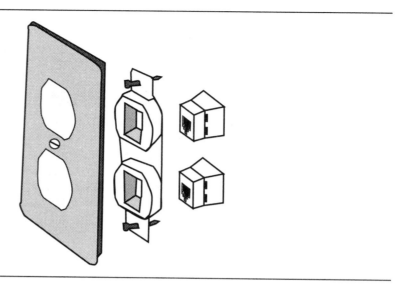

**Figure 11.2**  *A typical network wall plate assembly.*

the importance of a quality crimping tool in the next section. Figure 11.1 shows some typical modular connectors you're likely to encounter. Expect to pay (in U.S. dollars) $0.50–$4.00 each for modular phone-type connectors, and between $3.00–$7.00 each for coax connectors (and don't forget to buy enough terminators for your coax cables, either!).

Modular wall plates make attaching PCs to your network in an office environment simple and neat. Simply put, a modular wall plate supplies a network connection through the wall from a standard AC-style receptacle through a plate that looks very much like a normal light switch or power outlet wall plate, as depicted in Figure 11.2. The assembly includes more than just a wall plate, however; it also includes a face plate, and modular plug-ins for matching RJ-45 jacks. Expect to pay about $8.00 for each network connection that a wall plate supplies. For new offices, we recommend investigating wall plates that can deliver AC, telephone, and network connections through the same wall plate (this helps keep installation costs down).

## GET THE RIGHT TOOLS FOR THE JOB!

If you follow our earlier advice and eschew solder-on and screw-on connectors in favor of the crimp-on varieties, it's essential to obtain proper tools to build cables. A pair of instruments is commonly needed to build cables with crimp-on connectors: a cable stripper, which peels off insulation in just the right way to accommodate the

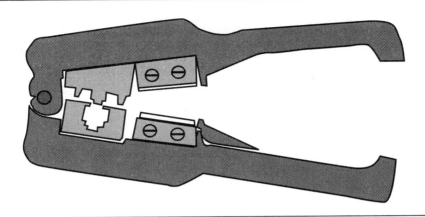

**Figure 11.3**  *A die-based crimping tool.*

connectors you'll use, and a crimping tool, which squashes the barrel of the connector in a precise way that ensures a good connection without damaging the cable.

When it comes to crimping tools, it's important to purchase those that use a "precision die" to do their squashing work. There are two ways to recognize a die-based crimper: First, when it identifies itself as such, and second, by its requirement for a die to be inserted for the cable and connector type you're using. A crimping tool's price is also a pretty good indicator: If it's under $100 (U.S.) it's probably not a die-based tool. We strongly advise you spend the extra money for a die-based crimping tool, like those manufactured by AMP or Shattuck Industries (these companies make excellent stripping tools as well). Figure 11.3 shows what a die-based crimping tool typically looks like (the size and shape of the die will vary depending on the type of cable and connector in use).

## THE BENEFITS OF MEASUREMENT

As you build and install your cables, it's important to keep tabs on how each cable segment winds up. If you're using pre-fab cables, or if you are building cables in a place that gives you room for easy measurement, so much the better. Our tip is to label each cable with some kind of unique name (like C001 or C2F301 for second Floor, Office 301) and to record the length with each name in some good place, like your network map!

If you have to make cables on the fly or are converting telephone cables over to network use, you'll want to rent a measurement device called a Time-Domain

Reflectometer (TDR) to measure the cables in your network. It acts like a kind of radar gun by sending out a signal pulse and measuring the time delay between when it sends and when the signal comes back after being reflected from the other end of the cable. The TDR is usually accurate to less than 0.1 cm, which makes it typically more precise than a tape measure would be. For existing networks or telephone conversions, it's an absolute must; for other networks, it's just incredibly convenient (expect to spend upwards of $200 (U.S.) per day's rental for a TDR).

Whatever you do, always label your cables and record each one's length!

## TESTING YOUR WIRING PLANT

As you're installing cables, it's standard operating procedure to test each one as it's completed. Here again, you can spend conservatively or resort to more expensive equipment. For metallic cables, you can use a volt-ohmmeter (VOM) to check conductivity and resistance, or you can rent or purchase cable test equipment that can check conductivity, resistance, and even make sure that the cable behaves to specification under a simulated network load. When we install cables, we use a VOM on the fly to check each cable as it's put in place; then, after we're through with basic cabling, we rent a cable tester and re-test each cable just to make doubly sure that everything works properly. We recommend that you adopt a similar approach.

Cable testers come in all sizes and shapes. Twisted-pair testers can typically be purchased for under $300 (U.S.), but coax and fiber-optic testers can cost many times that amount. For TP, therefore, purchasing a cable tester is more of an option. For other cables, we recommend that you find a rental source nearby. Or, you could hire a cable contractor to do your testing work for you—this will often cost the same, or only a little more than an equipment rental, and it lets you talk your installation over with a real, live professional to boot!

## KEEPING UP WITH THE TIMES

We've already preached the benefits of creating and maintaining an accurate, up-to-date network map. This is just another reminder that you should take care to record your cable labels and each cable's length (as measured) on the map as you're going through the installation process. Ignore this advice at your own risk!

# Summary

In this chapter, you've learned about what's required to be a do-it-yourself networker. We think this is a topic that has limited appeal, but we hope it tells you what you need to know to decide if rolling your own network is the right thing to do. Therefore, we've covered how to make the build-versus-buy decision, what kinds of connections need to be considered, the benefits of proper tools and rigorous testing during the installation process, and the need to fully document whatever work actually gets done. Even if you never lift a finger to install your network, all of these things are worth knowing, if only to make you a qualified superintendent of somebody else's work!

# Further Reading

Many vendors will be happy to send you test equipment or tool catalogs. For networking, two of the best we've found are Jensen Tools, Inc.'s *Master Catalog*, and Black Box Corporation's connectivity catalogs. As their names might indicate, Jensen is strong on test equipment and installation tools, while Black Box is strong on materials as well as test equipment and installation tools (Black Box even offers network consultation services for individuals in need of design or equipment selection assistance).

Jensen Tools, Inc. *1993–1994 Master Catalog*, 1993.

Jensen is located at 7815 South 46th Street, Phoenix, AZ, 85044-5399, and its toll-free fax number is 800-366-9662 (inside the United States, please call 602-968-6231 with questions; outside the United States, the number is 602-968-6241, extensions 316 or 347; the international fax number is 602-438-1690). If you write or fax, Jensen will send you a catalog and add you to its mailing list.

Black Box Corporation, *The Black Box Catalog*, March 1994.

Black Box is located at P.O. Box 12800, Pittsburgh, PA, 15241, and can be reached at 412-746-5500 for orders, subscriptions, faxback, or technical support. It also operates an electronic bulletin board, which can be reached at 412-746-7120.

# SITUATING NETWORK EQUIPMENT

# 12

Once you've conquered the cabling, it's time to start hooking things up. At this point, you should be ready to start installing networking equipment of all kinds so that the users can actually do something! Of course, you'll want to plan ahead where placement is concerned, because it's nice to have the cables end where you want your equipment to be.

Of all the equipment you'll start putting in place, the most important elements should include some or all of the following items:

- **Servers**, which provide shared computing resources like networked file systems, print services, database services, and the like
- **Hubs**, which act as central switchboards for individual networks, especially for networks that run on twisted-pair media
- **Shared peripherals**—primarily printers—which make themselves available to users over the network; other than printers, shared peripherals can include scanners, networked fax machines, and a wide variety of other devices
- **Network equipment**, which can include devices like repeaters that permit longer-than-allowed cable runs to be used, and routers, which direct traffic among local cable segments (and even across wide-area links, to tie remote networks together)

No matter what type of gear you're hooking up to the network, placement is always strategic: In some cases, the strategy is dictated by being where the wires are (as is the case for hubs and other network equipment), in others, by trading off security and control against convenience.

# THE THREE SECRETS:
# LOCATION, LOCATION, LOCATION!

Just as in the restaurant business, successful networking depends on judicious choices of location, especially for shared peripherals. Even for equipment that your users may never know exists—for example, a router that ties your local twisted-pair hubs together and links them to a fiber-optic backbone—where and how that piece of equipment is situated can mean the difference between a busy, working network and an idle, non-functioning one.

The first secret of equipment location is access. If it's a shared peripheral, the equipment has to be in a fairly public place, available to all of its intended users. Whether it's a peripheral, networking gear, or a server of some kind, the equipment has to be relatively secure, but accessible from the standpoint of letting you, or a service technician, get access to the hardware itself and to the all-important cables that hook it up to the network to do its thing. This means leaving enough room to maneuver around and with the equipment in the event that cables or the equipment itself have to be swapped out or moved (this also gives the added benefit of ensuring sufficient space for air to circulate).

The second secret of equipment location is convenience. If it's a shared peripheral, the smoking room at the other end of the building is not going to be an ideal place for your users to traipse toward to pick up printouts, faxes, or other output. Whether it's a peripheral, networking gear, or a server of some kind, the equipment also has to be close enough to its intended application to be workable.

For shared peripherals, this means no more than a one- or two-minute stroll away from its users' desks. For other types of equipment, this means relatively convenient for you and any other network administrators to get at, and also, conveniently situated for the equipment to do its intended job. In other words, hubs typically reside where the network cabling comes together, be that in a telephone wiring closet, or in a specially constructed wiring center. Similarly, servers need to be placed where you can get to them easily, whether it's to back them up, service them, or simply to start them back up after a power interruption. Likewise, routers have to be where the networking media they route come together.

The third secret of equipment location is workability. There's no point in putting any kind of equipment in the lobby, or any other common area where anybody can walk up and make off with your stuff. Even if you have to convert a broom closet, it's better to put your gear where only co-workers can get at it, rather than leaving it completely unprotected. It's also important to make sure that the resources your equipment needs can be adequately met wherever you decide to put that gear: These necessities include adequate AC power, sufficient heating and cooling, and enough space to set things up properly (even if this means putting in equipment racks to stack things up where you otherwise wouldn't have room).

# PRACTICAL RULES FOR SECURITY AND ACCESSIBILITY

In most office environments, there's a trade-off between security and accessibility. The more secure your equipment, the less accessible it will be, and vice-versa. If equipment needs to be shared, it can't be made completely secure. For this type of gear, we recommend one of two approaches:

1. Put the equipment near someone who can act as a part-time watchdog, who can keep an eye on what's going on. It's not a bad idea to train this person on replacing ribbons or toner cartridges, adding paper or other consumables, and the like—we're betting that in most cases, the shared device will be a printer or fax machine. Placement should be close enough for watching, but not so close as to prevent that person from being able to get on with their other duties.
2. Put the equipment in a dedicated public-access room, where other shared devices might already be located. At our companies, we're used to picking up printouts from the same rooms where our copiers and fax machines also reside. If these rooms are close to a trained key operator or someone else who's knowledgeable about the gear, you can adhere to the above approach as well.

Equipment that doesn't need to be shared should be secured within reason— remember, you might have to tell somebody else how to get to it when you're home with the flu, and you won't want to have to share your personal dossier or a retinal photograph with that person just to let them do you a favor! If you opt for the locked-room approach, make sure extra keys are stored in a safe place (with your security guard, HR manager, or someone similar). If you secure equipment with passwords, make sure those passwords are also recorded in a safe place as well (the same people will gladly keep a sealed envelope for you, and you can trust them not to look inside, or you can build yourself an emergency kit in a file cabinet that nobody will be able to find without your instructions as to how).

The important thing is to remember the secret of accessibility and honor that need as best you can.

# LOCKED UP, OR OUT IN THE OPEN?

In general, the more valuable something is, the more important it is to keep it locked up. On the other hand, the tighter the lock, the more likely it is that the need will come up to have it broken in case of some emergency. We strongly recommend that all equipment that doesn't have to be publicly accessible be discreetly stored, if not locked up outright.

As more and more organizations come to depend on their networks, their vulnerability to theft and accidents rises. Therefore, taking precautions to prevent such problems can be beneficial, but only if those precautions don't cause more problems than they solve in the event of an anomaly.

Whatever approach you take, be it open or locked, it's a very good idea to simulate problems with your network to see what happens when things go wrong. You want to make sure that you've trained your co-workers and staff well enough to know how to respond to problems, even if it's only to page you on the public address system to let you know that the network's not right. We recommend taking this one step further and training interested users (and there's no group more interested than the ones who have to have the equipment working in order to do their jobs) in responding to the most common types of problems. That way, when you're in Aruba relaxing on the beach, you'll be able to leave your beeper back at the office, where it really belongs!

## Perfect Printer Placement

Any piece of equipment that need supplies, like a printer, fax machine, or copier, has additional requirements over and above the big three of access, convenience, and workability. This kind of gear also needs additional storage space for consumable, including paper, toner, and possibly even spare parts. Its users also need information to be posted when the equipment malfunctions, or when they just can't figure out how to clear that paper jam in the sheet feeder or the collating bins.

The issue of what to do with output also needs to be addressed. Providing enough space for a set of mailboxes to stash printouts or faxes is a good idea, but it's often sufficient to set up a rack with slots labeled for each day of the week. That way, Joe from Accounting knows to look either in his mailbox or in the slot marked "Tuesday" if he wants to cruise by and pick up the print job he fired off on his way out the door last night, or to pick up the fax from Australia that arrived around midnight.

The moral of the story is: In addition to leaving enough room for storage of consumable and for giving the equipment room to be worked on, it's equally important to set up working room for that equipment's users, and to set up a storage system for materials that may have been consumed by the equipment, but not yet picked up by its intended recipients.

# SUPER SERVER SITUATIONS

Situating servers means setting up spaces where a computer, monitor, and keyboard can be set up, with enough space left over for external disk drives, tape drives, and other gear that might be necessary for your particular server's configuration. By the time the number of outlets and the amount of heat that the total collection of gear this can represent get taken care of, it may be obvious that a broom closet is not an ideal place to set up your servers. Make sure you've got enough electricity to do the job—plan for 20–30% more wattage and amperage than you currently need to leave room to grow—and that there's sufficient air conditioning to handle the heat that your equipment can generate.

Because continued server operation is highly desirable, we also recommend taking some extraordinary steps with the electrical power for servers. For one thing, it's a good idea to set up separate circuits for your servers, so that they don't have to contend with sags or surges that other equipment on the same circuit can cause. We've seen terrible things happen with cleaning equipment, like floor buffers, so make sure your cleaning staff knows better than to plug into the server room's outlets (or worse still, to unplug a server to plug something else in).

We further recommend investigating the purchase of an uninterruptible power supply (UPS) for all critical network equipment. A UPS can perform two important functions:

1. *Power filtering*, to supply clean alternating current to your servers, even if the local utility company experiences sags (power reductions) or surges (excess power). Most UPSs will also sacrifice themselves to lightning, rather than letting your equipment get fried (spike arrestors).
2. *Supplemental power*, typically from batteries, will supply enough power to your servers to permit a graceful shutdown in the event of an outright power failure. This is particularly important for database servers, where lots of files might be open and potentially damaged if the server just abruptly quit in the middle of operation.

When purchasing a UPS, you'll buy one that's rated to supply a certain wattage. You can calculate your wattage needs by adding up the rated power consumption for each separate plug-in device on your server (for simple servers, this would be about 400 watts for the server itself, and another 100 watts or so for the display). Expect to spend one to two dollars per watt, depending on the capabilities of the UPS involved. The more expensive the UPS, the better its power-handling characteristics and the more sophisticated its response to power outages will be.

Our last bit of server placement advice is to put them in an environment where you won't be afraid to spend some serious time. While it may be tempting to put a hub card into a server, and therefore put the server into a phone closet, think about what that means in terms of installing a new network operating system, or rebuilding the file system from a backup in the event of a crash. If you can't live there, don't make your server live there, either!

## Happy Hub Housing

Because hubs need to be where the wiring is, the temptation is nearly overwhelming to put them into the phone closet. That's just fine, but you'll want to make sure that there's enough electrical power and air conditioning available to keep the hubs working happily. For older buildings or installations, this can be a problem—phone wires don't need ventilation or electricity, and many existing phone closets offer little or nothing of either. Many of those for whom the costs of relocating a wiring center seem initially prohibitive find that the costs of bringing in electrical outlets and air conditioning aren't cheap either.

Whatever you decide to do, make sure you're not tempting fate by ignoring the need for clean, safe power and proper ventilation. Because a hub without power is a dead hub, we also think that UPSs for hubs are a good idea, too. Even though a UPS adds to the air conditioning load in any space, it adds something even more important—peace of mind!

## Summary

In this chapter you've learned the basics of positioning your networking gear. While access, convenience, and workability are important, don't forget that the network is an asset that has to be protected, and that a dead network is everyone's problem. Try to take adequate steps to keep things in the right hands and to keep things working.

# PLANNING FOR INSTALLATION

# 13

When you've decided what to install where, it's time to get ready to put your plans to work. In this chapter, we cover the preparations for installing your first network. Even if you've already set up your network these topics apply equally well to extending a network, or to changing out equipment, cabling, or other components.

Because you're now equipped to deal with the wiring (covered in Chapters 10 and 11), and know how to situate your equipment (covered in Chapter 12), this chapter will concentrate on the other factors that have to be considered when installing, extending, or changing a network. "Other factors," you ask? Yes, there are other factors indeed, all of which arise from your need to deliver a working network to your colleagues and co-workers. Some of these include:

- planning the order of installation and the steps to hook up people to the network
- observing the daily routine in your workplace to help figure out how to minimize the havoc that installation can wreak
- considering the advantages and disadvantages of three-day weekends
- pre-testing to make sure all the parts are working properly
- arranging a fallback position should the network fail to come together
- locating help before the inevitable crisis comes
- being ready for things to go wrong

No matter how small or simple the network to be installed might be, the chances of hitting a snag en route to network nirvana are better than 50 percent, especially for first-timers and other neophytes. Even the pros take care to work out a plan, simply because it gives them the opportunity to think things through before they have to get creative with the wiring and excited about the equipment. A plan is your road map through the installation process—if you're going to venture into unknown territory, a map is always a good thing!

## Careful Staging Leads to Good Production

A well-run network is a lot like a Broadway play or an amusement park. The users, like theatergoers or park visitors, only notice the play, or the rides and other entertainment; they seldom look closely enough to see all the behind-the-scenes effort that makes things happen so smoothly.

*Staging* is the process of figuring out what things need to happen to bring off a production, and then establishing the order in which those things must occur to achieve the desired results. It's just as important a process for installing a network as it is for any other complicated set of actions that are supposed to be unnoticed by an audience. As you get more familiar with networking, you'll become keenly aware of how desirable being unnoticed is; for now, just take our word that a lack of notoriety is the best thing a network administrator can hope for!

The similarity between delivering a network to your users and staging a play persists nicely, all the way through the process of getting ready for opening night (or day, as the case may be): The play must be chosen, the cast and crew recruited and trained, the sets constructed, and the production rehearsed before the audience ever gets a chance to see what's going on. In the same way, the network cabling has to be laid out on paper, and the equipment and connections positioned on your network map, well before anybody starts climbing around in your ceiling or hacking (small) holes in your walls.

The normal order of execution for installing a network works something like this:

- The whole network is laid out on paper, including cabling, network equipment, connections, and whatever else is needed to put it all together.
- Building plans, electrical plans, and other wiring plans (e.g., telephone system wiring) are consulted to check the planned layout.
- An inspection tour takes place to examine potential problem areas (elevator shaft access, fire wall penetration, potential interference sources, etc.).
- The network layout is revised to reflect what's been learned on the inspection tour (count your blessings if you don't have to revise anything).

- Wire run lengths are calculated, and overall wiring requirements are determined, including the type of cable, ensuring that applicable building codes are met, and the number of spools or length of cable are determined; connector needs must also be established: how many, what kind, and type of tools required.
- Equipment needs are specified, including networking equipment such as hubs or routers, and network servers are configured on paper.
- A bid, or request for proposal (RFP), is drafted. This document specifies what materials, equipment, and connectors you need, as precisely as possible; this kind of document can also request separate pricing for getting the installation done professionally—we recommend finding this out, even if you're a do-it-yourselfer, if only to find out what your time might be worth!
- Do-it-yourselfers will also need to order any special cable construction tools and arrange to rent or purchase appropriate test equipment for their wiring plant.
- Bids or RFP responses are evaluated, and one or more vendors is chosen to supply materials and/or perform the installation.
- Do-it-yourselfers must determine the order of installation for cabling and equipment, as well as establish the labeling convention (and purchase appropriate labels or tags) for their wiring.
- Wiring or cables are installed, labeled, tested, and measured (update your network map).
- Equipment is installed and tested (be sure to update your network map).
- The network is tested. This is also the point at which networking software would be installed and tested as well; up to now, things have been tested individually to make sure each component is working. (Here again, be sure to update your network map.)
- The network is advertised to users, and training commences.
- The network begins to receive everyday use.

As you can see, there's a lot of up-front work to do before anything resembling a network becomes available. For all intents and purposes, an installation plan is nothing more than a formal document that covers the steps we've just outlined, with all the essential details filled in. Our experience shows that the better the plan, the more positive the installation experience. We think that's what the common wisdom about prevention versus cure means, when applied to network installation!

## WORKING AROUND THE ROUTINE

Even the best-laid network plan will get you in trouble unless you recognize the need to work around your prospective users during the installation process. You'll endear yourself to no one if you're crawling around in the ceiling over their desks, while they're on the telephone, or otherwise engaged about their business. This introduces a sad fact about a network administrator's life: Because your job is to help other people do their jobs, you will often have to work when the other people aren't working, but you'll always have to be available when they are working, in case anything should go wrong!

The best way to work around your colleagues and co-workers is literally to work around their schedules. This means that the more disruptive your activity, the more imperative it is to conduct that activity during non-prime time. Schedule your ceiling spelunking for evenings or weekends, and you'll stay out of harm's way. If you're using a professional installation crew, this will mean paying overtime and often pleading for special treatment. If you can't afford the overtime, or the vendor won't oblige your need to keep them out of your co-workers' hair, schedule installation around a company holiday, an off-site meeting, or during a slow time of year (like the Christmas holiday season) to minimize the potential impact on the everyday work routine.

A bad experience during the installation process can sour potential users on the network before they ever have grounds for a real complaint. So schedule around the routine to keep your future (or current) users as blissfully oblivious to the hard work that's going on as you can, and everybody will be much happier and more open minded about the network! This rule also applies to any kind of network extension, enhancement, or change as well.

## GET A BACKUP FOR YOUR BACKUP

No matter how good your planning, how thorough and painstaking your installation, and how precise your evaluation of the needs of your future network are, it's always possible that you might hit a snag during the installation process. A measurement might have been faulty, an unforeseen obstacle encountered, or some of your materials unsatisfactory—it's always hard to say where and how difficulties can crop up. The only certain thing is that planning for trouble beats being caught by surprise nearly every time.

How does this apply to a network installation? In several ways:

- Order at least 20 percent extra materials for your network, just in case something isn't quite right or to compensate for minor mistakes in your estimates or installation (the latter is especially likely if you're building your own cables).
- Make sure your materials supplier has more stock on hand, or can obtain additional stock on 24 hours' notice (this will cover you should serious materials defects be discovered, or should your estimates turn out to be significantly short).

- Test all equipment as it's unpacked from the box. If a piece of equipment doesn't appear to be working, don't try to use it on your network; call the vendor and arrange for a replacement. If you have to return equipment by mail or shipping service, ask the vendor for a return merchandise authorization number or code, and also ask the vendor to "cross-ship" the replacement to you (this means replacement right away, rather than waiting for the defective unit to be returned first). Another alternative is to purchase spares, or to ask your vendor to have spares on hand in case any problems should show up.
- Set up a small-scale test installation of the network in a single room, to test the network software for servers and client machines. You'll want to build short cables (all the equipment can frequently fit on a single table for this kind of test) and put everything together to make sure you have all the pieces and knowledge needed to put the network together from a software perspective.
- Build an "installation cookbook" as you work with your cables, equipment, and the software installation. That way, you'll have access to all the details you'll learn and be able to avoid relearning bits of trivia with each repeated installation.

Once again, the basic idea is to expect shortages, failures, and missing pieces to crop up during the installation. If you're prepared for this, you'll be ready to deal with problems as they appear. Preparation will help to keep your blood pressure under control, too!

## Keep an Expert on Tap

Sometimes things will get really weird. That's when it's time to call on a real professional. If you're bound and determined to be a do-it-yourself cabler, do yourself the favor of locating a cable installer in the yellow pages before you get started. Call them up and find out their hours and how to reach a technician in an emergency. Then, if things get completely out of control, you'll know that help is just a phone call away.

The same thing is true for network equipment and software installation. Whether it's through a local networking user group, from a networking reseller, or a consultant who specializes in networking, make some contacts with experienced networkers in your community. You can often get free advice before you get started, no matter who you're working with. In fact, we think it's worth paying a consultant to look over your network installation plan and your network map before you start doing any installation yourself, just to make sure you have covered all the bases. The same expert who bails you out of a jam will typically charge a lot less to steer you clear of it instead!

Whatever you do, make sure you have the names and numbers of your safety-net people in an easy-to-find location before you start down the installation road.

## Summary

In this chapter we've tried to stress the benefits of prevention over cure and to emphasize the importance of planning your network installation in advance. The more you know about what needs to be done, and the problems you might face while doing it, the better prepared you'll be for a successful network installation!

# LIVING THROUGH INSTALLATION

## 14

With a firm understanding of networks, and a detailed plan for how to install or upgrade your particular network, you should be ready to knock it out with no effort, right? Just roll up your sleeves and do it.

Wrong! There's an Irish gentleman named Murphy—the putative creator of Murphy's Law, succinctly stated as: "What can go wrong, will"—who's never missed a network installation. No matter how good your plans, your preparations, or your intentions, don't be surprised when Murphy drops by just to make life more interesting.

We entitled this chapter "Living through Installation" because we're sure you'll have at least one opportunity to ask yourself if you really will do just that while you're working your way through the process. Take heart from prior experience: Everybody has asked that question, and most (if not all) of the questioners have lived to recount their missteps and tales of woe. What we'll try to do in this chapter is to steer you away from some of the well-known potholes and documented dilemmas you're likely to encounter, as we recommend some techniques to keep Murphy at bay.

To forestall such a visit, we recommend that you take your time when installing and that you continually check your work as you go. Follow your installation plan, and you'll at least be pointed in the right direction. We'll give you some rules of thumb to help you decide when you've gotten in too deep and need to regroup and try again, as well as when you're ready to go public with news about your new or improved network. Last, we'll help you with some guidelines about how to get the right word about the network out to your prospective users, so they'll be able to greet the network with more anticipation than trepidation!

## EXECUTING THE INSTALLATION PLAN

We spent a fair amount of time in the two preceding chapters outlining the contents and benefits of an installation plan. We hope the benefits of working your way through such a plan are obvious to you. If they're not, please take our word for it that an installation plan can spell the difference between a working network and a random collection of loose ends.

The two most important things about an installation plan are that it lays out all of the network's pieces and parts and that it spells out the order in which the installation must be completed. The first part should be your guide as to when it's safe to begin the installation process, which can happen as soon as you've received all of the materials, equipment, and software you need to begin putting the network together. The second part tells you how to proceed and what things have to be completed before other parts can begin.

In general, it's common practice to get the wiring installed first, the networking gear installed second, and any other equipment—servers, peripherals, and so forth—installed last, along with attaching your users' PCs to the resulting network. If any step along the way fails to be completed, it will halt further progress on the network until whatever problems are causing the delay get solved. That's why we recommend building a test lab, so that you can get some installation practice before going live. That's also why we recommend waiting until things are working properly before going public that there's a new or improved network available!

Working from a plan lets you monitor your progress and assess where and when you've reached the milestones that mark the path to a completed network. If you know what you're supposed to be doing next, and have a good feel for all of the tasks that have to be completed, you'll be much better equipped to install or upgrade a network than if you work haphazardly.

## TEST AS YOU GO

The proof that the network is working is when it behaves as it's supposed to. Along the way from a pile of raw materials and equipment in boxes to the consummation of your installation experience, you'll want to test individual pieces of your network as each one gets completed.

The reason why this "test as you go" philosophy is so important is that, whenever a network problem occurs, the problem has to be identified in order to be cured or worked around. Each new item in a network is a potential cause for problems, and the more untested components in a network, the bigger the resulting task of troubleshooting.

You could wait until you've put all the cabling in place and installed all of the equipment to test your network, but then if things don't work, how will you know where to start looking for problems? If you test each part of your installation at every step along the way, and something fails on the current step, the most likely culprit is in whatever step you've just completed. You don't have to back up and start checking things from the most basic levels, working your way through each component, to try to isolate causes and prescribe cures. You can recheck your most recent change with a fair degree of confidence that something's gone amiss during that step. While this doesn't constitute a guarantee that nothing else could have gone wrong in the meantime (where's Murphy?), it will help isolate the most likely causes or contributing factors.

Even if you try to do things any other way, the inevitability of problems, failures, or mistakes along the way will dictate that you test all your network components and materials whenever trouble crops up. Why not just head trouble off at the pass, and look for it at every step along the way? We also recommend keeping a working copy of your network map at hand during the installation process, so that you can check off each item as it gets tested to help you keep track of where to start looking when problems arise.

## Principles of Incremental Installation

When it comes to putting working networks together, the idea of "test as you go" actually has broader implications than just checking individual components as they are installed. We can extend this idea to the way installation itself proceeds, especially for larger networks that involve multiple hubs or cable segments. If circumstances at your company permit, it's not a bad idea to install the network in stages, so that you can gain experience with installing only part of the entire thing before having to complete it.

We call this approach *incremental installation*, because it lets you proceed with the installation process in discrete stages. For example, you might decide to install a single hub and server combination and only attach a small number of workstations at first to thoroughly exercise those pieces before proceeding with a full-blown installation. Or, you might proceed with the installation by bringing up the hub and server combinations for departments or workgroups in your office, with the installation order dictated by each group's or department's particular needs, or in line with a predetermined set of company priorities (e.g., "accounting needs the network more than human resources").

Living with a smaller version of the planned final network can confer significant advantages. By introducing it at first to a small number of users, including yourself, you'll have the opportunity to learn more about the network before having to deliver it in final, finished form. You'll also have the opportunity to observe others inter-act with the network, and to learn where the common misunderstandings lie and what typical pitfalls your users will encounter. Early familiarity with networks doesn't breed contempt; rather, it fosters a sense of confidence and understanding that will bolster your users and make your life as a network administrator easier as well!

Finally, living with a smaller version of the network for a while may alert you to problems that you can't do much about, but which can alert you to the need for changes in selection or plans. For instance, the super-duper electronic-mail package your boss insists be used might have some serious bugs that would make it unsuit-able, or you might discover that some of the networking hardware doesn't really work like it's supposed to. If everyone isn't subjected to these difficulties, or isn't champing at the bit to get things fixed, your life will be easier while you're figuring out how to cope with what you're learning.

## KNOWING WHEN TO PULL THE PLUG

Sometimes things get so seriously fouled up during a network installation that you simply can't get the network running as planned. Unfortunately, a lot of things can lead you to this sorry pass, but if you're prepared to rest and regroup, you can always try again another day. The key questions are: "How can you tell when it's time to abort your installation attempts?" and "What should you do to get ready to try again?"

If you have never worked on a network installation before, it's hard to predict how long particular activities should take. Nevertheless, it's still a good idea to try some educated guesses for the various activities involved, and the right way to get educated is to tackle the basic tasks—cabling, equipment installation, and software installation—in a test laboratory to give yourself a feeling for how long it takes to build and pull cables and to install equipment or software. We strongly recommend that real neophytes figure out a way to attend some networking training courses before getting really serious about an installation. That way, you can benefit from the wisdom and experience of others while you're learning, instead of having to do everything the hard way, over and over, until you get it right!

Step through your installation plan and do some simple arithmetic. If it takes four hours to install a hub, and you have four hubs to install, that means 16 hours; if it takes an hour per cable installation and you have 24 cables, that means 24 hours; and so on. Add up the totals for each separate activity. This will be your timetable to watch, as you proceed with installation, to see how you're doing.

To answer our first key question, "How can you tell when it's time to abort your installation attempts?" we can now refer to our timetable. If a given task is supposed to take four hours, and we've already spent two or three hours on that task and aren't getting finished, that's a warning signal that problems are cropping up, or that ignorance or inexperience is getting in the way. If three-fourths of the allotted time elapses and less than half of the task is complete, it's time to decide whether or not to proceed. Here again, training or test lab experience is a key factor in helping you to decide how you're doing. Unless there's a compelling reason to continue blundering ahead anyway, it's time to quit when you get to this point.

This, of course, raises the second question, namely, "What should you do to get ready to try again?" The simple answer is, "Figure out what's wrong and fix it before you do it again." What this really means is obtaining the right replacement parts, obtaining a new software driver, or working through the diagnosis of your problem to a cure (or at least a workaround) before wasting any more time making no progress. This will also give you the opportunity to consult one or more of the experts you're supposed to have on tap, as recommended in Chapter 13, to get their thoughts on the subject. You may even have to solicit their direct help, or get a referral for somebody to come to your site and do some troubleshooting with you, if you really get stuck.

As with gambling, knowing when to quit is just as important for network installations. Climbing the learning curve is one thing, but spinning your wheels is entirely another. By keeping tabs on how you're doing, you can make smart "go/no-go" decisions when things start bogging down.

## Going Public

Sooner or later, despite whatever misfortune Murphy may inflict upon you, you'll find yourself ready to announce the network to its users. We suggest you make this accomplishment an occasion, but not because you want to blow your horn about the hard work you've had to do to get things working. The real reason why going public with an announcement, or possibly even a meeting, is a good idea is to let your users know what to expect from this new or improved technology, and to give them a chance to ask questions or get additional information about what's new or changed.

No matter what the actual details might be, most people have to struggle to cope with change. If you're willing to work with your users, to tell them what they're going to encounter on the network, and to let them learn from you and each other, they'll be much better equipped to face the network by themselves. Working with users in groups gives you the benefit of being able to impart the basics all at once instead of over and over again in one-on-ones. It also gives everybody the opportunity to listen and learn from all of the questions that get asked, instead of just the ones they can think of.

Going public in an organized way also lets you get the word out about how to cope with problems, and to distribute information about whom to call with questions or reports of problems. Even more important, it gives you the opportunity to share what you have learned and to tell the users what you think they need to know in order to appreciate what a network can do for them.

For new networks or networks that have undergone major changes, we recommend setting up meetings for training and question/answer sessions on the network. This means planning ahead, scheduling a get-together, and taking the time to prepare training materials for the users to take away with them for additional information. The value of this kind of exercise is easy to belittle, but hard to overstate. Think of it this way: Isn't it easier to answer the common questions once or twice, rather than having everybody come up or call to ask those questions over and over (and over) again?

For routine upgrades or other minor changes, a memorandum or electronic mail message informing your users about those changes should suffice. Even if it's just a brief note, letting your users know that things have changed will help them feel more comfortable about working on the network, and might also help them to understand why some things don't work the same way they did last Friday (or whenever they last used the network). For that reason your message should also include some brief information about what actually has changed and should especially tell them what things they'll now have to do differently to accommodate those changes. Here again, working in a laboratory situation or with a small guinea pig group can be a big help in figuring out what needs to be covered in such communications.

## THOSE PESKY USERS!

An old joke about the restaurant business has one waitperson saying to another: "You know, this would be a great business if we didn't have to deal with customers all day long!" The same fate that befalls a restaurant with no customers will also befall a network administrator for a network with no users—some form of employment change is likely in the very near future.

Therefore, it's important to remember that taking care of users is ultimately what networking is all about. Sure, you'll get tired of explaining things ad nauseam, but think of the alternative. If you're prepared to tell your users what they need to know when they need to know it, you'll be able to keep them happy and be ready to handle the out-of-the-ordinary questions while you're taking care of their network for them. If they don't know what's going on, and keep having to relearn the same things over and over, don't blame them—blame yourself! A good network administrator has to be as much teacher as technologist.

Dealing with users is an important part of your job. Taking that part seriously means being prepared yourself, and it also means taking extra steps to make sure your users know enough about what's going on within the network, and enough about how things work, to do their jobs properly. Therefore, it's a good idea to think about building a "How to" manual for your network that explains how to perform basic, common tasks like those that follow:

- how to log on to the network
- how to write, send, and retrieve electronic mail
- how to access printers, fax machines, and other network resources
- how to access and use work-related applications (e.g., accounting software for accountants)
- what to do or whom to call when things don't seem to be working

This manual can be as simple or complex as you want it to be (or have time to put into it). Remember, though, that the effort you put into this will be repaid many times over by both the questions it saves you from answering later on and the message of caring and respect that it sends to your users.


## SUMMARY

In this chapter you've been prepped to deal with the glitches and gotchas that can occur during the installation process. You've also learned some important principles regarding testing your work as you go, proceeding with installation incrementally, and knowing when to pause in your efforts to solve problems that are getting in the way. Most important, we've tried to prepare you to deal with the people who'll be using the network, by keeping them informed and by empowering them to get the best use out of their network.

# MAINTENANCE BEGINS AT INSTALLATION

**15**

No sooner does your network get installed than your maintenance duties begin. If maintenance refers to keeping things up and running on the network, it's equally important to make sure that whatever you do during the maintenance process to change the network be recorded somewhere—that is, if it's added to the network map, it should be recorded in the database of information that you should be keeping that describes what's on the network.

It's also important to recognize that regular maintenance is a vital habit. It's essential to the health and proper functioning of your network and is often your only hope for continued employment. Since installation represents the startup phase for your network, starting maintenance at the same time will help you to establish the best networking habit there is!

## DOCUMENT AS YOU GO

By now, it may seem that we're lapsing into an incantation every time we stress how important it is to keep records about your network, especially as we repeat your need to maintain an accurate, up-to-date map of your network. As tiresome as it may sound, these concepts can really never be repeated too many times:

- Your ideas of what's on the network will originate primarily from what's on your map.

- If your map isn't accurate, you'll have to survey everything on the network to bring it up to date.
- A survey to rebuild your map takes time, costs money, and involves a fair amount of work.

The only alternative is to start out with a map, as part of your installation plans, and to keep altering the map to reflect what actually gets installed as the network comes together. If you keep up with all the changes as they occur, you'll never have to go out and re-survey to bring the map up to date. To butcher a phrase from Eric Segal's *Love Story*: "Keeping up with the map means never having to say you're sorry."

Assuming that you buy into the map maintenance mandate, what does that actually mean for the installation process? If you don't keep a copy of the map with you and use it to create a running record of what you're doing, it means recording each day's work before going home (and yes, that will be a pain at 2:00 A.M., but that's better than chancing a lapse of memory). To be more specific, here are the kinds of things you'll want to record.

For cabling:
- **Cable lengths**—estimates are okay, as long as you realize you'll have to go back and measure with a TDR at another time.
- **Cable identification**—write down the cable tag or tags and color-coding information for each individual cable, if applicable.
- Take note of the type of connector at each end of the cable (you can do this quickly by creating unique symbols for the types of connectors you use; we use alphabetic letters like "T" or numbers like "45" for RJ-45).
- Mark the location of each end for every cable, as accurately as possible.
- Trace out the route each cable takes, as accurately as possible.

For networking equipment (non-PC-based):
- Record the make, model & manufacturer of each piece of equipment.
- Record the equipment serial number or other unique identification (for example, an asset tag number).
- Record the software or firmware name and revision level.
- Create a list of port-to-cable match-ups (for example, on a combination fiber-optic/twisted-pair hub, you'd record the cable labels from the fiber-optic ports with their corresponding port numbers, and match up twisted-pair cable labels with their RJ-45 ports).
- If you can get a copy for your files, it's also a good idea to get a copy of the invoice for the equipment and a record of payment; sometimes these things are necessary to get technical support from a vendor later on.

For computers (PC-based or otherwise):

- Record the make, model, and serial number of the computer; also include the machine's base configuration (RAM installed, floppies, type and speed of CPU, etc.).
- Record the type and revision level for the machine's operating system (for example, DOS 5.0 or 6.2 for PCs, System 7.1 for Macintoshes, etc.).
- Record the type of network interface and software drivers it uses (or operating system revision level, for network-ready computers like Macintoshes).
- Make a list of the peripherals or accessories for the machine (number and size of hard disks, tape drives, CD-ROM drives, modems, keyboard, and display).
- As with networking equipment, get copies of invoices and proofs of purchase whenever possible (again, for technical support questions, proof of purchase is sometimes required).
- Record an inventory of the software installed on the machine, including name of program, revision level, and serial number where applicable (for example, Word for Windows 2.0a).

It's going to be hard to capture all of this information directly on the network map; that's why we recommend sticking with basic identification and length information on the map, with a reference number to a paper file or database record for the rest of the details.


## KEEP THE MAP UP TO DATE!

Just a forceful reminder that any changes, additions, alterations, or other tangible activity on the network deserve to be recorded somewhere—either on the physical map of the network itself, or in the paper files or database records that record the remaining details. Don't forget!


## WHEN IN DOUBT, WRITE IT DOWN!

Sometimes you'll find yourself wondering if a particular change is worth recording on the map. If there's any chance that you'll ever need to dredge information up about that change again, the answer is an emphatic "Yes!" That's why we say, "When in doubt, write it down."

We've gotten in the habit of keeping a maintenance diary while working on our network. It's really just a spiral ring notebook that we carry with us everywhere we go. Whatever we do, we write it down, even if it's just to say something trivial like

"Replaced RJ-45 connector on cable number 23, hub side." Then, if cable number 23 starts acting up in the next few days or weeks, we'll know to check that connector at the hub first thing. You could (and should) do the same. (This also makes it easy to answer the question, "What did you do at work today?" even if your significant other really doesn't want to know all the gory details!)

## Capturing Real Configurations

A map is a small-scale representation of reality, convenient enough to be portable and easily accessed. By keeping track of what's out there on your map, you're making sure that what's being represented is an accurate model of the cables, equipment, and computers that make up a typical network. The problem is that many of those computers on the network are not directly under your control, and they keep being changed all the time. What's a responsible network administrator to do?

The main thing to do is not to worry about things too much. Chances are, the really important equipment, the hubs, routers, servers, printers, and other network gear, can't be changed that easily with your involvement. The real issue then becomes: What are your users doing at (or to) their desktops? Here again, the answer is to relax, secure in the confidence that if something they do breaks or disturbs their connection to the network, you'll be hearing about it anyway!

A good approach is to document the configuration fully, including both hardware and software for a computer, when it is turned over to a user for the first time. Then, with each change you're involved in, you'll want to do two things:

1. Record whatever change or upgrade you're making.
2. Make copies of each PC's AUTOEXEC.BAT, CONFIG.SYS and relevant .INI or other configuration files, and print directory listings from its disk drives, so that you'll be able to refer to this information later. We call this "making a snapshot" of the PCs you're working with, because it gives you a current idea of what's on each one, and how it's really configured.

Number 1 is standard maintenance procedure; number 2 reflects your desire to capture whatever state your user's machine is in at the time you pay your visit (which, by the way, could be electronic, over the network rather than in person). For number 2, you'll want to capture the following information:

- Recheck the basic configuration: Is it still the same machine, and if so, have there been any changes to the RAM or CPU installed?

- Obtain the current revision level for the operating system.
- Print a copy of the machine's disk directory structure; this will tell you what applications are installed and, with a little detective work, the revision level (you can check this by date and file size, if no other way).
- Get copies of important configuration files (for a DOS PC, this would include CONFIG.SYS, AUTOEXEC.BAT, and any relevant memory management and network driver configuration files).

Even if you don't make the effort to collect regular snapshots of your users' configurations, this technique will give you a good starting point for troubleshooting. We know of many companies where taking snapshots monthly or quarterly is part of the maintenance routine. Maybe it should be part of yours, too!

## HANDLE WITH CARE: TWEAKING AND TUNING

With any new network, or after any appreciable changes, there comes a settling-in period immediately thereafter. During this period, you'll find yourself adjusting equipment or configurations to better fit your users' needs, or to better match the actual fit among the pieces that make up your network. To go out and make a quick fix is hardly worth recording, right?

Wrong! This is the period when it's probably most important to keep track of the network's configuration and components. Most tweaking and tuning is a mixture of inspiration and wild-haired guessing. Sometimes this produces exactly the right results, but mostly it's a process of fiddling and fudging, as you grope your way to a new and hopefully fairly stable dynamic equilibrium. Knowing where you stand before and after tweaking is the only tool you'll have to figure out where to go when it's time to tune or tweak again. Therefore, it has to be recorded, if only in your maintenance diary.

Once more, with feeling: If it changes on the network, it has to change on the map!

## SUMMARY

Here we've tried to stress the idea that you need to develop careful, attentive habits for taking care of your network from the very day you begin installation. This includes updating and annotating the network map whenever you install anything or make any changes, so that what's on the map reflects what's actually out there on the network. It also includes the need to capture as much information about the equipment and software in use on the network's machines and the need to proceed carefully while working through a network's shakedown period. The bottom line remains: If anything changes, write it down!

# MANAGING UPGRADES AND REPLACEMENTS

# 16

Surviving a network installation certainly gives you the right to pat yourself on the back, and when you've brought your users up to speed on their new capabilities you might even be able to relax a little bit. But if you think your challenges as a network administrator are behind you, think again!

Sooner or later you'll get a package in the mail from a hardware or software vendor, bearing a new and hopefully improved version of something you're already using. Either that or you'll have to swap a piece of equipment for something bigger or faster, or simply have to replace some piece of gear that has to go into the shop for service.

All of these things mean changes to your network. Change is good, because it represents growth and progress, but change can be challenging because it represents a continual grappling with the new and unfamiliar. Change can also be troublesome because networks are most likely to fail right after changes are made.

When it comes to network maintenance, managing change is a critical key to success. There will be no escaping the occasional need for upgrades and replacements; these things are an integral part of what it means to manage a network. If you expect and plan for change, it will be less difficult to deal with. If you give yourself leeway to cope with the unexpected, and to recover from the occasional glitch that change can bring, it will be much easier to master the art of networking, and your users will remain cheerfully oblivious to your efforts. Remember, their ignorance is your bliss!

## THE BENEFITS OF LONG WEEKENDS

As we mentioned when discussing installation, it's best if you can work around your users' schedules, that is, to avoid interrupting service during peak hours or peak times of month. Minimizing disruption will let you minimize the number of complaints and will help your users to maintain a positive attitude about the network. That's why it's become accepted practice for network changes to happen at night or over the weekend.

We certainly don't recommend that you become a creature of the night, at work only when everybody else isn't around to bother you (although we do know a few network administrators who seem to operate continually in this mode). What we're saying is that things which do disrupt your users, or which have the potential to limit their access to the network, are best handled when the users aren't around, or at least when they're not up against a deadline. For instance, it's a really bad idea to start replacing the accounting department's server the day before the monthly sales reports and financial statements are due!

Here are some approaches to working around your users that you might want to consider when it comes to performing upgrades or changes.

- Get an estimate of how long the procedure should take. If you haven't a clue, ask your vendor for an estimate; if the vendor doesn't know, call the company whose software you're upgrading, or whose equipment is about to be installed, and ask its technical support staff how long they think it should take. Add 25–50% to that estimate to compensate for having to climb the learning curve (or to do it more than once, if necessary).

- If it's a critical piece of software or equipment, you might even want to practice on a test network first before doing things live. That way, you'll have plenty of time to get help and to solve any problems that might crop up along the way. This will also give you a more accurate estimate of how long it should take to do it for real.

- If the upgrade or replacement takes longer than four hours or so, plan on doing it over a weekend instead of some weeknight (even network administrators need their sleep). Plan to start on Saturday so that you can come back on Sunday and try again, if you have to.

- If the upgrade or replacement takes longer than a day to complete—and fortunately, not many of them do—you have two options: First, you can plan to do the job on the next three-day weekend; or second, you can work with your management to decide a good time to take the network out of service during working hours. For instance, during routine employee training, an off-site meeting, or a slack period around the Christmas holidays would be less disruptive than during peak times.

All of the tips we offered for installation in Chapters 13 and 14 apply equally to replacements and upgrades: Don't forget to arrange for spares (if applicable), make sure you have an expert on tap (personally, we couldn't live without round-the-clock technical support from some companies), and above all, know when to quit and roll back to your original configuration.

What does all this mean? It means that you should take the time to create an upgrade or replacement plan whenever you have to change your network. This need not be a lengthy or incredibly detailed document (most of them are less than a page long). What such a plan does need to tell you to do is the following, though.

- If the activity consists of or includes adding new software to a computer, make sure the first step of your upgrade is to create a full backup of that system, before you make any changes.
- Prepare a checklist of all the items you need to have on hand to complete the replacement or upgrade (don't get started until you've checked everything off, either).
- State your time estimate for completion, along with a list of all the tasks that have to be completed (for instance, if you're replacing a hub this would include detaching all cables, removing old hub, inserting new hub, reattaching all cables, testing new hub).
- Include names and contact information for your expert(s) on tap, and for the upgrade or replacement vendors' technical support lines.
- State your fallback position if the upgrade or replacement fails (restore backup on server, replace new hub with old, etc.).
- No matter what else you do, your last steps should be to test whatever it is you've just replaced or upgraded, to make sure it works as it's supposed to.

This may seem completely obvious, but it will help you to monitor progress and to make sure you don't forget anything essential along the way. Look at it this way: Every time aircraft mechanics work on a plane, even the 20-year veterans, they are required by law to prepare and complete a checklist for its maintenance and repairs. Their performance record is enviable by any standards, so we'd all do well to emulate them!

## WHY A SINGLE BACKUP IS NOT ENOUGH

Any time you make software changes to a system, you take the chance that this change might be the straw that breaks the proverbial camel's back and brings the system crashing down. This leads us to two essential questions:

1. What can you do to avoid or prevent a system crash when upgrading software?
2. If you do suffer a system crash, how can you recover?

We're firmly of the opinion that avoidance beats cure every time, but especially when it comes to system crashes. So first, let's examine how to avoid the problem before we discuss how to fix it if and when a crash occurs.

## Crash-Avoidance Techniques

The most common cause of system crashes from upgrades or maintenance is the dreaded "operator error," in other words, due to some mistake or improper setting, you might accidentally render your system inoperable. We *hate* when this happens, and so will you! But rather than losing sleep over the possibility of such a dire event, try to head it off at the pass.

The best cure for mistakes is information, so before undertaking any upgrades or replacements, tap into whatever expertise you can about the product or item you're getting ready to change. We're especially fond of the on-line bulletin boards as a source for such information and have learned to check out vendor forums on CompuServe as a vital step, not just to get ready to do an upgrade, but even to decide if the upgrade is worth doing. Alas, another cause for unhappy upgrades is that software vendors have been known to release products that don't quite work as well as they should, or which have as-yet undiscovered conflicts with certain kinds of hardware or with other software that you might just happen to have running on your system already.

Talking to people who have been where you're going is ultimately what you're about when it comes to avoiding crashes. Whether by reading the on-line message traffic about a new product, reading company bulletins about the new upgrades, or talking to the vendor's technical support staff, you can get answers to some key questions that can help avoid the dreaded system crash.

- Does this upgrade work as it's supposed to?
- Are there known problems that other installers have discovered?
- Is this upgrade the most current version of the vendor's software, or are new patches and fixes already available?
- Are those who have upgraded happy with the upgrade? If not, why not?
- What are the most common questions that other installers have asked (and what are the answers), and what are the most common complaints (and their cures)?

Armed with this information, you'll be able to proceed with much greater confidence. You may even decide that the upgrade isn't the good idea it may have at first seemed to be. We've skipped several versions of programs whose bad reputations preceded them, and we recommend that you consider following suit should similar news about your intended upgrades reach you!

## Curing the Common Crash

The best-accepted method for curing a crash is to restore your system to the presumably pristine state it enjoyed before you started messing with it. How do you actually do that?

The key is called a *backup*, which is a snapshot of your entire system's software, taken some time before you've started making the upgrade. Since the value of a backup is akin to the value of a fish—the fresher, the better—we recommend making the backup the first step to changing software on any of your systems. This means, among other things, that you have to have backup software for the system you're about to change, and that you know how to use it, before you can proceed. If you don't have backup software for your systems—and industry studies show that an astonishing 60 percent of systems don't get backed up regularly—do yourself an incredible favor and get some right away.

There are two kinds of backups that you should become familiar with. A "full backup" is a complete copy of whatever is on the system being backed up, while an "incremental backup" is a snapshot of only what's changed since the last backup. Many companies are in the habit of doing full backups once a week, with incrementals at the end of each day to capture that day's work, as a way of protecting the value of the information stored on their computer systems.

When it comes to making changes to a system, the full backup is the right kind to do. Because software changes can have so many subtle side effects on a system, it's usually easier just to blow the whole changed software away and replace it with a prior version, than it is to figure out everything that's been affected and replace only changed files. For this kind of wholesale replacement, only a full backup will do.

In fact, we recommend making two backups of your system whenever you're contemplating major software changes, such as a network operating system replacement, or when moving over from one application to another (for example, when changing over from a flat-file database to a more powerful relational database). Is this paranoia at work or a necessary protective measure?

Here's why we say that two backups for major changes are recommended: If one is corrupted or damaged, you can use the other to get back to where you started. Even though the chances of this happening are slim, the chances that two backups will be unusable are even more remote. This is only recommended for major changes, but it could be a lifesaver someday. Obviously, we can't make you do anything to your system that you don't want to, but we ask you to think about having a backup for your backup when major changes or replacements are in your future.

## Test Before You Leap

By now the concept of trying things out in an experimental or laboratory setting should be familiar. Remember, the idea of testing things in such an environment is to:

- become familiar with the installation and set-up of what's being tested
- isolate and identify potential problems whose solutions will permit a successful installation, and whose lack of resolution could prevent one
- test configurations and usage of the upgraded or replaced element instead of assuming that the users will do that for you
- protect users from unnecessary disruptions or loss of network service

The real value of testing prior to actual installation for a network administrator is that it makes that procedure go more smoothly and promotes confidence that all will go as planned. Since things that don't work in the laboratory seldom work in real life, testing changes in a controlled environment lets you manage if and when such changes are inflicted on users. While no amount of testing can completely predict what users will actually do with hardware or software once they're allowed to use it, our experience tells us that some testing is clearly better than none!

## Test After You Leap

Okay, so you've been through the grind of upgrading or replacing a part of your network, and everything seems to be working fine. How can you be really sure, though, that there's not some little detail that you've overlooked that will keep the change from having its desired effect? Worse yet, how can you be sure that the network isn't just about ready to come crashing down around your ears?

The answer is, of course, to perform at least some cursory tests. If you've tried a lab or pilot installation and that worked okay, cursory tests should be enough. If you're trying something out for the first time, sit down and run through part of your normal network routine to see how things are working: Use the printer, send an e-mail message, load and run some networked applications. If everything's working, you can call it a night (or a weekend, or whatever); if it isn't, you'll have to figure out why not. If it can't be fixed, it's time to use your contingency plans and get back to your starting point.

## THE PROS AND CONS OF SCHEDULING

Upgrades and replacements have their own timing. You can never say exactly when a new software release will show up at your desk, nor can you be completely sure precisely when an old piece of gear will have to be replaced with something newer and more capable. Unless an emergency drives the timing for either activity, we recommend a more measured approach to upgrades and replacements than the "whenever I get to it" philosophy.

Since you know in advance that upgrades and replacements will occur, why not schedule a regular time to perform them? We handle this sort of thing once a month on our own systems, and that appears to be a reasonable interval for most other companies that we've talked to about this subject. Since a backup is always a good way to start, why not plan upgrades and replacements to follow immediately after you perform a full backup of the system or systems you'll be working on anyway?

The worst thing that can happen with this kind of planning is that a scheduled maintenance period will come and you'll have nothing to upgrade or replace during that time. If so, you can go home with a clear conscience, knowing that your workload has been temporarily reduced. Our experience has not been too encouraging in this regard, however; there's enough hardware and software on a typical network that something is always in need of attention during these periods.

Be warned, though, that this approach doesn't work for adding users to the network. If Sam Spade shows up for work on Monday, and your next scheduled maintenance period isn't until a week from Thursday, neither Sam nor your boss will be too glad to hear that you won't be able to get him attached to the network until then.

It's a good idea to build yourself a checklist for adding users to the network and to practice that activity regularly so that you can accommodate new staff members, visitors, or temporary employees at the drop of a hat. "This is different from maintenance," is what you'd hear if you tried to stall servicing new users, and whoever told you that would be right. Once the network becomes a part of the work routine for users, it's no longer an option whether or not to connect them—it's a requirement for them to do their jobs. Be prepared, and you'll prosper!

## NOTIFYING USERS

We believe in the old three-times approach ("tell 'em what you're gonna tell 'em, tell 'em, and then tell 'em what you told 'em") to handling user notification of replacements or upgrades.

That is, a warning note should go out a week before any changes are scheduled to occur, especially if the network will be going down (or slowing down) as a consequence of making those changes. This note should also briefly cover what's changing, why, and what impact it will have on your users afterward.

The day of the change, another warning note should go out to remind users that things are getting ready to slow down or go down at a predetermined time (remember, you're not the only person who has to work weird hours to meet deadlines, or to work around your colleagues' schedules). Repeat the what, why, and impact information from the first note. Shortly before beginning your work, repeat the message again, with a dire warning about getting off the system if that's what's required (we recommend sending it 15 to 30 minutes beforehand).

Immediately after working on the change, send a note to indicate whether the change occurred or not. If the change was successful, explain in as much detail as necessary what its impact will be. If necessary, you might even want to schedule a brown-bag seminar at lunch that day, or hold a meeting for interested parties to come and ask questions.

## PAMPERING POWER USERS

If there's one group of users who can make or break a network, it's the so-called power users. Don't be surprised if you find a dedicated cadre of computer jocks in your organization whose lives are immeasurably enriched by the magic they can create with their workstations. In fact, don't be too surprised if some of them turn out to be more knowledgeable than you are about your job. While this might make you defensive, try to get over that feeling: Your power users are an incredibly valuable resource. The care and feeding of power users is a delicate and important task but, done properly, can lighten your workload and make the network a better environment for everybody.

The first thing you'll notice about power users is that they ask highly complicated questions and press you for details that no one in his or her right mind would care about. The second thing you'll notice is that they really understand how the network behaves and how to work with and around it to do lots of interesting and sometimes important things. The third thing you'll notice is that they have an incredible appetite for information and are always ready to tackle something new, in the hopes of learning still more magic. Finally, power users have a constant craving for more: more horsepower, more peripherals, more doodads, and more of anything else you could think of.

Power users can run you ragged, in fact, but don't let them. Co-opt them instead. They can become the test staff for your test or laboratory network. You can go to Paul Poweruser and say: "Paul, I've got the latest version of MegaSpreadsheet here. How'd you like to look it over to see if it's worth putting on the network?" If Paul lives up to his name, he'll become transfigured with lust and will probably lunge forward to rip the box out of your hands. He'll also take the time to read the manuals and work through the installation, all the while thinking of ways to make things run more smoothly.

The moral of the story is that as long as you share information and early exposure with your power users, you can make them an effective part of your networking team. If you try to put them off, or starve them for goodies, they'll simply ignore you and do things their own way. Pampering power users isn't just a way to keep them off your back (which it will help to do); it's also a way to put their talents to work on your behalf.

## Seeing Double: Running in Parallel

The more complicated a system, the more things that can go wrong with it—consider this a Murphy index, if you like. Any time you're making major changes to a system that people depend on to do their jobs, or that the company depends on to meet its bottom line, extra care and caution is well advised.

If a new system is being brought in to replace an aging or ailing older system that remains critical to company operation, the prudent thing to do is to leave the old system up for a while and to bring the new system up alongside it. This will provide an easy way to migrate information from the old system to the new, since they'll both presumably be on the network (or at least within walking distance of each other). You should also continue to run the old applications and procedures alongside their new replacements, until you feel comfortable that the new system is working properly.

The crux of the matter is that the old system works. No matter how slow and decrepit it may be, no matter how painful to use, or ugly to look at, it can still do the job it's been doing. The new system will be questionable until you've put it through its paces once or twice. If you're processing payroll, accounting information, order entry, or something else equally important to your company, you don't want to have to go to management and say, "We can't process everyone's paychecks until we can figure out how to get the new system working."

That's why we recommend running old and new systems in parallel until the new system behaves properly and successfully completes the critical jobs it's supposed to take over from the old system. In fact, it's a good idea to go through the cycle with two successful runs: The first time, let the old system take the lead, while the new one chugs alongside (this also means no immediate changes to check printing, invoice creation, etc.); the second time, make the new system perform the tasks for real, knowing that the old one's ready to take over should any problems appear along the way.

## SUMMARY

Here you've learned some approaches to accommodating changes on your network. You should be prepared to upgrade or replace hardware and software as necessary, and know how and when to move forward with the new, or go back to the old as circumstances dictate. Above all, you should now appreciate the value of preparation and testing whenever things have to change on your network, as well as the value of keeping your users informed.

# GROWTH CAN BE PAINLESS

## 17

Maintenance, upgrades, and replacements are all part of the networking routine and will be part of your duties even if you're running the network in a five-person outfit that looks like it'll stay that way for the rest of all time. For most of us, though, the network has to adapt to keep up with changing business conditions.

In many cases, change comes from growth, as well as from other factors. Typically, growth strikes a network for one or more of several reasons. Here are a few of the more common causes for network growth you might encounter:

- The company grows and adds people, who in turn need to be added to the network.
- The company acquires another company (or is acquired in a merger or an acquisition), and the non-networked portion wants to emulate the networked side.
- A small group of individuals within a company gets on a network and over time other people within the company see what it can do and want to partake of the benefits.
- Use of the network leads to increased demand for services or capabilities from the network (or, sometimes growth is necessary even without adding more people).

Whatever the particular cause or causes for growth in your environment might be, it's a good thing to be prepared for the changes that growth can bring. A key ingredient is to be aware that growth is a highly likely outcome for your network, if not an outright eventuality. That's why we've tried to counsel you to think about growth and extension as you install your first network, and why we think it's a relevant topic for a book on network design.

In fact, many of the habits and practices we've counseled for managing your network's installation, and its subsequent maintenance, will prepare you to deal with growth. In particular, learning how to plan for and execute changes will be helpful, as will developing the practice of training new users, and keeping all users up to date on the network. But there are some issues peculiar to getting ready to grow a network—some political, others technical—that we want to warn you about so that you can grow gracefully, not hurriedly or forcibly.

Then too, there's your responsibility to be able to deliver the services and support that your users will need in order to get the best use out of the network. Growing pains are indeed tough, but they're always toughest on the person who's running the network!

## BUILD A BETTER BASELINE

One of the premier symptoms of growing pains is when the network starts to get bogged down in its own success, as it struggles to accommodate the rivers of data flowing amongst the user community. One of the more important tasks involved in running a network is to keep tabs on how it's behaving, and to keep an eye out for problems, abnormalities, and congestion patterns. Think of yourself as a highway designer whose job it is to make sure that there's enough roadway to accommodate all the traffic that's needed to support your users. You can also think of yourself as a community planner for computing communities, which may have to be subdivided and spun off, as needs increase and network usage grows.

In any case, you have to know what's normal to be able to recognize what's not. Once your network is up and running, and your users have started to settle in to their relationship with the network, it's time to start measuring all kinds of things that happen on it. Assembling this collection of information and measurements is called "building a baseline," because it represents the collection of traffic levels, error counts, and other things that constitute a healthy, properly functioning network.

### Pulling Your Baseline Together

How should you go about collecting this information? The good news is you have lots of choices for tools to help with this task. The bad news is that most of them aren't free, and that all of them take some effort to learn and to understand what they're telling you. The tools used to gather this kind of information are sometimes called network monitoring or management programs, or even network or protocol analysis software, but whatever they're called, you should use them to tell you some or all of the following details:

- The amount of traffic on the network cables, called the *utilization rate*. This is normally expressed as a percentage of the medium's overall bandwidth, so that an Ethernet network running at 50 percent utilization would be moving five megabits per second over its wiring. This might sound like you have a comfortable margin, but in fact Ethernet tends to start bogging down in performance at between 56 and 60 percent utilization, so an Ethernet network with 50 percent utilization is in need of further analysis, because it's being fairly heavily used.
- The amount and kinds of errors on a network can also tell you a lot about it's health. High percentages (over 2–3% of total utilization) for short packets or collisions on an Ethernet network can be the warning signs of congestion or hardware problems.
- The number of users logged in, and the resources they're consuming, can also be illuminating. We've encountered several networks where management's idea about who was using the network was literally years behind the actual usage patterns. If you don't find out for yourself, how will you know?
- The storage space consumed by users, including some information about who's using what, can be important.
- The number of legal application licenses versus the number of people using those applications (if the number exceeds the license limit, pray you don't get a visit from the Software Publishing Association until you set things right— remember what we said about prevention being cheaper than cure?).
- Plotting usage over time can also be revealing, because it points out periods of peak usage (which typically occur both daily and monthly, because of various business and personal cycles).

Some of the information we suggest collecting can be obtained from the software that makes your network run (for instance, Novell's NetWare will report most of these statistics, except for error information, if you know where to look and how to interpret what you're seeing). All of this information will be supplied by programs specifically designed to monitor or analyze networks, along with lots of other data that describes your network.

## Network Monitoring Aids

For pure monitoring, network management packages will be overkill (and probably too expensive as well). For smaller networks, we recommend looking at these or other network monitoring software:

- AG Group's EtherPeek, LocalPeek, or TokenPeek for AppleTalk networks on Ethernet, LocalTalk, or Token Ring, respectively (list prices range from $495 to $995 US)
- Azure Technology's LANPharaoh (wide range of protocols and technologies, lists for $2,995 US)
- Dolphin Networks Dolphin ESP (wide range of protocols and technologies, lists for $995 to $1,995 US)
- FTP Software's LANWatch (wide range of protocols and technologies, lists for $1,200 US)
- General Software's Etherprobe (Ethernet only, but a wide range of protocols, lists for $995 US)
- Intel's NetSight Analyst (Ethernet and token ring, but a wide range of protocols, lists for $995 US)
- Novell's LANalyzer for Windows (broad range of protocols and technologies, lists for $1,495)

There are plenty of other options available, though, and administrators for larger networks will want to investigate the features and functions of more full-blown network management packages. (One word of warning. Read about these products sitting down—most of them cost in excess of $10,000, and many cost significantly more than that.) Please consult the *Further Reading* section at the end of this chapter for sources of more networking product information.

Whatever approach you end up taking, remember that the focus of this exercise is to understand what a healthy network looks like in general and to establish a set of measurements for your own network. This baseline will be helpful to let you track its performance and usage over time. It will also help you to establish what's normal for your network, and what's not, and will let you observe how your users are interacting with it. We recommend a minimum of monthly baseline checks, but weekly reviews are better still.

## TRENDING POINTS TO YOUR FUTURE

In some ways, your network will grow over time even if you add no users nor equipment. As your initial users climb the learning curve and begin to incorporate the network into their daily work routines, usage will climb. As they become more familiar with the network, they may even surprise you by inventing new and innovative ways to make it work for them. By observing the traffic patterns, and keeping up with what your users are doing, none of this should take you by surprise.

Regular monitoring should alert you to increasing demand for services, capacity, or storage space. Growth is often as much a consequence of Parkinson's Law (colloquially best stated as "the more you have, the more you'll use") as it is an effect of an ever-expanding sophistication on the part of your users. If you observe a regular increase in network usage (steady growth in network traffic at both peak and non-peak times), it may be time to start thinking about splitting up the network. If you see that disk usage keeps increasing, both overall and per user, it may be time to request money for additional hard disks, or to think about installing a hierarchical storage system. If more and more people want to start using electronic mail, you may need to replace the current e-mail server with a newer, more powerful machine.

Comparing network information over time lets you look for trends in actual usage. There's no better indicator of where the action is right now, and consequently, where growth is likely to occur. Think of this exercise as a positive kind of preemption: Anticipating users' needs before users become acutely aware of them not only keeps them from turning into problems, but it also has the pleasant side effect of keeping you out of the hot seat.

## PLANNING FOR EXPANSION

As trends develop, you can start thinking ahead about what strategies to enact to grow your network, be it to add more computing capacity, to increase storage, or to subdivide your cabling to lower the amount of traffic on any given segment. Planning for expansion simply means going through the exercise of building yourself the installation plan for meeting the requirements that your trend analysis tells you to anticipate.

Here again, you'll want to follow the guidelines covered in Chapters 13 through 16. That is, start out by designing on paper what it is you need to do. Use that information to build checklists for the materials and activities you'll need to have ready in order to implement your network expansion. Follow the safety precautions for backing up, arranging for support, and creating a fallback position. Above all, keep your users in the know, and be prepared, if necessary, to start working with the new group of networking neophytes that expansions can easily create.

If you do your homework, growing the network will be a lot like your initial installation, in that you'll be adding new capabilities. But because you'll have become more familiar with your network and its components, it should have some of the feel of a replacement or upgrade operation as well. This may not be the best of all possible worlds, but your previous successes will make you better equipped to do more of the same!

## Working within the System

It's not unusual for networks to start small, occupying relatively modest niches in odd, but technologically advanced, backwaters of their parent organizations. Such trifles can easily be ignored, but when they start growing large enough to attract upper management's attention, or when they start forcing interaction with corporate MIS staff, the political side of growing pains can make itself felt.

Political problems typically occur when "turf" gets violated. Problems can occur when you cross outside the boundaries of your own group or department and want to network with another group or department, which will typically involve facilities managers and possibly, local MIS staff. Problems may also arise when you need to network multiple sites together, which will typically require involvement from your facilities and telecommunications staff, if you're lucky enough to have them. As the networking thing gets bigger and gathers momentum, it becomes more visible, and more and more interested parties will start to get involved.

Then, too, there are monetary implications to continued growth and success (these, too, can attract the attention of upper management and MIS). When you're spending thousands or tens of thousands of dollars on technology, that will often be beneath corporate notice. But when the numbers climb into the hundreds of thousands or higher, it's a whole new (corporate) ball game. The rule of thumb here is that when your ability to sign for expenditures is exceeded, you'll have to start educating your boss about this networking stuff. Sooner or later, his boss will have to get involved, and you'll get to start all over again, and so on. (A sense of humor—and of technology's manifest destiny—is really helpful for times like these!)

While we're sorry to say there's no cure for these kinds of difficulties, there are some palliatives available. The most important instrument on your side is information: If you've been keeping track of usage and demand, you can justify the need for growth. If you can get the users who want more resources or who want to be part of the network on your side, you'll become a spokesperson for a potentially powerful group.

If you freely share information about the network, its trends, and anticipated requirements with the other organizations (management, MIS, facilities, etc.) that start getting involved, you'll be much more likely to garner cooperation in return. If you approach them early and often, you may end up building strong working relationships with those groups (which we highly recommend that you do). Finally, if you present them with clear, well-thought-out plans about how to proceed and can show them your track record in managing your own network, they may even end up offering you a job!

## Forewarned Is Forearmed!

Except under exceptional circumstances, growth is an inevitable consequence of networking. If you plan for it, build for it, and train your users for it, you'll be able to survive and prosper, even as you grow. If you ignore it, or let it become unduly painful, you and your users will suffer.

There! We've warned you. Now, what's your game plan going to be?

## Summary

In this chapter, we've explored the reasons that networks grow, and we've outlined a number of coping strategies. The most important idea you should carry with you from this exercise is to expect growth and therefore be willing to plan for it to avoid unnecessary growing pains. As the network grows in size and scope, you will probably end up learning more about your company's politics and procedures than you ever wanted to know. But growth seldom occurs in only one dimension, so the best thing you can do is to be prepared for it when it hits you.

## Further Reading

During our discussion of network management and monitoring software, we had occasion to mention a plethora of related products. Following the adage "Give a man a fish, feed him for a day; teach a man to fish, feed him for a lifetime," we'd like to share some of our favorite product research tools with you, to help you research networking products for yourself.

These particular tools come in the form of buyers' guides published by two of our favorite networking publications. Before we give you the bibliographic information on each one, here's a little information about what's in a buyers guide: These magazines are published as special issues yearly and provide comprehensive listings of networking products by category. Each covers thousands of products and provides short descriptions for each one, along with information about how to contact the vendors of each offering. They're not going to help you ultimately decide what you need or what to buy for your network, but each of them is a great place to start looking for stuff. They'll also help you to get a feel for what's available on the marketplace by way of networking technology, which makes them interesting reading for that reason alone. Their citations follow below.

*LAN: The Network Solutions Magazine, Buyers Guide*, September, 1993.

   *LAN Magazine* is published monthly by Miller Freeman, 600 Harrison Street, San Francisco, CA, 94107, 415-905-2200. An annual U.S. subscription costs $19.97. This magazine also provides coverage on a broad range of networking topics, including technology overviews, user tutorials, and product reviews.

*LAN Times Buyers Directory Issue*, August 16, 1993.

   *LAN Times* is published 25 times a year by McGraw-Hill, Inc., 1221 Avenue of the Americas, New York, NY, 10020, 415-513-6800. The magazine is free to qualified subscribers. *LAN Times* also provides coverage on a broad range of networking topics, including technology overviews, network industry news, product reviews, and includes editorials from networking industry leaders and personalities.

# RULES TO KEEP THINGS RUNNING

# 18

G iven that you have a network, we can say with confidence that there's been at least one such installation in your past (or at least someone's past, anyway). We'd also like to think that you've already gotten into the habit of regularly scheduled maintenance and have worked your way through some replacements and upgrades. If this describes you, reading this chapter from start to finish may be unnecessary, but the only way you can decide that for yourself is to skim it over, skipping over the parts you're already familiar with. If none of this applies to you, it's even more important that you read this chapter, because it can give you a jump-start on success as a network administrator.

However, it's a sad fact of networking life that many people who are responsible for networks do it as a sideline in addition to their "real jobs," whatever those may be. If that's the case, you may have never been formally trained in network administration, and you may have not had the luxury to learn the subtle distinctions between the recommended ways of running a network as well as the chaos that so often results when networks are left to run themselves.

No matter how hard your "real job" might be, or how little time you have for wearing your network administration hat, we can't overemphasize the importance of regular network maintenance. Maintenance often makes the difference between a network that works and a network that doesn't. More important, maintenance keeps the crises fewer and further between, and those are what will always rob you of your precious time, whether network administration is your main role or a sideline.

In this chapter, we cover the elements of a good maintenance routine. We'll also try to explain why each of the activities we recommend is a good idea and what the potential consequences of skipping an activity might be. Our goal is not to scare you into doing what we recommend—far from it, we understand that you alone can make the decisions about what's essential and what's not for your environment.

## Routines Are Boring, But Safe!

Let's step back from the hubbub of your busy network and think about what maintenance is supposed to do in a general way. From a purely physical standpoint, the need for maintenance is dictated by entropy, or rather, by the tendency of things to get run down over time. What maintenance does is to keep those things up, to make sure they're in good repair and running properly, and to police the environment to keep it clear of the detritus that time and usage will inevitably deposit.

How does this generality about maintenance apply to a network? Interestingly, it applies in lots of ways that you might find useful to consider. If we pick apart our informal definition of maintenance and look at the pieces, they tell some interesting stories about what's involved in maintaining a network.

1. **Definition**: "Keeping things up" refers to dealing with replacements and upgrades; that is, to staying current with hardware and software revisions and not let the network lapse into an outmoded or obsolete state.

   **Justification**: If you've ever tried to get technical support to help you on ancient revisions of software, you'll know why keeping up with what's current is a good idea, even if it's painful to achieve. If not, take our word for it that the quality and quantity of help and information about products diminishes substantially with each new release that follows.

   **Warning signs**: If you get responses such as, "Oh, you've got one of those. I wondered if anybody still had one," or "Gee, I'm not familiar with that release. Maybe Joe remembers back that far," you have lapsed into the outmoded zone.

   **Fix**: Ask about the cost of an upgrade to the latest version and about availability and potential problems with upgrading. It's time to bite the bullet and upgrade!

2. **Definition**: "Make sure things are in good repair and running properly" refers to the need to inspect and test equipment from time to time, and to stay in touch with utilization and error statistics (these can often warn you of impending disk drive failures, network interface card problems, and the like). It also refers to the need to service equipment with moving parts or frequent use (and even to plan on occasional replacements for things like keyboards, which are usually cheaper to replace than to repair).

**Justification**: If things aren't running properly, it's just a matter of time before they break. A failing component is still working, but a failed component typically is not. Because failure of a component can sometimes cause total network failure, it's better to be proactive and handle things before immediate reaction is required.

**Warning signs**: These include user complaints about slow or erratic network performance, increasing error trends from hardware, and unreliable software performance.

**Fix**: Remove and replace the failing part, service regularly for moving parts. Paying attention to the network is the master key!

3. **Definition**: "Police the environment" covers the need to keep cleaning up trash and excess, to monitor activity and performance, and to watch out for violations of safety, courtesy, or usage.

**Justification**: Trash piles up over time, in the form of old or duplicate files, old e-mail messages, unused applications, etc. Violations of safety, courtesy, or usage can occur when users consume too much disk space, supplies, or hog the network, limiting its availability to others.

**Warning signs**: These include user complaints about slow or erratic network performance, signs of impending exhaustion of storage space, and even, sometimes, outright network failure (what we could call a "stress-related crash!").

**Fix**: Clean up the trash, throw away the old stuff, and publish and enforce appropriate levels of resource consumption.

What's really interesting about our definition is that each of its pieces revolves around activities that are recurring, not one-shot deals. The fundamental principle of maintenance is that it's an ongoing activity. We think it's because "rust never sleeps" that maintenance never stops. Because the passing of time and the constant actions of your users keep wearing away at the magnificent network you've constructed, there's nothing to counter those forces except for regular maintenance work.

Any type of regular task is best served by establishing a routine that incorporates that task into the daily, weekly, monthly, and yearly round of business or work. As our section title indicates: "Routines are boring, but safe." The problem with maintenance is, literally, when it doesn't happen. Making it part of the routine lowers the degree of consciousness required to ensure that maintenance happens, and for most of us mere mortals, this is a good thing!

Throughout the rest of this chapter, we'll take a look at some healthy network maintenance routines, and try to recommend what to do, when and how often to do it, and why it needs to be done.

# WHEN IN DOUBT, BACK UP!

Believe it or not, despite the incredible investments in time, money, and energy you can make in putting a network together, most of its value is represented by what's on it, not what it's made of. Let's put this another way: It's the data that gets moved, stored, and used on the network that is the most valuable thing about it, not the wires, or the networking equipment, or even the sometimes staggeringly large number of computers that it can tie together. The data represents the efforts of your organization's workers, and the information that they have painstakingly gathered. Everything else can be replaced relatively quickly by spending money, but the only way work can be replaced is by doing things over!

What this diatribe is leading up to is the need to back up the data on your network. Because it does indeed represent so much value, keeping that value safe from harm should be a high priority for any network administrator. Alas, though, more than half of the networks in use today never get backed up in any way, shape, or form. Despite these odds, we want you to understand more about backing up, because we think it's the right thing to do!

## Backing Up: What to Do

The purpose of a backup is to create a copy of the software and data on a network server or on individuals' machines (or on both, to be completely safe). Many companies opt solely for backing up servers and try their best to ensure that all important information gets stored on their servers. This happens simply because servers constitute a smaller number of machines to keep track of, and servers are easier to manage than end-user workstations, which can be subject to all kinds of gyrations (including being taken home on the weekends, which is a favorite backup time as well).

Backing up is typically accomplished with the aid of software designed specifically for that purpose, and backups come in two flavors. A total snapshot of a system's contents is called a full backup; because a full backup supplies everything necessary to recreate a system that's failed, it is the best kind of backup to have. However, making a copy of everything takes longer than making a copy of a subset of what's out there on a system. The other flavor of backup is called an incremental backup, or incremental for short, and it represents a snapshot of only those things that have changed since the last backup. Because it has to be combined with other backups to fully recreate a system, it's not as efficient as a full backup, but because it typically consists of far less information than a full backup, it's a lot faster to complete an incremental backup than a full one.

The flip side of backing up is called *restoring*. This refers to copying the contents of a backup onto a system to recreate its contents at the time the backup was performed. When a full backup gets restored, it will supply you with a completely operable system, just as it was when the system was backed up. When a restoration requires incremental backups, you will first have to start with restoring a full backup, and then proceed to restore each additional incremental backup you have, in the order in which they were performed (that is, Tuesday's incremental should be restored before Wednesday's, and not vice-versa—but don't worry, the backup software will handle this for you).

## Backup: When and How Often to Do It

The down side of restoring is that whatever work has taken place since the last backup was performed, whether full or incremental, is lost forever. This should help you to figure out how often to back up—all you have to do is answer the question: "What's the largest number of hours of work that my company can afford to lose for this system?" As for when to back up: If you recognize that copying a large number of files from the hard disk of a system to a tape or other backup device takes time and consumes lots of CPU cycles, this should remind you of the "workaround" principle of maintenance we first mentioned in Chapter 13. That is, backing up can cause noticeable network delays and can adversely impact server performance. Therefore, you'll want to do it when the users aren't around, if possible, or during non-peak usage periods if they never go away altogether.

In practice, the need to work around users ends up providing a more practical answer to the how often question we raised earlier. Backups tend to be performed most often at night, or on weekends, simply because those are the times when the users are most likely to be out of the way.

The really interesting issue to figure out is what flavor of backup to perform when. The deciding factor will inevitably be the amount of time it takes to back up your system: If it takes longer than six to eight hours, you'll have no choice but to perform full backups only on the weekends. This inevitably leads to daily incrementals being performed at night. If you can back up the whole shebang every night, doing so will make restoration a one-step process, and therefore both faster and easier. These days, however, with many systems sporting 10 or more gigabytes of storage, this approach becomes purely wishful thinking!

## Additional Backup Tips

All backups do is to provide a form of data insurance, to make sure an additional copy of your precious data is still around and available if for some reason the original should become inaccessible. All backups are therefore preambles to restorations. But backups will get performed far more frequently than restores and will be much more familiar. We insist that if you do take the step of backing up your systems, that you occasionally (at least once per quarter) practice performing a restore. Whenever a real restoration is called for, it's typically because of some system failure or other disaster and is usually a pretty stressful situation. This is no time to be climbing the learning curve, or looking for the backup program's manuals to read up on just how restoration works. If you perform regular "restoration drills," you'll be able to concentrate on reassuring your freaked-out users (and management) that relief is just a matter of hours away. If you join in the general panic, things will get really strange in a hurry!

Another benefit of a backup is that it provides extra copies of files that may be deleted by accident. Some backup programs offer the ability to do what's called a selective restore or a file-by-file restore, which will give you the ability to retrieve missing files from the backup by name. We recommend that you purchase only backup programs with this capability because in practice this will be the most common use of your backup software.

Finally, backup programs offer varying degrees of automation and capacity. We strongly recommend purchasing backup hardware—be it a DAT drive, optical disk, or whatever—whose storage capacity exceeds your system's hard disk capacity by at least 20% (more excess means more room to grow), or one that is capable of swapping media without human intervention (there are a variety of tape and disk changer units on the market today). For the same reason, we recommend buying only backup software that offers easy-to-script unattended operation. As for why, think about it: We've already told you that prime time for backup is on evenings and weekends. If you have to come in to run the equipment, or to change media, you'll have to be in the office on evenings or weekends too! Our advice is to avoid that like the plague, unless budgetary forces compel you otherwise. The best backup is the kind that happens while you're asleep.

In fact, for those with larger budgets, there are other, more advanced approaches to backup available. These usually fall into two categories: first, so-called archival systems, which automatically create copies of data every time something changes, and second, hierarchical storage systems, which can let previous versions (or duplicates) migrate from your hard disk to tape or optical storage automatically. These options are costlier than more conventional backup systems, but they provide a greater degree of data protection and security, because the only work that gets lost with one of these systems is the work that's occurred since the last time an open file was saved.

## Management by Walking Around

While you can rely on network management or monitoring software to give you a picture of how your network is performing and behaving, there's another source of information that's always on tap, if only you'll avail yourself of it. We strongly recommend using it regularly, and making it a part of your maintenance routine. This section's title, "Management by Walking Around" (MBWA), refers to taking the time to visit with some users to ask them how you're doing and what they like and don't like about the network. MBWA is also a fairly useful theory of business management, in that it forcibly propels managers out of their sanctums into the offices, assembly lines, and hallways where the work really happens. For both business and network managers, MBWA has the benefit of providing the opportunity to listen to and watch what's going on out there, and to talk to the people involved.

While you, as a network administrator, might be inclined to pay most attention to the feedback that touches most directly on the network, you'll be surprised by how much you can learn about your organization with this exercise. Regular contact with users also provides additional benefits: It gives you the chance to solicit and answer any questions they might have (thereby avoiding additional time for support calls), it lets you observe how people are actually using the network, and it can often alert you to problems that not even your management and monitoring tools have noticed yet. This is especially true of your power users, who may be the most sensitive network monitors you've actually got!

### When and How Often to Go on a "Walkabout"

The short answer is, as often as you have time. Since many network administrators will probably feel like they never have time, the long answer needs to be at least once a month, with at least two or three users, preferably not all from the same network neighborhood. A quick way to check in on some of the same information is to ask the same kinds of questions you'd ask on this maintenance mission whenever you talk to users, or whenever they talk to you. Every contact with users is an opportunity to learn, and to "take the temperature" of your network, so to speak.

### Why MBWA Is a Good Idea

MBWA is a useful form of network maintenance, not just because it gives you the opportunity to see the users in their native elements, but also because it's a regular reminder of why the network is there in the first place: These users you're talking to and working with are the network's sole reason for being. If they're not happy—and they'll be anything but bashful about letting you know—it's just a matter of time before you're not happy, either. Staying in touch is the best form of public relations there is, but it's also an honest indicator of how well the network is doing and, by extension, of how well you're doing your job.

### Tips for Quality MBWA

Be sensitive to the work habits and free time of the users you'll be checking in with. Don't come calling when they're extremely busy; try to hit them when they're less preoccupied, and you'll get better information. If your workplace is more formal than informal, you might even want to schedule your visits. Before sitting down to chat, be sure to ask if they've got time. Pay attention to their interest level and to their affect: You'll do much better talking to people who want to talk to you, than with those who don't. If you're sensitive and respectful toward your users, they'll return the courtesy in all kinds of positive ways.

## SCHEDULED MAINTENANCE IS A WAY OF LIFE!

We've already talked about the benefits of scheduling installation, replacements, and upgrades around your users, to minimize the impact of these sometimes monumental tasks. The same approach works as well for routine maintenance: Establishing and publishing a routine will let your users know what to expect and should also boost their confidence from how smoothly and professionally their network is being run.

### What to Do about Scheduled Maintenance

The basic concept here is to share information about your maintenance schedule with your users and to follow the "tell 'em three times" approach to routine maintenance activities, especially if they will adversely impact users' access to the network (backup is a prime example here, because it can often slow the network considerably). It's a good idea to make a discussion of your maintenance routine a part of the information you impart to network users during their training and in any handbooks or handouts you might put together to document the network.

The foundation of all this activity is to establish a regular maintenance schedule. Then, publish and describe that schedule, and stick to it as best you can. If you make it a part of the routine, you can extend some maintenance intervals to include additional installations, or replacements and upgrades, without unduly disrupting your users' working lives.

## What Kinds of Scheduled Maintenance Should You Be Doing?

The answer to this question depends so much on the details of your particular network that we can't answer this question as directly as we'd like, but the keys to the answer lie in our definition of maintenance and its discussion at the beginning of this chapter. The guiding principles are:

- keeping things up
- making sure things are in good repair and running properly
- policing the environment

What this means in practice is that you should be checking up on your systems no less than weekly, by examining information from management software or consoles and/or monitoring software. It also means that you should physically inspect the hardware at least that often, and should make cleaning up file systems, printer areas, and other places where network trash accumulates a part of your weekly routine as well.

## Additional Scheduled Maintenance Tips

Backup media do wear out with time, so you'll want to create a media rotation schedule (see the Further Reading section for some good references on that subject). While you're at it, it's a good idea to store at least some backup media off site, in case a fire or meteorite strike wipes the whole place out! If you use tape or optical drives for backup, consult your hardware manuals for recommended cleaning schedules, and add them to your list (monthly is fairly typical). During your MBWA walkabouts, checking on network cabling and connectors is usually a pretty good idea, too. Other details will come to you, as you get in the habits of keeping your network up and running properly and of cleaning up after your users.

## COPING WITH FREQUENT CHANGES

There's no doubt that routines are disrupted by change, and that frequent change is hardest on maintaining any kind of regularity to your routines. In these ever-more-frequently changing times, how's a network administrator to cope?

The key is to be insistent on the need for maintenance, no matter how you might be pulled in other directions, or how often you may be called in to cope with personnel, location, or software changes. Just as the show must go on, the network has to keep working, and that means regular maintenance. Your best ally will be a positive attitude, along with a willingness to continue working around your co-workers' and users' schedules, no matter how crazy that may occasionally be.

The secret to successful maintenance lies at the heart of the subject: No matter what happens, your job is to keep on keepin' on!

## SUMMARY

In this chapter we've made an impassioned plea for the value of regular network maintenance. We've also pointed out some of the more essential activities you should consider making part of your maintenance routine, along with how often, when, and why these activities should happen. In the final analysis, maintenance is up to you. Just remember that entropy is always lurking out there, waiting to erode all of your hard work as soon as you let down your guard.

## FURTHER READING

There are lots of interesting resources that mention maintenance in passing, but very few devoted entirely to that subject (none that we could recommend, in fact). However, we'd still like to point at a few gems that expand on the topics covered in this chapter. (We swear that it's only a coincidence that two of the three books listed below have an author in common!)

Frederick P. Brooks, Jr., *The Mythical Man-Month*, Addison-Wesley, Reading, MA, 1982 ($19.95).

Fred Brooks was one of the principal architects of the IBM 360's operating system, and everything of value he learned in surviving its completion is covered in this book, including some pretty inspired thinking about maintenance. Chapter 11,

"Plan to Throw One Away," is probably the most germane to the issues we've discussed here.

Patrick Corrigan and Aisling Guy, *Building Local Area Networks*, second. edition, M&T Books, Redwood City, CA, 1993 ($29.95).

Even though this book is largely focused on Novell's NetWare network operating system, it also contains more useful network design and maintenance information than we've ever found anywhere else (except this book, of course). For those with NetWare on their networks, it makes a great complement to this book, in fact.

Patrick H. Corrigan, *Backing Up NetWare LANs*, M&T Books, Redwood City, CA, 1992 ($26.95).

Even though this book is completely focused on backing up systems built around Novell's NetWare network operating system, it includes the most detailed descriptions of the backup process (if you thought we sounded insistent on the subject, wait until you see this book) and of related issues that we've ever encountered. If your management balks at backup, make them read this book—they'll be changed for life!

# DEALING WITH DISASTER

# 19

What will you do if your building ever catches fire and burns down, or if something else equally catastrophic should occur? Even though the loss of the network may not be uppermost in your thoughts upon hearing of a cataclysm that's befallen you and your organization, dealing with the aftermath will quickly become a top priority for anyone who's responsible for running a network.

Unfortunately, this is another one of those cases where some planning ahead is the only thing that can offer even a remote chance of putting things back together in a reasonable amount of time. Unless you have arranged for off-site storage of your backups and have some kind of contingency plan for putting a replacement network together, there's simply no hope of getting your network back in business without rebuilding it from scratch. But rebuilding can only replace the hardware and the software that made the network run; it does nothing to recapture the data that represents the prior work your organization had stored on the network.

In many cases, organizations that haven't planned ahead have had to spend enormous amounts of time and money recreating data from paper records—often obtained from customers or vendors, if paper backups aren't available either, and from the imperfect memories of its employees. If the loss of your network and facilities is a pure and simple disaster, then being caught unprepared raises it to the level of a total disaster, from which recovery will be slow, painful, and perilous. Some organizations have declared bankruptcy in the wake of a loss of their facilities and networks, rather than face the task of resurrecting previous business, while still trying to keep up with current activity.

The real problems behind disaster recovery are business related, not technology related. As long as the technology side of things is planned for, and proper precautions are taken, recovering from disaster is merely difficult and mildly painful. Acquiring the ability to recover in this fashion, however, is not a trivial expense—many organizations would rather deny the possibility of disaster, or avoid confronting it directly, than pay for something that the odds dictate they will probably never need. The funny thing is that most of them would scoff at the suggestion that they similarly forgo taking out insurance on their property, key personnel, or other business assets.

In this chapter we'll cover the technology aspects of disaster planning and recovery and deal with the business issues that can also be involved. Because disaster recovery is a relatively expensive item, you'll have to involve your organization's management in setting up some kind of response to the topic, if not to the possibility of disaster itself. Brace yourself—this could be one of the most interesting aspects of your job as a network administrator!

## Planning for the Unthinkable

We've used the example of a fire (and elsewhere in this book, of a meteorite strike) to portray vividly the idea of a disaster for your organization. The unvarnished truth is that most disasters are far less dramatic, and more mundane, but all have the effect of separating the people who work on the network from the network itself, preventing them from using any of the information or services that the network can provide. In other words, being locked out by a disputatious landlord or evacuated by a bomb scare also qualifies as a disaster, following the idea that separation of the people from the network is what really matters. Even though we've called disasters unthinkable, the fact is that they're merely unpalatable and therefore often ignored or avoided.

This points out an additional consideration regarding the need for disaster planning: No matter how carefully you plan to avoid or forestall the conditions that could contribute to a disaster, there's no way to guarantee that you've eliminated the possibility that a disaster could strike at any time. Fires, earthquakes, and meteorites are forces of nature that often can't be avoided which makes them such sterling examples of things that no amount of planning can completely defeat. Given the unshakable possibility of disaster, it's only prudent that it be planned for. Providing that the costs can be born, enacting the plan is all that needs to be done should the unpalatable occur.

## What to Plan For

Disasters come in various shapes and sizes, so it's wise to think your way through the kinds you're willing to deal with, and the kinds of reactions that are required to surmount them. Equipment failure can cause the loss of the network, be it a partial or complete failure of a critical system, of a collection of systems, or the whole network. These kinds of failures don't imply the complete loss of your facilities, so they can be planned for through a series of contingency plans involving the repair or replacement of existing equipment.

Let's examine these possibilities in a little more detail, and suggest some possible plans to accompany them.

1. **Disaster**: Failure of a critical component or subsystem—for example, a disk drive, RAM memory, a network interface card, or a network hub—is the least catastrophic and the most likely type of failure that's likely to bring a network down, at least for a while.

   **Recovery requirements**: Prudence dictates that arrangements to replace failed components like these are essential. Larger organizations commonly keep a cache of spares on hand for emergency replacement; smaller organizations should make arrangements with local network dealers or service providers for specific emergency response service (this means that you will be guaranteed a response from the vendor within a stipulated time period; the shorter the time, the more you'll pay).

   **Recovery plan**: Review your collection of spares, or your service provider arrangements, and make sure that replacements for common components can be delivered and installed within a day, at most. Self-recovering organizations should practice disaster drills once per quarter or so, and organizations using outside service providers should request drills at least once a year.

   An important alternative to consider is to compare these costs to those for the purchase of a fault-tolerant system that can handle component failures without causing the system to fail. The rule of thumb here is: The more important the information or services that a system provides, the more affordable this level of protection will be.

2. **Disaster**: Outright failure of a network server or other critical system on the network—for example, a file, print, fax, or other kind of server on the network—is more catastrophic, but the next most likely type of network disaster you'll have to confront.

   **Recovery requirements**: A system backup for the failed system, and a replacement for that system, are what's needed to get back up and running. Some organizations keep spare servers around or buy their network administrators desktop machines that can double as servers for this contingency. Similarly, organizations that rely on outside service providers can make arrangements for spare machines to be delivered and installed on site, within stipulated time frames (remember, though, that a backup is essential to implementing this strategy).

**Recovery plan**: Proceed as for component failures, that is, make sure that you or your service provider have adequate spares, and that the network can be restored to operation in no more than a day. Practicing backup/restore drills will prepare for the most important aspect of this exercise, so additional drills need only ensure that replacement machines can be moved into place and set up within a reasonable amount of time. A drill frequency of twice a year is adequate. Here, too, fault-tolerant systems can obviate the need for such planning and practice.

3. **Disaster**: Total loss of multiple critical systems or of the connections that tie them together—for example several servers might be incapacitated by a transformer outage, or construction work may result in the break of critical network links—are relatively more catastrophic, but still likely enough to be the cause of potential network failures.

**Recovery requirements**: The failed servers must be restored to operation or replaced with equivalent equipment, or the broken network link must be restored. Either scenario could extend the recovery time to more than a day, but making arrangements for replacement equipment, and for emergency network repairs, should keep the number of days to an absolute minimum. If prolonged failures are possible under these circumstances, you'll want to consider proceeding as for scenario 4.

**Recovery plan**: For multiple equipment failures, check availability of a varying number of replacement machines, ranging from two of your servers, hubs, or whatever, to the whole collection. Get firm estimates on how long it will take to get those machines delivered to your site, and installed and tested before going live. For cable breaks, get a firm estimate of how long it will take to run a replacement cable versus repairing the broken one (it's often much faster to run the replacement out in the open, while simultaneously beginning the repair of the broken one, from the standpoint of restoring network operation). You'll also want to build a recovery budget for this kind of disaster, to include additional personnel costs, materials, or equipment purchase or rental, and service provider costs to assist with restoring multiple backups, installations, and testing.

4. **Disaster**: Total loss of access to the facilities in which the network is housed is the most extreme disaster you'll ever confront. The key to a successful recovery is the existence of backups for the systems and data that will have to be recreated at another location. This underscores the need for off-site backup

storage—if your building is inaccessible and the backups are in the building, too, they might as well not exist! Many companies make arrangements to courier weekly full backups to special fire-proof storage vaults for just this contingency. If you want to be able to recover from this kind of disaster, you should consider doing the same (at the very least, take a set of full backups home with you once a week).

**Recovery requirements**: You'll need to make arrangements to recreate the barest minimum approximation of your original network somewhere else. Because this includes space, furniture, equipment, power, and supplies, many companies contract this out to recovery services that specialize in providing a home away from home for your network. You'll be trading time and effort against expense to do this, but if getting your network back to work soon is an issue, the extra cost will be worth it. If you try to do this sort of thing yourself, you'll have to make sure that there are available personnel to manage simultaneous acquisition of all of these resources.

**Recovery plan**: A full and formal plan of action should be created for this scenario. If you're working with a recovery service, they'll help create such a plan and manage drills for you, all as a part of the services they provide. If you're doing this yourself, which we expect to be the case for most smaller businesses, you'll want to draft a plan that includes specifications and orders for equipment, furniture, and materials, for acquisition of replacement office space, for delivery of all materials, and for installation, testing, and restoration of the network at a designated site. Even if you can't afford a recovery service, hire a consultant with recovery expertise to review your plan just to make sure nothing important has been overlooked. The expense may be unpalatable, but the alternative is far more so!

The key to planning for a successful disaster recovery is identifying the resources and equipment that need to be replaced or repaired and obtaining firm information about how long recovery will take under a variety of circumstances. Then, you and your management can proceed to the next step, balancing costs against losses, to decide what recovery plans make most sense to implement.

# BALANCING COSTS AND LOSSES

The business element in disaster recovery enters when you start dealing with the concept of sustainable loss. As a network administrator, a failed network tells you that it must be restored as quickly as possible, so that the users can get back to work. A business manager or owner will have to weigh the costs of recovery against the losses incurred while the recovery is underway. It's important to understand that cheaper alternatives will have to be found if the cost of recovery for a particular alternative exceeds the losses that would be incurred thereby.

This difference of perspective means that you may end up implementing a disaster recovery plan that takes three days to restore your network to operation at another site, even though you might have been able to finish the job in less time. The element of time is certainly important, but the opportunity costs will balance out your recovery options.

When it comes to calculating costs, it's important to consider that existing staff will have to handle their usual workloads under trying circumstances that will range from operating at an unfamiliar location to working very long hours. At the same time, additional help will be needed to manage delivery, set-up, installation, and testing of an entirely new network under extreme time pressure. It's also wise to trade the costs and advantages of setting up shop temporarily in another location, versus setting up shop on an indefinite basis, especially if a recovery service is involved. Many of these companies offer temporary sites for immediate move-in right after a disaster, but can only supply these locations for a fixed (and typically short) time. If it looks like your main location will remain inaccessible for an appreciable amount of time, you'll also have to manage the acquisition and construction of a more permanent replacement for your network while the temporary version is up and running.

The bottom line for all of this can be scary, but it's important to remember that the costs of doing without a network can be even higher. More important still, the costs of being out of business for any length of time over a week can be downright prohibitive! For that reason, you'll also want to check to see if your organization is covered by any kind of business interruption insurance; if it is, chances are good that the policy will cover some or all of your disaster recovery costs.

## Where Does the Money Go?

Even though disaster recovery services come in many shapes and sizes, their cost structures are all pretty much the same. The actual charges they levy will vary from firm to firm, which is why asking competitive bids is a good idea, but the basic types of charges you'll encounter look like this:

- **Subscription fees**: These are levied yearly, quarterly, or monthly, depending on the details of your contract with the disaster recovery service, but they basically cover the provider's cost of acquiring, maintaining, and being ready to deliver a replacement network for you at a specific period of notice. You should try to negotiate regular drills as a part of this charge.

- **Declaration charge**: This is a one-time fee that is levied each time you declare that a disaster has occurred when you call on the recovery firm to make its equipment and services available to you. It's designed to cover their start-up costs, which may differ, depending on which day of the week and what time of day the declaration occurs.
- **Daily access charges**: These are levied for each day you use the recovery service's facilities, and are intended to cover equipment and facilities usage costs.
- **Technician fees**: These are levied to cover costs for the recovery service's technical staff, and may be charged on an hourly or daily basis. These will vary according to how much help you'll need from the service to supplement your own staff and technicians. It's worthwhile trying to negotiate a certain level of technical support from the service as a part of the other charges, to help minimize these costs.

By the time you add all these charges up, the total may seem overwhelming. When that happens, just consider the alternative, and you'll be glad that a disaster recovery service provides a strong guarantee that you can get your network back in operation within a short period of time.


# BENEFITS OF OFF-SITE OPERATIONS

Beyond a certain point of failure, another location for your network becomes a necessity. Loss of access to your normal site is the obvious case for another location, but loss of access to enough of your normal site, or enough of the equipment and information in it, might also make moving to another location justified.

Moving your network anywhere—even down the hall—is a major pain, so it's important to think of the benefits that moving can confer, if only to motivate yourself enough to survive the ordeal. Here's a list of reasons why moving off site may not be as bad a deal as you think:

- It gets you out of the way of whatever recovery activities may be going on at the original site, not to mention whatever chaos and confusion may ensue.
- It lets you concentrate on restoring the network, and on delivering necessary information and services.
- It gives you the opportunity to rethink your network's operations, organization, and contents.
- It provides an opportunity to try out newer, more powerful equipment and options in the replacement network that gets put into place (and the older the equipment on your original network, the more likely and pronounced this effect will be).

- It lets you see what real "crisis management" is all about, so you'll be better able to appreciate normalcy whenever it returns!

Because your off-site operation may persist for some time, or become the new site for future operations, don't lose sight of the opportunity a move confers to rethink and redesign your network. At first, you'll be much too busy to have time to deal with the big picture, but as things begin to establish a new equilibrium, do yourself a favor and try to take advantage of this radical change in operations and environment.

## Never Bet Your Business Unless You Plan to Win!

Dealing with disaster is difficult and time-consuming, and it requires substantial effort to make sure all the bases are covered. Even worse, the normal workload will not diminish one iota while you're going through this exercise! Because the possibility of disaster is always lurking in the future, the bet that it will strike has already been placed, whether you recognize it and plan for it or not.

However, the benefits of proper planning for disaster can't be overstated. To be able to get back to business in a reasonable amount of time after a total loss of the network is the most amazing thing an organization can do for itself. As with many other forms of insurance, the biggest benefit of such preparation is the comfort that it can confer. In many cases, though, going through the disaster recovery planning exercise provides a much-needed opportunity to review how your organization's information and systems are designed and how well they're functioning.

By forcing you to recreate your network environment, even if it's only on paper, you'll be granted the opportunity to examine in detail what it is that has to be replaced and restored. While you're in the process of identifying all of the network's critical components, and deciding how to build a reasonable facsimile, you'll be able to reconsider and rethink the familiar and the obvious. Although this comes from the "no pain, no gain" vein of benefits, it's still entirely worthwhile!

## Summary

In this chapter we've cogitated on the unthinkable and have tasted of the unpalatable. Planning for a disaster whose chances are remote may seem like the least important of your concerns, but that remains only untrue until the unthinkable happens. So, to prepare you for the worst, we've covered the need for disaster planning and the types of disasters that need to be planned for, and we have tried to outline the costs and contingencies for each of them. If you ignore our advice to plan for disaster, at least now you should know more about the potential downside!

# TRAINING USERS

## 20

Throughout this book, we've repeatedly suggested that training users is a good idea, not only because it will arm them with useful information and improve their confidence and ability to use the network, but also because it should ultimately help to lighten your support load. This may sound like an extra burden to an overworked network administrator, but it's the classic case of prevention versus cure: If you can work with your users before they really get confused, you can head off a lot of support issues before they can even get formulated.

One of the more interesting factoids that's emerged in the networking marketplace in the 1990s is that as much as 40 percent of the overall costs of owning a network, including all hardware, software, and maintenance, over the period of its productive life, will be spent on training and supporting users. Since those numbers can result in expenditures of thousands of dollars per year per user, maybe training isn't quite the small potatoes it at first appears to be! Properly applied, training can be a boon to everyone who interacts with a network, ordinary users and network administrators alike.

Like any kind of education, you and your users will get out of network and computer training more or less what you put into it. This means that planning and preparation will continue to pay off, and that the more energy and thought you put into the training phase, the better off you'll be in the support phase.

In this chapter we'll talk about what training can do for you, along with a variety of ways to develop and deliver training materials. We'll also address alternative resources, including custom manuals, technical support options, and the benefits of advanced training from outside vendors. Our goal is nothing less than to educate you about your network education options, in fact!

## Who's the System Really For?

This is just a reminder that network administrators—and networks—exist to serve users, not the other way around. The most profound benefit that training of any kind can confer is to empower its recipients to perform better at their jobs. Any computer- or network-specific training, therefore, has to be worth something to its attendees to justify taking them away from their jobs to participate in it. We know of several companies who routinely pilot-test all their training, internal and external, and who quash any training from which less than 50 percent of the attendees emerge with positive reviews, or if the majority doesn't rate the training as worthwhile. This is probably a good rule to apply to any training that you develop yourself or that you pay someone else to deliver to the users.

We've also counseled you to habituate yourself to the "tell 'em three times" approach to notifications and information sharing with users. Many companies never go beyond that level of training internally and, if you do a good job of keeping users informed and supplying them with sufficient detail to cope with new and changing network elements, this may be as close to training as you and your organization need to get.

Increasingly, though, companies are coming to rely on their networks to link up all of their employees, many of whom have had no prior contact with computers, let alone networks. Especially for total neophytes, training is an important tool to help overcome people's natural tendency to avoid change and to concentrate on what they already know, no matter how out-of-date or inappropriate that might be. This is particularly true for long-time employees who have considerable expertise in their particular jobs, but who may have had no reason to fool with anything so newfangled as a networked computer in the past. In these circumstances, the role of training is to help overcome fears and prejudices, and to inculcate in new users an appreciation and maybe even respect for what technology can do for them.

Another circumstance that demands training is when a particular position requires extensive knowledge of a particular system or program. Even if the users are minimum-wage, order-entry personnel, they're still required to know what they're doing. And no matter what claims a software vendor might make about how "intuitive" or "natural" its products might be, those feelings invariably come with time, not immediately upon first exposure. This is another case where training is a must, as it would be for any other employee whose primary function is based around some kind of computer system.

There's one final and critical justification for computer and network training in the workplace, and that's to inform its beneficiaries about what's possible from these modern technologies. Even upper management can benefit from systems training and computer familiarization, because it can help them to rethink how its business processes work. In these days of "business reengineering" this is a far more critical task than many organizations are willing to grant.

## AN OUNCE OF TRAINING BEATS A POUND OF TROUBLE

When it comes to being able to cope with the network, whether for first-timers or for more experienced users who are faced with changing systems or software, a little training can often go a long way. Some of the most interesting training classes we've ever attended have taken the time to acquaint users with the fundamentals of what computers and networks are, how they work, and why they behave in the sometimes mysterious ways that they do.

Even though this kind of information may not be germane to any particular position or to learning the details of a particular system, it helps users to know what kind of world they're working in. Thus, we strongly recommend offering an occasional Computing 101 and Networking 101 to your users, or as a part of orientation, to better familiarize new employees with what systems and networks are and can do. This need not even be a class; it could be something like a favorite magazine article or book on the subject, loaned to employees with a recommendation to read it during their first few days at work.

When it comes to introducing new systems or software, hands-on training is best. This need not be structured as a formal class, with all the trappings; it can be delivered one-on-one or several-to-one, with attendees clustered around a PC that you're using to show the important details. In fact, your power users can be a valuable resource to other users if you'll train them first, because they usually function as experts in their local communities.

Whether training is formal or informal, make sure you give plenty of handouts to your attendees, as a memory aid for the important points of what you've covered. Even if it's just a handful of photocopies of screen captures from your demonstration system, with handwritten notes about what's important and how things work, this will still help them to remember what's been covered after the class is over. Don't overlook the information that you can find in manuals or third-party books on software and systems, either: You can use these materials to help structure your training efforts, and they can provide valuable information for handouts, even if you can't afford to give everyone his or her own copies.

Pilot-testing any training you develop is a good idea, too, because it will help you tweak your materials to reach your audience better, and you will be able to use the questions your guinea pigs ask to build a list of commonly asked questions to which you can then provide answers. These kinds of materials make the best handouts for training encounters, simply because they both help users to feel free to ask other questions and usually cover the details that users need to know.

## THE BENEFITS OF BROWN-BAG SEMINARS

A common management objection to training sessions, especially for telemarketing or production-oriented operations, is that they take employees away from their desks during prime-time hours. This is a valid objection, but you shouldn't let it stop you from getting users trained. There are lots of ways to work around schedules—you should be used to this by now, anyway—such as the following:

- **Brown bag seminars** are training sessions held at lunch time (or during the mealtime that hits during the shift being trained), where employees bring their own food (in a brown lunch bag, get it?). These work well for subjects that can be covered in one hour or less, or which can be successfully cut up into one-hour segments. Just make sure each attendee has enough room to spread out his or her meal in addition to whatever training materials might be handed out. Because there's usually drink where there's food, brown bags are not recommended for hands-on computing classes (liquids and keyboards don't mix very well).
- **Evening classes** can work well for subjects that require one- to three-hour periods, provided that a free evening for attendees can be negotiated in advance. It's a good idea, in fact, to meet with attendees a month or more before the seminar is held to let people work out a good time to meet, and to give employees with dependents enough time to make arrangements for baby sitters or caregivers.
- **Weekend day classes** are difficult to sell, but sometimes necessary. Our experience has been that if management will pay attendees for showing up, the bitter pill of losing a weekend day is somewhat mitigated. Like evening seminars, lots of advance notice and a negotiation meeting is the right approach to take for scheduling such a training session. Because of religious obligations and beliefs, some attendees may be unable to participate in either Saturday or Sunday meetings; be prepared to be sensitive, and to repeat the session if necessary, to accommodate your users.

The nice thing about training is that most employees are so grateful to get any amount of it that they will understand the need to work through lunch or on an occasional evening or weekend day to get the information they want and need. As long as you don't waste their time, you'll be able to use non-prime-time encounters to build rapport with your users as well. Don't just roll over and play dead with management if it doesn't initially approve of prime-time training, however—it's worth a little "cussing and discussing" before going with one of the alternatives we've mentioned here!

# BUILDING BETTER MANUALS

Most users build up a repertoire of system knowledge and behaviors over time, as they become more familiar with and accustomed to working in a particular networked environment. If you subscribe to our Management by Walking Around theory (see Chapter 18 for the details), you should try to explore what your users have in their repertoires, as a part of what you discuss when you visit with them.

Although most software packages come with copious documentation, in the form of manuals, quick reference cards, keyboard templates, and even training videos, most of this information never gets used. Why? Because it's often irrelevant to what users need to know when they're sitting at the keyboard doing their jobs. Those hard-earned user repertoires would make much better manuals if they could be captured on paper and distributed to all of your users, wouldn't they?

This task would be a daunting one if you tried to capture this information for all of the programs and systems that your users have to use every day. For the most common programs and the most basic network details, this will prove to be a worthwhile task. If you set yourself a length limit such as "less than five pages," you'll be forced to distill the information down to its bare essentials. Then, make sure that your handouts of these mini-manuals include blank pages so that your users can record additional things they think are important, and you'll make them happy while creating a powerful resource for future revisions!

We also see a growing trend in the marketplace for software products or third-party vendors to offer customizable manuals for systems and software. We applaud this trend and wish it were already more widespread. Today, an excellent example of this technology can be found in *Kits for Creating Customized NetWare* manuals, published by M&T Books (see the Further Reading section at the end of this chapter for all the details). Customizable on-line help for some Windows-based applications offers similar capabilities and may also be worth investigating (Blue Sky Software's RoboHelp program, advertised as a "Microsoft Windows Help Authoring System," is the best product we've seen in this category).

The bottom line is to capture and distribute information that users deem useful or helpful, not to recreate an encyclopedia of seldom-used facts about their network and computing environment.

# REMOTE CONTROL:
# THE NEXT BEST THING TO BEING THERE

Occasionally there's no substitute for sitting down with users and taking them through a series of menus, or showing them exactly how to enter a particularly tortuous series of commands at the screen. Unfortunately, getting together can be a problem (especially if you're in Dubuque and your user's in Des Moines). Here's where the network can be a big help: There's a large category of software utilities, known collectively as *"remote-control software,"* that will let you attach to a user's computer over the network and turn it into a slave of your own. Then, everything you do on your own desktop automatically shows up on the other user's computer. Some remote-control programs will even let you slave multiple users to your machine at the same time, so that you can take a gang of them through a hands-on demonstration, no matter where you and they might be. We think this is actually better than getting everyone clustered around a single system, as long as you can conference your users over the telephone at the same time (your commentary is almost as important as the demonstration, after all).

For helping the hopelessly addled, or for training users on new programs, features, or functions, remote-control software can be a valuable tool. Because there are so many different varieties of such software available today, for different kinds of hardware (you will have to have the same type of computer—PC clone and PC clone, or Macintosh and Macintosh—and a common network link, for remote-control software to work) and different kinds of networking, we can't really give you a meaningful list of potential candidate products. However, if you check either of the buyers' guides we referenced in the Further Reading section of Chapter 17, you can quickly find the programs that meet your hardware and networking software requirements.

Check out remote control capability for your network—we're sure you'll find it a worthwhile training and support tool!

# ADVANCED TRAINING:
# PROS, CONS AND COSTS

Some of your users may need to get serious about training, especially if your organization requires them to work with specialized systems in their jobs. This could be as mundane as a page-layout program for your marketing relations staff, or as exotic as the control program for a Magnetic Resonance Imaging (MRI) machine. As a network administrator, you can't expect to know everything about all of the systems and programs on the network, so don't be surprised when users ask for help in finding outside training courses to meet more advanced needs.

The pros of outside training are many: They include high-quality classroom training, hands-on exposure to state-of-the-art systems and technologies, access to leading authorities in the field of training, and opportunities to watch professional trainers at work. The cons can seem daunting, though, even when there aren't any viable alternatives to outside training: Travel and lodging may be required, significant time away from the office may be involved, and the selection process for training may not always produce results that meet the needs of the individuals being trained.

Last, but by no means least, there's the cost factor of training. Most quality classroom training costs at least $200–$300 per day of instruction if your attendees go to scheduled classes off site; on-site training from outside sources will typically be an option only if you plan to send 10 or more employees to a given class, since normal rates for such training is $2,000 per day and up. Add travel and lodging to this—it's an add-on for most on-site instructors and required for your employees if they're out of your immediate area—and costs can seem downright prohibitive.

The key to selling training to management is to justify it by its returns. It's easiest if the person who needs training simply can't function without going to a class, but that's seldom the case. You'll need to resort to your company training policies to help figure the value of the benefits that training can supply, and be ingenious in your arguments if you encounter resistance when it comes to justifying training, whether it's for yourself or your users. Another useful approach is to consider training someone to be an in-house trainer, who can then spread the information, and the cost of training, across a larger number of employees. This is yet another benefit you can propose to your power users, who will probably learn the most from such training anyway.

One last tip: If you have to arrange for outside training, for either yourself or others in your organization, shop around for training companies. The more basic the topic, the more options you'll have. Take the same approach to training companies that we recommended for selecting cabling contractors in Chapter 8: Ask for referrals, talk to previous customers, and always, always check references. If you're a member of a local network user group of some kind (like NetWare Users International), these organizations are an invaluable source of information and feedback about your training options.

## ADMINISTRATOR, TRAIN THYSELF!

When it comes to training, don't forget your own needs. Your network probably consists of a sizable collection of systems, network equipment, and software. The more you know about how each piece works, the better you can use it. The more you know about networks in general, and yours in particular, the better you can make it for your users and your organization.

Given the mix of technologies available today, and the rate of technological change that networks are experiencing, on-going training has to be part of any responsible network administrator's job. By all means, try the same justification techniques for yourself that we recommended for users in the preceding section, but understand that since your responsibilities are greater, your need for knowledge—and hence, for training—is also greater.

Don't take no for an answer when it comes to training yourself. If your company won't fund classroom training, look into self-study courses, computer-based training, and make regular visits to your local computer-aware bookstore. Obtain and read network-focused trade publications (see our Publication List in the Resource Guide at the end of this book for a good list of candidates), and do what you can to keep in touch with the ebb and flow of network technologies. The more you learn, the more valuable you'll be (and if your company won't pay for training, you can set yourself the objective of becoming knowledgeable enough to appeal to a company that will). Remember also that training you pay for out of your own pocket may be tax-deductible if it's job-related (please consult a tax professional before trying to write anything off, however).

## SUMMARY

In this chapter we've investigated the costs and benefits of training, both for you and your users. By remembering that your role, and the network's role, is to serve your users and to enhance their abilities to do their jobs, you'll automatically develop an attitude that promotes the free exchange of information and ideas that good training represents. If you can work within the constraints of your organization to deliver training and information, you'll be meeting the ultimate goal of serving your users. And while you're about the training task, don't forget your own needs to learn and grow, so you can keep up with ever-changing and expanding computing and networking tools and technologies.

## FURTHER READING AND INFORMATION

There are plenty of sources for network training information, if you know where to look or how to get on the right mailing lists. In fact, if you end up subscribing to one or more of the networking publications we recommend in the Publication List in our Resource Guide at the end of this book, you'll start getting lots of potential training advertisements in the mail! We've had particularly good luck with several training companies in the United States, but only one of them operates nationwide. For local references, check with other network administrators, user groups, or on-line bulletin boards for recommendations for quality training companies.

The NetWare Manual Makers series information is as follows:

Christine Milligan, *The NetWare 286 Manual Maker*, M&T Books, Redwood City, CA, 1989 ($49.95).

Christine Milligan, *The NetWare 386 Manual Maker*, M&T Books, Redwood City, CA, 1989 ($49.95).

Kelley J. P. Lindberg, *The NetWare for Macintosh Manual Maker*, M&T Books, Redwood City, CA, 1989 ($49.95).

Unfortunately, these books are out of date and aren't worth acquiring unless your NetWare is equally obsolete. However, they can serve as a model for how to build customized documentation for your system, and they even include a disk that offers templates and prewritten information to help with the task.

American Research Group, Inc., is located at P.O. Box 1039, Cary, NC, 27512, and can be reached at 919-467-8797 (Fax: 919-380-0097). They are one of the preeminent network training companies in the United States, whose curriculum includes every-thing from introductory networking classes, to wiring system training, through advanced network protocol analysis, system administration, and internetworking training. Their rates average $300 a day, but their attendee satisfaction rating is among the best we've ever seen. They teach classes all over the United States, typi-cally near large metropolitan airports to facilitate access to attendees, and may be teaching something interesting in a town near you soon. A phone call will get you their course catalog.

# PLANNING FOR THE FUTURE

**21**

Planning is a consistent theme in our discussion of network design, but that's only because planning and the research that typically precedes it are key ingredients to delivering quality networks to any organization. While we've already discussed the need to plan for growth and to be ready to expand and support the services that your network offers, in this chapter we'll examine some of the more important aspects involved in planning for an uncertain future.

As always, the main ingredient for a successful future network remains the same as that for a successful present network: *information*. The more you know about your organization's activities or business, the better prepared you'll be to assess up-and-coming technologies. The more you know about those technologies, the better you'll be able to determine their fit to your anticipated needs.

When it comes to deciphering the promises that technology makes for the future, it's also important to apply a little bit of everyday product savvy to the hype. Most vendors paint pretty rosy futures, both because they want to grab "mind share" well in advance of product delivery these days and, even more important, because they want to have a place in your budget planning as well.

If you remember that delivered products seldom match their pre-release features, functions and costs as touted by vendors talking up unfinished products, you'll be better armed to evaluate realistically what network professionals call "slideware" (so-named because the only place the product under discussion typically runs right now is on the slide you're looking at). The relationship between promises and reality weakens further as the time gap between the planned delivery you're hearing about and the actual release date increases.

The other thing to remember is the old adage: "If it sounds too good to be true, it probably is." Beware of vendors whose next product or release will "solve all your problems" or do "everything you want it to." Chances are nearly 100 percent that the person who's making those promises doesn't fully understand all of your problems, nor have a firm grasp on the things that you really do want your systems to be able to do. When it comes to systems and software, the sad truth is that one size never fits all, and no one solution solves all problems.

The bottom line is that nowhere else does caveat emptor ("let the buyer beware") apply so forcefully as it does to buying futures. Use your common sense and believe no more than half of what you're told, and you'll be much less likely to be disappointed at what gets delivered. It's okay to expect great things from the future, but it's not okay to bet your organization's continued success on systems, software, or products that have yet to see the light of day.

## WHERE'S THE BEEF?

The most important thing you'll need in order to evaluate your future networking options is a firm grasp on today's networking reality. This means understanding as much about your organization's activities and work procedures as you possibly can. It's entirely possible that you may be able to revamp and upgrade your network entirely from systems, software, and other products already available today, without having to wait for the opportunity to try out systems, software, or products currently under development.

Here again, we feel compelled to remind you what a network is really for and who it's supposed to serve: A network's primary role should be to improve the productivity and capabilities of its users. Only by knowing as much as possible about what users do with the network—and what they do without it—can you understand what's missing in your current implementations and services. Sometimes, recognizing the gaps that the network has failed to fill, and providing solutions that fill them, can be the biggest and most obvious benefits that the network can provide.

This puts you in an interesting position, but one that should be keenly felt by technologists of any kind: The role of technology is to enable, empower, and energize its users, not to be an end in itself. Admittedly, there's so much "neat stuff" involved in networking that the temptation is always there to dive in and lose yourself in the oceans of available information and interesting facts. The link back to your users, and to your organization's activities, is what helps you stay real. The key to finding solutions is to know the problems that drive them, and to understand that these problems keep changing and shifting over time. The marketplace is littered with products whose epitaphs read: "A great solution in search of a problem."

This points to the other side of the solutions picture, namely, the need to stay in touch with current networking developments and emerging network technologies.

The only way to find the best possible solutions for your users' needs is to know what options are available and to develop a feel as to how they compare to each other. This means keeping up with on-going technology developments, emerging industry standards, and looking for other organizations who have come up with solutions to problems that have something in common with the problems you're trying to address.

If you know what problems you need to solve, and the kinds of solutions available to meet them, you'll be well on your way to finding the pot of gold at the end of the technology rainbow.

## What's Hot and What's Not?

Keeping up with technology could be a time-and-a-half job if you were willing to get completely sucked in. There's so much going on in the networking marketplace, and so many aspects of the technologies involved—from hardware, to systems, to software, to communications, and much, much more—that the real issue is to establish and maintain a focus on what's most important to you and your organization's needs.

The secret is to let your problems drive your search for solutions. Sure, there's lots of interesting things happening with multimedia applications for networking these days, but is that something you really need to know about. While new technologies and products may have lots of sex appeal, or even be of genuine technical interest, they don't matter very much if they don't apply to the problems you're trying to solve. A print shop is probably not going to need much multimedia capability in the near future, but a research hospital can probably realize immediate benefits from its use.

There's always lots of "hot stuff" being discussed in the trade rags, and some of it may even have significance for network computing. But it's really only "hot stuff" in truth if it can be a contributing factor in solving problems that you're dealing with today, or that you can see coming at you in the relatively near future. While it will be difficult to rein in your enthusiasm and curiosity, this is the only way to separate the futures worth watching from the many futures that keep popping up every day.

## Networked Software: Licensing, Legality, and the SPA

Networking does bring some interesting issues to the fore, however, and sometimes those issues can have profound implications whether you find them fascinating or forgettable. Because the tendency is to use the network to distribute and deliver applications to users, you'll want to consider the legality of how you're using and delivering that software. The Software Publishing Association (SPA) has been doing a good job of cracking down on companies who use copyrighted software illegally, and you'll want to review your current set-up and methods in light of the potential liability that illegal use can incur.

Networking makes it so much easier to move copies of applications around to multiple users that it takes the temptation to spread copies of software around nearly irresistible. The network map can be invaluable in monitoring this tendency, because it tells you which applications are installed on what machines. If your count of legal copies—with master diskettes, the software license, and other materials—equals or exceeds the count from your map, you have nothing to fear. Otherwise, you'd better start moving toward getting legal, or a visit from the SPA may compel you to do so and sock you with some substantial fines for copyright violation as an unwanted bonus.

As more and more software becomes *network-aware*, meaning that it understands that it's being used on a network and is monitoring its own usage (looking for duplicate serial numbers, or some equivalent self-check), this problem will abate over time. The other positive trend is for companies to provide networked versions of their software, which include a license for a fixed number of simultaneous users, that can do their own policing.

But since so many software packages do not offer built-in license management, you should consider some of the license management products available for that purpose on the market today (these products are also known as "software metering" applications). These packages act as sentries that keep count of the total number of simultaneous users of an application, and refuse entry to any who ask to use the application as soon as the legal count is filled. This may frustrate some users when it happens, but it will keep you on the right side of the law. We strongly recommend that you research your options for this kind of software for your network and that you use the SPA as a club to get permission to buy one, should your management balk at the outlay (you can find lots of candidates in either the *LAN Times* or *LAN Magazine Buyers Guides*; see the Further Reading section in Chapter 17, for the details).

## Watching the Trades, Catching The Trends

The number of network-related publications continues to grow, and the amount of network coverage in other computer industry periodicals is keeping pace as well. Given an ever-larger mass of details to wade through, how's a responsible network administrator going to cope with all this information? The answer, as we indicated earlier in this chapter, is "focus, focus, focus." Focus on your immediate and anticipated problems, focus on what you've already got in place and where it's going in the future, and focus on your users' and your organization's needs. Believe us, this will probably be more than you can handle by yourself anyway—you've got a real job too, remember?

## Battling the Buzzwords

Nevertheless, there are some important networking trends being covered in the trade press that may have relevance to your organization and that could even help with some of your problems. None of these is fully baked today, so don't expect magic solutions to leap right out at you, but all of them could have an impact on the ways every one of us does business in the future. Here's a list of emerging technologies that you might want to keep an eye on in the future.

- **Groupware** refers to an emerging class of applications that builds group coordination into their basic capabilities. Examples available today include group scheduling and calendaring programs that can coordinate meetings and the use of shared facilities, such as meeting rooms. We expect more and more programs to become groupware-oriented in the future.
- **Imaging** confers the ability to incorporate, store, and move image-based data around a network. This includes legal documents (bank signature cards, contracts, etc.), but also enables all documents to be stored electronically on the network. Imaging is essential technology for better integrating most work processes (which are mainly paper-based today) into the electronic age.
- **Workflow** refers to the ability to use software to route information among co-workers (and someday, even between organizations). An example might be at an insurance company, where a mail processor would open a claim form and scan it into the network. It could then be routed electronically to a claims processor, to the adjuster, back to the claims processor, and on to accounts payable to be paid out. The benefits of workflow are that it matches paperflow's ability to be dispatches around an organization, but includes built-in tracking and archiving, so that it's always clear who has possession of a particular document, thus nothing ever gets lost. Workflow will be an important step toward reducing the staggering amounts of paper used in most organizations today.
- **Networked Telephony** refers to the ability to link telephone and data networks together, so that users can look up phone or fax numbers on-screen, and then instruct the computer to place a call or send a fax immediately. Telephony

applications also promise to integrate telephone and data network management much more tightly, and should ultimately allow voice and digital communications to be interleaved (remember our example of the remote-control training in Chapter 20), Since many workers use a telephone and a networked computer in their jobs today, telephony technology should offer interesting productivity improvements (if it lives up to current vendor claims for the future, that is).

- **Digital Signature** refers to the ability to attach a unique, legally binding, and secure identifier to network communications that acts electronically like your signature does on a check, credit card slip, or other legal document. This technology will enable users to conduct business over the network. In tandem with Electronic Data Interchange (EDI), this technology should facilitate transfers of funds and orders between companies. It is an impetus to take networked companies and attach them to public networks and, ultimately, to the emerging digital superhighway touted by the Clinton administration.

In some ways, this is just a sample cross section of emerging technologies that could impact your organization. We just happen to think that these are some that have a better-than-average chance of being fully realized and of showing up on a network near you soon. You will undoubtedly discover others as you try to stay focused on what's of most concern to you. The main thing is to remember that need to focus, so keep asking yourself about these new technological wonderlands as they shimmer invitingly before you: "What's in it for my users?"

## Summary

In this chapter we've tried to arm you against the lures and lies you'll sometimes hear when you encounter technological futures. While it's important to stay in touch with networking technologies that could impact your organization, it's equally important to recognize that the future is never all that it's cracked up to be. If you know what problems you need to solve, and what processes you need to move onto the network, your knowledge will guide you through the maze of future technologies that vendors will cheerfully try to sell to you. The important thing is to maintain a focus on what's relevant for you and your organization, to help you attend to those things that will be of the greatest use.

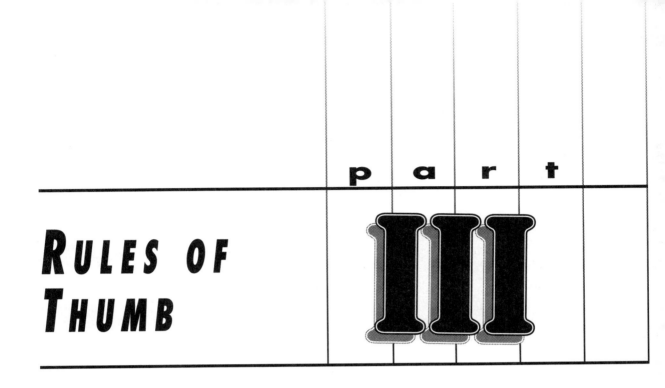

# RULES OF THUMB

**part III**

**B**y now, you should be familiar with the procedures and practices for running a network, as well as with the underlying concepts and components for networking. We sincerely hope that you've acquired an appreciation for the ordinary activities involved in feeding and caring for a network and its users and that you've also learned how very extraordinary the job of a network administrator can occasionally be.

This book has tried to acquaint you with the value of networking technology, but in the context of how to make it work to the benefit of your users and your organization. At this point, you should have some idea about how to lay out a network, how to ensure that one can be put in place, and what to do with it when you've got one.

You should also have an idea about how to document what's out there on your network (or at least what's planned to be out there). Armed with this information, you've also learned about how to plan for growth, how to budget for installation or growth, and how to spend money and hire talent to help you do what needs to be done with your network. You've also learned to anticipate the new products and technologies that networking can bring, but to look with a jaundiced eye at vendors who promise you the world.

If any of this material sounds unfamiliar or strange, dig back into the chapters in Parts I and II and refresh your memory. At this point in the book, we've covered all of the material that we feel is needed for a general book on designing and running a network. This section is devoted to a collection of rules of thumb, and includes checklists, how-tos, gotchas, and other information, organized around specific topics or activities that you will encounter as you confront your network. Use it as a reference tool before you go out to tackle the network, or as a guide back into Parts I and II. We hope you find it informative and useful!

# PRINCIPLES OF EFFECTIVE LAYOUT

# 22

I f you've been charged with building a network, you'll have to decide where the elements of the network—the cabling and the equipment—must go. As you consider the awesome responsibility involved, review our tips for deciding how to lay your network out. We'll try to make sure that you balance convenience for your users against the need to keep the cabling and equipment safe from harm, and from light-fingered larcenists who might otherwise lend a new poignancy to the term "mobile computing."

## START AND END WITH A MAP

Chapter 25 covers the details of building and managing a network map, but we'd just like to point out that the best way to lay things out is on a set of plans, or a to-scale drawing, of the space your network is going to invade. If you start with a realistic idea of the space you're working with, your layout will make more sense, and will keep more with the version that ultimately gets built.

Plus, if you start out with a network map and keep up with all the work on that map, you'll be able to keep track of everything in one place, starting with layout through installation, and afterwards, as you fiddle with and tweak your network and begin the process of growth and evolution.

When it comes to planning cable runs, it's also a good idea to find out where the other wires in your space are. These could be electrical wiring, telephone wiring, or other communications media (closed-circuit cable TV for security systems, distribution wiring for mainframes or other pre-networking cabling, and more). By studying where the wiring already runs, you can learn some valuable information:

- Look for cases where the straight line between two points isn't used; this will often point out obstacles or impediments that had to be wired around, rather than through. You may have to do the same thing yourself.
- If existing wiring is running in cable trays or conduit, you may be able to pull your cables through the same carriers. This can save time and money during the installation process.
- Check out the kinds of cable and their coatings; this will often alert you to specific building code requirements and may ultimately help you select which type of cable to use for your network.
- If you're thinking about using modular wall plates, look at how other wiring is placed in the walls; this may help you find easier access spots for your wiring than you might otherwise pick for yourself.

When it comes to layout, the path of least resistance is very often also the path of least expense. That's the real reason why it's worthwhile to look over the wiring that's already been installed at your site.

## GET CLOSE TO THE USERS

Networks are for users; that's why the layout you design should bring the network as close to them as possible. For new build-outs, this means working with your facilities staff or office manager to decide where desks, cubicle walls, or other office furniture will be positioned. You'll want to bring the network connections right to each user's desk, credenza, or wherever else they put their computers. For installation into existing offices, you'll have to balance access versus aesthetics, and both will undoubtedly end up suffering! However, remember that close is better!

For those of you considering a star topology, the idealized pictures we presented in Chapter 2 don't do justice to the way things typically get wired. In fact, unless your hub is centrally located in the middle of a cluster of offices, it won't look anything like Figure 2.2 (p. 16). Rather, wires for offices in proximity to one another will typically follow the same path until they branch off to feed into the particular office that they service.

The implications of this arrangement are that you should decide on a common wall over which the cables will run, and make sure that you can get from that area to wherever the network connection needs to occur, while still staying within the distance limitations for twisted-pair media. For widely dispersed offices, this may increase the overall number of hubs you'll need, since the limiting factor will be the

Hub

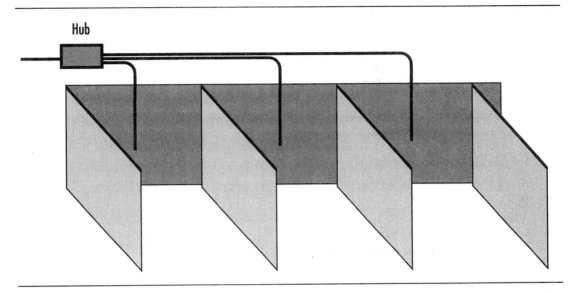

**Figure 22.1**   *A typical as-built office twisted-pair wiring scheme.*

length of the hub-to-office cable runs, and not the number of ports per hub. A typical installation of a star-wired network for offices on a common hallway is depicted in Figure 22.1.

Even though coax-based networks use a different distribution metaphor, it's still a good idea to use a common wall as the way to route the network cable if that's at all possible. Coax cables have to run something like a river that has to pass by all the points where there's a network attachment, as shown in Figure 22.2. The cable has to loop around to all of the connection points in order to get to all of the nodes along the way. This also explains why coax installations are more likely to result in visible cables dangling from the ceiling than twisted-pair installations.

## BRING SERVICES WHERE THEY'RE NEEDED

Planning a network layout is, at least in part, an exercise in bottom-up design. If you take a floor plan (your prototypical map) and mark all of the offices and areas where network connections are needed, you'll have most of the information you'll need to play the "graphing game." From a mathematical standpoint, a network is a kind of connected graph called a tree, where each piece of equipment is a node in the graph, and the cables are the branches (the lines that connect all the nodes together). A hub or router is like a link from a major branch to the trunk of the tree, and the cable or cables that link hubs or routers together is the trunk itself.

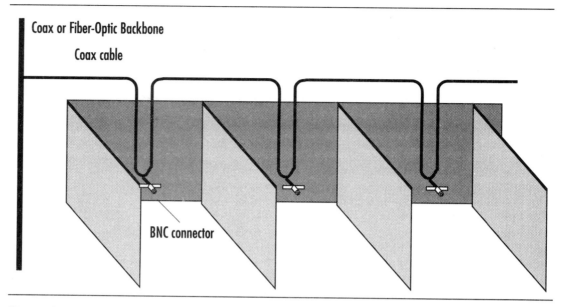

**Figure 22.2** *A typical as-built office coaxial wiring scheme.*

Why are we swinging in these metaphorical trees as we talk about network layout? It's not because of a Tarzan fixation, it's because this type of organization works very well for matching networks to buildings and offices. If you think of the cable that links multiple areas or floors together as the trunk, the individual hubs or cable segments served by routers are the branches, and the cables that pass by or extend into offices are lesser branches that finally bring the network to the workers, as depicted in Figure 22.3.

Physical limitations on your chosen media will dictate how the farthest ends of the network get laid out, simply because they'll lead to natural groupings of computers around the cabling. The links between groupings will define the next layer of the network, which feeds into higher layers as branches get closer to the trunk. Most network technologies support only three or four layers of branches anyway, so your network trees won't even begin to approach the giants of the forest floor in complexity!

## USE WHAT YOU'VE GOT—OR NOT?

If you make a decision to use twisted-pair cabling for your network, questions about reuse of already installed telephone wiring will inevitably come up. To resolve this issue, the best thing to do is to find out how much unused cabling is available and what the distribution scheme for that unused cabling might be.

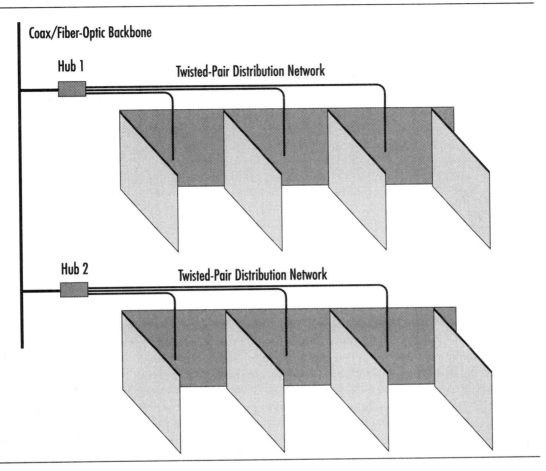

**Figure 22.3** *A hierarchical, as-built network "tree."*

The best possible scenario is to learn that two or more unused pairs are available for each and every office (or wall jack) that you need to access. This might mean that all of your network cabling is already in place, just waiting to be hooked up and used! The problem is that you'll have to test this wiring in order to determine if it's suitable for network use or not. Our advice is to hire a professional cable installer to come in and test your wiring for you. The job will be far less than the cost of an equivalent installation, and no matter what you learn, you'll never have to wonder if the telephone wiring was right for your network or not.

Even if you learn that this wiring isn't suitable, the premises' wiring equipment for the telephone system may still be worth investigating. If the system is new enough to be built around standard punch-down blocks and there's sufficient unused connections in the equipment, you'll want to investigate using that equipment to do double-duty—that is, to determine if the same wiring control centers can service the network as well as the telephones. Here again, a cable installer can answer that question quickly and cheaply, so you'll be able to proceed with dispatch.

Given that network bandwidth requirements are increasing steadily with time, we recommend bidding out the cost of using newer shielded twisted-pair cabling for your network, unless that type of cable is what's already available for your use. Unless you're dealing with a new building, many of which are prewired for networks these days, or you are extremely lucky, you may not be able to use the installed cabling for anything but Ethernet or token-ring networks, if that.

## POOLING RESOURCES

Don't forget that a good network layout plans for unused capacity to leave room for growth, and that you need to plan for connections for network equipment, peripherals, and servers, in addition to your end-user machines. Many a network layout has had to be scrapped because all the ports in a hub were filled before the designer realized that a printer and a fax server had to be installed along the same hallway as the offices needing network connections. A good rule of thumb is to leave two ports unused on every hub and to buy expandable routers that can add at least one more port, whenever you plan out a network layout. That way, unexpected needs can be serviced without redesign, and there'll still be room to extend the network, if need be, to accommodate future growth.

## SUMMARY

In this chapter we've looked over the principles for effective network layout. If you stay aware of how your design stays within the limits of the technology you're using, and leave some slack left over for surprises and growth, you'll be able to live with your work for at least a while. If not, you'll have the joy of doing things over (and over) as you make the changes needed to make the layout right.

WIRING
ESSENTIALS

# chapter

# 23

After the layout comes the installation. The cabling typically comes first, as the skeleton of your network begins to take shape. In this chapter we'll cover the information that's essential to wiring that works well, and share some techniques to help you cope with constant change. As people and machines move around, you'll thank us for these tips for keeping track of which end of the wiring goes where!

## DECREASING WEAR AND TEAR

No matter what kind of media you use, the most important thing to remember is that cable does not respond well to physical stress. Loose connections are, by far, the biggest cause of network difficulties, and physical stress causes the most loose connections that we've encountered in the workplace. So much for general guidelines. What does "avoid stressing the cabling" mean to you, when you're placing wiring?

First, it means that you have to educate your users about the media limitations. It doesn't hurt to tell them to leave the cable alone as much as possible. For bus-based topologies, it may even make sense to tell them not to touch the cable at all (remember, the wrong kind of disconnection on a bus topology will bring the whole cable segment down. We *hate* when that happens!). A word of warning to the users is in order, at the very least.

Second, it means that you should avoid running cable where it's going to be subjected to any kind of stress. This means keeping cable off the floor as much as possible. This especially means keeping cable well away from rolling desk chairs, dollies, or anything else with wheels on it (wheels do a marvelous job of concentrating lots of weight onto a small point of contact, which works entirely too well at beating up cable). It also means keeping cable out of doorways or anywhere else it's likely to be stressed.

Third, it means that you should be very careful about yanking or pulling on cables in general, even during the installation process. It's better to pay out cable and pull it gently over its intended path than to force it to pay out from a spool at the same time it's being pulled out. That also means that the cable selected to be pulled through conduit has to be rated to handle the torque it will be subjected to during that process, and that the torque level needs to be monitored to make sure it doesn't get overstressed. For coaxial and fiber-optic cable, this also means knowing the bend radius limitations for cable and being careful not to exceed them. Broken cables will make themselves known almost immediately, but damaged cables are worse, because they may not identify themselves readily for years to come (while causing intermittent network problems the whole time).

To sum up: Be careful, be gentle, and stay within the installation ratings. Keep cable away from traffic, pressure, or impact. If you keep your cable free of stress, it'll do the same for you!

## Make It Easy to Get Things Right

Each type of networking medium has its own set of rules and regulations for what it can and can't do. There are too many different kinds of cables and wiring for us to document each one, but here's what you need to find out for each type of networking medium that you use:

- **Maximum permissible length for any single cable segment**
  This will help you to estimate the reach for the areas that can be serviced by a single cable segment on your network.
- **Insertion loss for each device on a segment**
  Every time you plug in a device on a cable segment, it shortens the actual permissible length that the segment can reach from the maximum by a fixed amount. Use this figure to deduct the number of connections, times the insertion loss, from the maximum permissible length to calculate the actual permissible length of the segment. This calculation is only necessary for coaxial media, because both fiber-optic and twisted-pair are point-to-point media (only two connections per cable are legal).

- **Maximum number of devices per segment**
  This tells you what the ceiling for the number of devices on a cable segment will be (again, applies only to coaxial media).
- **Maximum number of segments between any two devices on the network**
  This is sometimes listed as the maximum number of repeaters per network. It will allow you to calculate the maximum span of a network based entirely on this medium (most conductive wiring systems are too limited for larger installations, which also helps to explain the growing popularity of fiber-optic network backbones. The maximum circumference of an FDDI ring is about 66 *miles*).
- **The medium's termination requirements, if applicable**
  These will tell you if terminators are required, and what kind are needed, if applicable. This applies to most coaxial media, and to daisy-chained, twisted pair media (like Apple's LocalTalk) as well.
- **The medium's impedance rating, if applicable**
  You'll need this value to test your cables.
- **The medium's signaling characteristics**
  You'll simulate these to stress-test and communications-test your cable.

Some manufacturers will offer you products that exceed some of these values. This might sound like a great deal, but their guarantees are only good if their equipment and interfaces are the only kind in use on your network. This might be too much of a commitment to be worth it!

# Spending Money Versus Spending Time

When it comes to installing cabling, if you're inclined to be a do-it-yourselfer, go through the exercise of determining the cost of your time, and compare it to the bids you get from the professionals. Unless you're a real cabling professional, plan on it taking you two to three times their estimate to finish the job yourself. Add to the cost of materials, tools, and test equipment the value of the time it's going to take you to cable up your network (which you can calculate by multiplying your hourly rate times the number of hours it's going to take). We think it's only prudent to do it yourself if the number for that option comes out lower than the professionals' estimate, or if you can't afford to put in a network any other way.

Remember, if you install the network, you're the one they'll call to fix it whenever it breaks. The best thing you get from a professional installer is a warranty and access to trained repair personnel!

## Tooling Up for the Trade

If you end up doing the wiring yourself, be sure to spend the money it takes to buy good tools. This means you'll probably spend at least $200 to $300 on tools. We also recommend buying extra cable and connectors to practice on, and to practice building cables for your network until you can build a working one every time, before you start crawling into the ceiling with your miner's helmet and lamp.

Tooling up also means arranging for the use of proper test equipment during the installation process. For conductive media, buy a good-quality voltage/ohmmeter (VOM) for your tool kit and take it with you everywhere you go to install cables (it's also what you'll need to use to check your work during the practice phase we recommend). Other test equipment you'll need (to rent, at least) during the installation process will include a TDR (time-domain reflectometer), a protocol analyzer, and possibly an oscilloscope/signal generator for load-testing. Most of this equipment is too expensive to buy unless your organization can justify paying for a full-time cable installer as a part of its networking department.

Our last word on tooling up: Don't try to build your own fiber-optic cables unless you really are a trained professional. The test equipment is pretty exotic and expensive, too. We think this exercise is nowhere near worth the grief and expense it can incur. Proceed at your own risk!

## Always Label Your Cable

The best reason we can think of for beginning your network map at this stage of the game is that it is where you'll want to record the cable labeling information. For absolute clarity, we'll say even more strongly: Never, never, never lay out a cable segment without attaching a tag to each end that bears the same unique identifier. It's worth taking the time to think ahead to come up with a good labeling scheme before you start. It's even more worthwhile to follow our advice and put label tags on each cable end. It's most worthwhile if you also record the tag ID on your network map, to identify the placement of the cable's ends and to trace its route from end to end.

This does involve extra planning and work, it's true. But when you have to move people or equipment around, you'll know exactly what you're dealing with, and how things get from here to there. If you're not convinced, take our word for it: This is worth doing!

## SUMMARY

In this chapter we've examined some rules and tools for dealing with wiring. We talked about what media limitations you'll want to establish and observe, and about the difference between hiring your network out versus building your own. We've stressed the importance of acquiring the right tools for the job and of making sure that cables are properly labeled. Throughout this material, we also stressed that the difference between gambling and network design is that in one, cheating will only get you killed; but in the other, it will get you killed over and over again! We hope you can guess which is which.

# PLACEMENT PRACTICES

## 24

A statistical analysis of most networks reveals that of all the equipment that a network interconnects, 10–15% is intended to be a common resource for the entire network. This kind of equipment falls into three broad categories:

- **Shared peripherals**: These include input or output devices, such as scanners, plotters, printers, fax machines, film recorders, image setters, and other pieces of gear that users need to get things from (or put things into) in order to complete certain tasks.
- **Network servers**: These include the computers and systems that provide services to users on the network, including print queues, network file systems, message handling, and shared applications.
- **Network equipment**: These include the hubs, routers, wide area network links, satellite links, or other equipment that help to tie the network together and that let the many pieces of a network function as an integrated whole.

The rules of placement are different for all three because of the way in which each one gets used and the kind of proximity and access it must supply. In this chapter we'll examine the placement factors you should consider for each class of equipment, while reviewing the needs for physical security, for making network facilities convenient for users, and for managing the difference between your perception of perfect placement and your users'.

## PROXIMITY AND ACCESS

One of the main differences that separates the three classes of equipment is proximity. Stated as a question, this would be: What does this piece of equipment have to be close to, in order to be optimally placed? Here are some answers:

- Shared peripherals need to be close to their intended users. This virtually mandates placement in a public area close to those users' offices, cubicles, or wherever else they hang their hats.
- Network servers need to be kept away from the public eye but have to be easily accessible—especially for you. For this type of equipment, you'll want them in your neighborhood, but you'll also want to make sure they're located where adequate electrical service, proper cooling and ventilation, and enough room to accommodate the tape drives, disk farms, and other server gear can also be housed.
- Network equipment needs to be placed where the branches in your network tree come together. Approaching the limits of permissible distance on cable segments can force you to put this gear in some mighty strange places, unless you plan for some slack to let you decide where this stuff should go. Remember also that this equipment needs adequate electrical service, and proper cooling and ventilation as much as your servers do. Because its job is both subtle and critical, this equipment is seldom housed in public areas.

If you consider these factors when placing your equipment, you'll be more likely to meet the needs of your various constituencies. Sometimes, you'll have no choice but to violate these principles, but be prepared to take the heat if you put shared peripherals in hard-to-reach or out-of-the-way places!

## SECURING YOUR ASSETS

No matter what kind of device you're placing on the network, it pays to be aware of physical security. Just because a shared peripheral, say, a printer, has to go in a public place doesn't mean that it should be placed in an area that is completely insecure. In other words, you'll want to pick a table or a room near an administrator or a file clerk who's usually around, rather than putting the equipment in the break room, where you never know who's going to be around (and where, for example, vending machine personnel enters freely once or twice a week).

The more critical the asset, the more steps you'll want to take to safeguard it. Expensive peripherals might need to be secured to a tabletop with a cable locking system, or have a custom base built that allows easy access but prevents theft. For servers and network equipment, whose loss means loss of the network, physical security has to be a more pressing concern. Unless the users need direct access to this equipment, it is best locked away in a separate room to which only you and your security staff have keys. If direct access is required, we recommend setting up a locked laboratory where access is controlled through a pass-card or combination lock. That makes it easy for authorized personnel to get access at any time, but keeps everybody else away.

Stressing security with your users is also a good idea. Let them know how much this stuff is worth and how long it will take to get it replaced or returned if it wanders off. If you tell them that such a loss will deprive them of network access, they'll gladly work with you to keep the "bad guys" away. It's not necessary to be paranoid, but it is a good idea to control access to your assets, as the most basic form of protection.

## DELIVERING OUTPUTS AND INPUTS WHERE NEEDED

Printers are by far the most often used peripherals on a network. Your biggest concern should be to put printers where users can get to them quickly and easily. You'll also want to make sure that they're housed in an area where paper, toner cartridges, and other supplies can be neatly stored. The consumables for these devices often end up costing more, over their useful lives, than the devices do themselves, so planning to accommodate them is important.

It's also a good idea to recognize that output needs a place to live, after it's been created. Not everybody gets up right after queuing up a print job to retrieve it immediately. It's not uncommon for printouts to sit around for hours, or even days, before they're collected by their owners. Therefore, you'll want to set up some kind of storage rack or mailbox system to store unclaimed printouts. You'll also want to establish rules for how long aging materials will be stored—for most organizations, this means that old printouts get tossed on Monday morning, or once during some other time of the week.

The same thing is true for fax machines or scanners. That is, they need space for consumables or materials, and room to queue up incoming materials, and to store materials that have already been processed. Sometimes a table will be enough, other times a whole room will have to be dedicated to service a number of these devices. Many organizations, in fact, set up rooms where the copying machine, the fax machine, the printers, and the scanner are all housed together, with a common set of storage racks for incoming and completed materials.

## WORKING WITH YOUR USERS

Whatever kind of setup you select for your peripherals, make sure you check with your users to see how well it's working. If they don't like it, they'll be unhappy; if they're unhappy, they'll complain; and it will all come back to you eventually. Why not take the tack of announcing a test configuration, explaining the layout, and soliciting user feedback, as part of the process of placing shared network peripherals where you work?

This lets users know you're aware who the equipment is really for and should encourage them to let you know how well things are working. If you make it easy for them to suggest changes and improvements, they'll end up making your job easier. That's why we strongly recommend that you consider taking this kind of open-ended approach.

On a technical note, this is another reason why it's a good idea to leave unused capacity available from your wiring plant, and unused ports on your networking equipment—it gives you the flexibility to move things around until you get them right. Room to breathe is as important a concept for a networked group of users as it is for any other living population.

## MAKING SURE THINGS ARE WORKING

While a network layout may appear to be just what the doctor ordered when it's first delivered, don't forget that users' needs and perceptions change over time. It's not enough to satisfy yourself, right after installation, that your equipment placement is satisfactory, especially if it's a new network or a newly networked group of users.

Keep checking in with your users, following our suggestion to practice management by walking around (MBWA; see Chapter 18 for the details). Needs and priorities will change over time, so what worked fine yesterday may begin to chafe today and become a crisis by tomorrow. If you keep your ear to the ground, you won't end up beating your head against a wall!

## SUMMARY

In this chapter we've reviewed the technical and human factors that need to be considered when placing equipment for networked use. The basic rule is: The more people who need to access a piece of equipment, the more important its actual placement becomes. For less popular gear, we also introduced a series of precepts to help guide you in their proper placement, including security, accessibility, electrical service, cooling and ventilation, and adequate space for access and storage. As you've worked your way through them, we hope you've also figured out how best to place your own equipment.

# MAPPING MAGIC

## IT'S MORE THAN JUST A MAP

When you first think of a network map you probably imagine a top-view picture of the building, showing offices, hallways, cables, and computers. When we use the term, though, we mean much more than just that picture. Your network map is the pictures plus a database describing every component of the network. The following is a checklist of everything you need to include.

### PC Hardware

- ✔ PC type
- ✔ PC brand name, model name, and serial number
- ✔ processor type and speed
- ✔ amount of RAM
- ✔ keyboard type
- ✔ monitor type
- ✔ monitor interface card type, configuration, and serial number
- ✔ network interface card (NIC) type, address, interrupt level, and serial number
- ✔ hard drive brand, size, and configuration information (this means number of heads, sectors, everything)
- ✔ diskette drive sizes and brands
- ✔ any other devices attached to the PC, along with their interrupt levels, addresses, and serial numbers

## PC Software

✔operating system
✔applications
✔network drivers, redirectors, and shells
✔drivers for any other cards in the workstation
✔workstation configuration files
✔version numbers for each piece of software

**Note**: Also keep count of the number of valid licenses for each piece of software.

## Cables

✔name, number, or whatever label is on the cable
✔length of cable
✔end points—where the cable begins and where it ends
✔attachments—what's at the ends of the cable (a printer, workstation, or server?)
✔intermediate connections, if any

## Hubs, Routers, Concentrators, and Other Network Equipment

✔brand name, model, and serial number
✔size of item: number of ports, for instance
✔software the item requires, with current version number and date

## Printers, Plotters, and Other Peripherals

✔brand name, model, and serial number
✔configuration options, such as RAM
✔any drivers the item requires, with current version number and date

## Miscellaneous Information

✔phone numbers of vendors and support people
✔problem report lists (useful for historical tracking)
✔anything else you can think of

# USING COMPUTER TOOLS FOR MAPPING

Obviously this is a lot of information to keep track of, and a lot of detail. This makes it a perfect task for a computer, so don't try to put it all on paper! If you're handy with a fairly flexible database system and you have your own system for tracking all this data, you might want to put together your own database and archive your network map that way. If not, no problem! There are a number of companies who already make this type of software. Try one of the following:

- LAN Auditor, by Horizons Technology
- Heaven Nodes!, by dtech
- LAN Directory, by Frye Computer Systems, Inc. Gives you pictures as well as database tracking (for Novell networks).
- Network Management Services, from Novell (for Novell networks, of course).

# INTEGRATING ENGINEERING PLANS

You have a lot of resources to help you create your network map; be sure to take advantage of all of them. Start with the building blueprint, if possible, and don't forget the following:

- **HVAC plans.** These are the heating/vacuum/air conditioning diagrams. They show ductwork, vents, and climate controls. Your map should show them too, because you'll have to work around them.
- **Electrical plans.** Look here to see where all the electrical wiring in the building runs, the wiring loads, and the circuit breakers are located. You'll need to know these things if you'll be sharing conduit with the electrical wiring, or to give some electrical elements a wide berth (motors can hopelessly garble your network).
- **Telephone installation diagrams.** These show all the phone wires in the building, along with their punchdown blocks and patch panels, and are especially useful to you if you're using the phone system for your network. Even if you're not, use these drawings to see what to avoid.

Your best bet is not to try to incorporate all this information into a single diagram, but to keep it all together, so that when you need additional levels of detail on a particular building system, you have it right there at hand.

## KEEPING CURRENT

Keeping your network map up to date is a two-part process. The first part involves training yourself to record every change as soon as you make it. Good network management software can be a big help here; you're more likely to record the information if doing so is easy and quick. The second aspect is training everyone else to keep you informed of changes. Get the word out to everyone, including:

- Users: If they change their workstation configurations, make sure they let you know (so you can help them fix it if the change causes problems).
- Purchasing or Receiving: When software arrives, have them notify you so you can record its type and version number before anyone installs it.
- Building Maintenance: Make sure they inform you of any changes to electrical, HVAC, telephone, or any other systems that might affect your network.
- Cleaning crew: If they need to move or unplug something, you'll want to know about it.

## MAKE THE MAP YOUR FIRST AND LAST RESORT

Yep, we'll say it again: The network map is your faithful sidekick no matter what's happening to your network. When you're planning any kind of a change to the network, check the map first. It might show you that your planned change will add too much capacity to a hub, or that you'll need a new revision of software for some of your workstations. It's the first place you should go if anyone reports a problem on the network, too; you need to find out the type, revision level, and configuration of the offending equipment.

If you have a network problem and you just can't figure out what's going on, go back to the network map. Could you have two pieces of software with mismatched revision levels? Is some piece of equipment in need of an upgrade? Are you close to the limit in number of users on a server? Your network map will tell you.

## SUMMARY

With the checklists and reminders in this chapter, you now have everything you need to create a thorough network map. You know what to include in this collection of network data and how to pull it all together, and you even have some tips on how to keep it all up to date. In short, the map contains everything anyone could possibly want to know about your network. You'll congratulate yourself every time you use it, and if anyone else ever has to use it when you're not around, they'll appreciate you even more.

# BUDGETING BONANZAS

# 26

## KNOWING WHAT THINGS COST

Forewarned is forearmed, as they say. This is especially true when you're about to spend money; the more educated you are about the choices you have and the relative costs involved, the better you'll be able to shop. By studying typical costs before you buy, you'll be much more able to spot both good deals and bogus bargains.

You have a number of sources from which to get information about networking equipment costs. To start with, try the following:

- CompuServe Information Service. CompuServe has a number of forums dedicated to PC equipment and its support, maintenance, and sources. Check for a forum dedicated to the type of network you plan to install, and for forums on networking in general. There's a good chance that a forum library will have the information you need. For more on connecting to CompuServe, see the Resource Guide at the end of this book.
- Networking periodicals, such as *LAN Magazine*, *LAN Times*, and *Network Computing*. These general networking journals will have ads that often list prices. At the very least, the ads will give you addresses and phone numbers of vendors whom you can call.
- PC periodicals, such as *Computer Shopper*. While primarily devoted to PC issues, these magazines also have ads that list networking equipment and software, and many of the ads list prices as well. A great place to start.

- Periodicals devoted to your specific type of network. Check your local discount megabookstore for these; they're likely to have a large selection of computing magazines.
- The Internet. This collection of computer networks has thousands of electronic bulletin boards, and many of them are devoted to buying and selling computer and networking equipment. Often these messages are organized by region, so check for one that connects people who live near you. For more information on connecting to the Internet, see the Resource Guide at the end of this book.

## THE FINE ART OF JUSTIFICATION

Before you can put together a budget, you have to have money to spend. If you have sympathetic management who easily sees the benefits of networking and writes you a blank check to fund the project, you're set. You are free to devote your attention to the other matters that demand it. But the more likely scenario is that, while it may be supportive of the concept of networking, management will need some convincing before it's willing to spend the kind of money required to build a good, productive, stable network.

In order to make believers out of them, you need to convince them that by spending the money that you're requesting for the network, they'll be saving even more money in the long run. Simply convincing management that everyone will be more productive will probably not be enough; you'll need to talk in terms of cost-benefit trade-offs. Some benefits to emphasize:

- Network users will be able to work more effectively.
- Networking will lead to a higher volume of work.
- The network will bring improved working conditions.
- Sharing devices through the network saves equipment costs.

A common strategy is to compare the present dismal state of communications in the organization to the streamlined, productive, elegant state of affairs that will exist after the network is up and running. The trick is to tailor this presentation to the particular pet issues of your audience. If your manager is an advocate of a highly ordered workplace, be sure to stress how much more organized everything will be after the network is in place, and how much more easily things will stay organized with it. If you have a manager who is big on maintaining a high degree of communications between various members and groups within the organization, be sure to emphasize how the network will facilitate communication and bring it to the group in ways that were not possible before. Go back to Chapter 3 and review the benefits of networking when preparing your presentation.

Negotiating for funding is basically a political process. You need to figure out the hot buttons of the people holding the purse strings, and turn that knowledge to your own ends!

# Trading Real Money against Future Funding

By "real" money we mean money that's in your current budget; these are the funds you can actually spend right now, as opposed to future funding, which is the money you expect to get in next year's budget. The trick is to do what you can to make sure that you actually do get that money in next year's budget. It's a sad fact of budgeting, but if you don't use all of your budget this year, the powers that allocate money are likely to conclude that you don't need as much next year (even if the company, and the network, are expecting a 20% increase in size next year). On the other side, if the economy or your industry is experiencing a downturn, the holders of the purse strings are going to be searching hard for areas of the budget that they can trim. You want to make sure your allocation doesn't make their list.

Therefore, if you have money, go ahead and spend it now to shore up whatever area you've been planning to address with a future budget—education, equipment, or expansion of the installation. Push ahead on infrastructure spending, such as cables, routers, and hubs, so that when that growth spurt does occur, you'll be well prepared.

It might sound odd, but it's possible that your own budget is not your only source of money. In many companies, a good-sized chunk of funds gets allocated every year to office supplies, such things as stationery, pens, and markers. Frequently the definition of these items is loose enough that you can use it for many other things, possibly including network expansion. Check around before you try to dip into this pool, though, and make sure this is accepted practice in your organization. We are certainly not suggesting that you try to find ways to divert funds from their legitimate purposes!

# Planning How to Spend

The more money you plan to spend, the more angles there are from which to approach the process. This section describes a few of the things you'll need to keep in mind as you get into the more rarefied atmosphere of large expenditures.

In most organizations of more than just a few people, you'll encounter a signature structure in getting funding approval. Usually, the more money you want to spend, the higher up the command chain you'll have to go to get the right people to sign off on the expenditure. Keep in mind that if you need a vice president's signature to buy a big chunk of equipment, the approval process will probably take longer and require more justification than did the network expansion for which you required a director's signature. This time lag means you'll have to plan ahead on your orders, allowing more time to keep the company's credit rating pristine. In other words, don't order equipment for which you must pay in 30 days unless you're positive you'll have the required approvals and the funds will be released when the bill comes due. Otherwise you could antagonize your vendors, which could strain your future dealings with them and give your company a bad name.

Planning also means breaking up large expenditures into stages, so that some money gets disbursed up front, a little more along the way, with a chunk held in reserve until the end. This helps labor- and material-intensive purchases get started, helps to keep them moving along, and provides the suppliers an incentive to make sure you're happy with their quality and service at the end of the project. For large equipment purchases, a similar approach demonstrates intent at the beginning, helps vendors cover shipping and incidental costs along the way, and helps keep vendors' own suppliers at bay at the end.

Get in touch with the financial managers at your company to find out how they like to do business. In the case of large expenditures, you might want to arrange for financing. This provides you a way of spreading costs across multiple fiscal quarters or years. Your finance department calls the shots here, so work with those personnel to figure out the approach that makes most sense for your company.

## THE SPEEDY ART OF OBSOLESCENCE

Computing technology is changing so quickly that it's pointless to try to keep up. As soon as you buy a computer, some say, it's obsolete. This doesn't mean you need to buy a new one immediately; it just means that there are faster, cheaper, and better ones out there than the one you have.

Dealing with this rapid obsolescence cycle means striking a balance. The key point to remember is that once your equipment is truly obsolete, you won't be able to find anyone to work on it anymore. Make sure you replace equipment before you start having trouble finding people to support it.

The rate of obsolescence will depend to some extent on how widespread and standardized that technology was in the first place. You can still find people who can work on the first IBM-PC clones, introduced in the early 1980s, because there were so many of them and so many other computers based on them. But if you buy a JiffyData FiberLink hub today, one that does not adhere to the FDDI standard, you may well find yourself in trouble a year from now if it stops working.

# STAY BEHIND THE BLEEDING EDGE!

You need to strike a balance here between museum equipment and equipment that is still warm from the development shop. As we discussed above, you don't want to be saddled with a bunch of equipment that no one supports anymore, but it's also possible to go too far in the other direction. Some people get a certain thrill out of being what's known as "early adopters," those folks who always opt for the latest, coolest new equipment as soon as it's available on the market. We recommend that you resist this temptation, for several reasons.

1. **Expense**. This latest and greatest technology doesn't come cheap. Because it hasn't had the chance to become the commodity that some of the older and more common technologies are, you'll pay a premium for the privilege of being among the first to use it.
2. **Lack of testing**. Once a product has a large user base, many people have tested it and reported problems back to the developers, and those developers have fixed the problems and released the fixes. A few of these cycles increases reliability of a product tremendously. Many industry experts adopt the maxim, "Never use Release 1.0 of anything."
3. **Obsolescence**. The newer the technology is, the faster the equipment will become obsolete. Unless you have a compelling need, protect your investment by selecting equipment that you will be able to service at least until you've fully depreciated it.

This ever-advancing line of state-of-the-art technology is usually known as the "leading edge," but these traps we've just described have led to the more descriptive term in the title of this section.

# SUMMARY

With the tips and advice in this chapter, you will be able to put together a solid budget and plan ahead for changes in funding availability. You also are aware of the pitfalls of buying equipment that is too far ahead or behind the curve of current technology, and with this information you are equipped to make the financial decisions that will maximize your network funding.

# RULES FOR WORKING WITH CONTRACTORS

## 27

## WRITE IT DOWN!

Consultants have experience and special knowledge that you don't have and that you don't want to acquire—that's why you hire them. But their expertise doesn't come cheap. In this chapter we'll go over some techniques to make sure you get the most for the money you're spending on your contractors.

Be sure that every aspect of your agreement with the cabling contractor is in writing, from the type of cable you want to use in your network to the total amount of money you have agreed to pay. If some aspect of the network changes during the course of the installation, put that in writing, too.

Don't leave anything to guesswork! The requirements document that you present to them before they make their bid should show the network layout and describe every detail of the network, including:

- type of cable to use—fiber, twisted pair, coax
- beginning and end points of all cable runs
- types of connectors
- style and location of wall plates
- instructions on how to label the cables
- deadlines.

Furthermore, the contract should state that the contractor is responsible for testing every cable and for cleaning up after the installation is done. This cleanup clause ensures that you don't have bits of wire, food wrappers, and empty cable boxes lying around after the installers leave.

## ALWAYS CHECK REFERENCES

You're not in the business of educating someone on network installation; make sure you're not paying a contractor to learn new skills on your network. Once you find a contractor whom you think you might like to hire, ask for at least two references, preferably three. Make sure the contractor's work with each reference was long enough ago that any problems have had time to show up. In other words, if the references you get are all from work the contractor did within the last six months, find a different contractor. You simply won't have enough information on which to base your decision.

The network technology affects the difficulty of the installation, and the harder the installation, the more carefully you will want to check references. Fiber-optic cable, for instance, is extremely tricky to install. The cable breaks if bent too sharply, and attaching the connectors requires special tools and some practice. Coaxial cable is the next step down in installation complexity, with twisted-pair wiring being the easiest.

Here are some questions you might want to ask when checking references.

- Was the work completed within the estimated time?
- Were the workers considerate of others in the building?
- What type of requirements did the reference provide the contractors? If the contractors did not have clear instructions, this could account for some problems during and after installation.
- Did the installers clean up after themselves? This includes cable boxes, unused materials, and wire ends as well as food wrappers and soda cans.
- Was the installation completed within the budget?
- What problems came up during the installation? How were they resolved?
- What problems have they seen since the installation? How has the contractor handled them?
- Would they use that contractor again, for expansion or to install another new network?

## ESTABLISH LOTS OF LITTLE DEADLINES

In any big project, it's helpful for everyone involved to be able to see progress. It's helpful for the morale of the folks doing the work to see that they're getting closer to completion, and it's helpful to the people paying for the work (you) to see that your money is being well spent. For these reasons we recommend breaking the project up into smaller sub tasks, each with its own deadline. Frequent checkpoints also help you spot any problems or misunderstandings before they develop into big, expensive mistakes. Finally, structuring the project as a series of small projects gives you the opportunity to tie compensation to work actually completed, which can be helpful to your budgeting process.

For these reasons, we recommend that you divide the installation into steps. Write down what each phase of the installation contains, and, most importantly, get agreement with all parties about how to determine that each phase is complete. Write all these requirements into the contract so there are no misunderstandings. We show an example of such an arrangement below, but your requirements will depend on your installation.

1. Review requirements document; agree on a plan of action.
2. Run all twisted-pair wiring and test cables. Check for labels.
3. Run fiber-optic backbone, test cables.
4. Test connections between fiber and twisted-pair segments.
5. Install wall plates in each office; test.
6. Wire and test patch panel.
7. Clean up: Pick up all unused or discarded material, and make sure all cables and wall plates are secure and every cable is labeled.
8. Hand-off. Receive a network map that documents the new installation.

## PAY FOR PERFORMANCE, NOT FOR TIME

Different people work at different speeds, but there's no need for you to have to budget for this. Professional installers are accustomed to bidding projects according to the total completion price, rather than on a price-per-hour basis.

Paying your contractors per task has a big benefit: You can tie their compensation to their execution of the contract. You'll give them a chunk of the total figure up front, when they begin the project—between 20 percent and 40 percent is common. From there, give them 10 percent at a time with the completion of each subsection of the project, after you have satisfied yourself that the subsection is complete and tested. Once the entire installation is finished and tested, and everything is cleaned up, you'll pay them the remainder of the total.

If you find a contractor who looks just great, has the right experience, and has great references, but insists on billing by the hour, be sure to get an estimate of the number of hours the project will take, and get them to commit to that estimate. Also, write a clause into the contract stating that if the installation takes longer than the estimated time, they pay a penalty for each day (or eight-hour period) it runs over the allotted time.

## Think about Building a Business Relationship

Network installation is not a one-shot project. Your network has a life, and will need maintenance, expansion, and repairs. Keep this in mind when working with your contractor. Carefully document the installation process so that you have records for the contractor to reference in the future, or for another contractor to use if you work with someone else next time. Also, if someone calls you checking the contractor's references, careful documentation means you'll have specific information to give.

The most important documentation you'll need to get from the contractor is the revised network map. It should show:

- location of every cable, indicated by the label on the cable
- location of every repeater, with all configuration information about each device.
- location of every wall outlet
- diagram of the patch panel, if any, with all connections labeled

## Never Assume

Before you sign off on any portion of the network installation, be sure to test it completely, or have someone you trust do so. Contractors can overlook things, or misunderstandings can crop up, and you don't want to find out about these issues after the installers have packed up and left the building. Specifically, make sure of the following:

- The number of cables they installed is the same as the number you requested.
- Every cable is labeled, and the name or number appears on your network map.
- Every cable works (get a helper and some test equipment and make sure a signal travels from one end of the cable to the other).
- Every wall outlet works (perform the same test as above, but through the wall outlets instead of the cable ends).
- Every patch panel connection works.
- All of the patch panel cables work (this is an easy one to overlook!).

# Summary

This section arms you with everything you need to know to arrange a contract with a network installer and to manage that contract throughout the installation so that your network goes in smoothly and efficiently. You know what to put in your requirements document, what to watch out for when working with contractors, and how to get the most value out of their expertise for your money. The next chapter gives you tips and reminders on saving money on other aspects of your network installation.

# SPENDING WISELY ON NETWORKING

# 28

## MAIL-ORDER MADNESS

Just browse through the back pages of one or two networking periodicals and you'll become convinced that there is a boggling number of mail-order sources of networking equipment and supplies. The prices, too, might astound you, especially when you compare them to what your local "one-stop, we-do-it-all" shop is charging for the same items. But be aware of what you're giving up to get those savings! Spending wisely means spending for now and also for the future. If you save a little money now but incur huge expenses later by doing it, you haven't really saved anything.

When you buy your equipment from a mail-order supply house, you are taking on burdens of maintenance, service, and research that you would not if you bought from a local supplier. They might offer some support, but it will probably be over the phone, and there are a lot of problems that are very hard to diagnose over the phone. If you have the background, interest, and time to support the network equipment yourself, then the apparent savings of the mail-order route are truly savings for you. If you'd like to be able to plan on a little more help from the vendor, though, read on.

## FABULOUS FULL SERVICE

If you buy your equipment from a full-service supply shop, you can expect to spend somewhat more than you would if you had bought it from a mail-order house. But you can also expect to get something that the mail-order devotees can't: Full local support, possibly including installation and maintenance. The folks at a full-service supplier will be able to advise you in every aspect of your equipment selection and installation, and if you do ever have problems, they can come out to your site and investigate. Those who opt for the mail-order route must find a local contractor when they need a service call.

It's almost certainly true that equipment from a full-service provider will be more expensive than mail order, at least for the initial expenditures. But evaluate all the costs involved; if you don't want to do a lot of support yourself, or just don't have the time, the extra outlay might turn out to be a bargain.

## FLUSHING OUT HIDDEN COSTS

Certain costs of your network installation won't show up on any of your invoices, or at least not on those invoices for installation or equipment. These hidden costs fall into the categories of time, training, and materials. The more aware you are of these costs, the better you can budget for them. A complete account of all the costs of your network also helps you justify expenditures.

Recall the adage from Economics 101: There's no such thing as a free lunch. Keep this in mind and you'll be able to spot hidden costs before they bite you.

### Where Does All the Time Go?

Once the network is running, or probably some time before that, you'll find that a large chunk of your day is spent in maintenance chores related to the network. If your job description says that all you do is deal with the network, this won't be a problem; the cost is already identified and your managers are allowing for it. But if you're a departmental resource with a job besides network maintenance, the time cost of keeping the network going is one that you'll want to be aware of, and get your manager aware of, right away.

### Uninformed Users Cost Everyone

Another cost of the new network that might not be immediately apparent is the time it takes to get everyone up to speed on using the network, including yourself. Nobody is likely to know how to use it as soon as it's running; someone will have to explain the services to them, how to access the shared resources, solve problems, and utilize the network to its full capabilities. This person is likely to be you, so you need to allow for this time in your budget too. Also plan on spending some money on training materials, such as books or handouts. And don't forget the users' own time; the time they spend learning about the network is time they won't be spending doing their regular jobs. The immediate cost of this slight slowdown is a trade-off against the future benefits in increased productivity once everyone has learned to use the network.

## More Supplies, Again?

It's obvious once you think about it, but it's easy to overlook the fact that sharing devices means the costs associated with those devices will go up. A networked printer will generally get used more frequently and more steadily than it did before it was shared on the network. This means that you'll find that printer requiring more paper and toner than it did before; expect these costs to go up. It also means that the printer is getting more wear and tear, so you need to allow for higher servicing costs than it needed before. The same goes for most other devices that are now available to a wider range of users by the introduction of the network.

# MATERIALS, EQUIPMENT, SOFTWARE, AND SERVICES

You'll need to watch for hidden costs from a number of areas. When budgeting for a network, these categories—materials, equipment, software, and services—are important to consider in light of how the network will increase usage, requirements, licensing types and fees, and the kinds of services needed to make everything work. To be more specific:

- Materials whose consumption goes up after you install a network include all kinds of consumables, as described in the section on supplies above; they also include costs for spare parts like connectors, cables, and network interface cards.
- Equipment costs for the network include all direct items like network gear, cables, connectors, hubs, and whatever else is needed to put the network together and to let it grow over time. Equipment costs also include beefing-up or replacement costs for PCs that must now fulfill a network server's job, and add-ons (like large disk drives, tape drives, UPSs, etc.) typically needed to let a server perform reliably.

- Software costs include license management over standalone software whose increased accessibility promotes use (and abuse, under the wrong circumstances); it also includes costs for converting standalone software to its networked equivalents (like XTree Gold to XtreeNet, for instance).
- Services costs include those for network training for administrators and users, for repair and maintenance on network equipment, and for troubleshooting or extending the cable plant (for instance, costs paid to the phone company for extra lines for a modem server should rightly be considered service costs, as should be the monthly connect and usage fees).

## SUPPORT IS NEVER FREE, NO MATTER WHAT THEY SAY

Free support is getting more and more rare, in part because more and more people are needing support. As demand for their product goes up, vendors and software manufacturers are finding that in order to keep up with the questions the new users are asking, they must charge for support. Most vendors who do charge for support do so in a tiered structure, so that the more responsiveness and access to their experts you want, the more you pay.

But some vendors still advertise free support. What this means is that you don't have to send them a check before you can call them up and ask them a question. It does not, however, mean that getting support is free. The costs they incur in running their support line are built into the price of your package. Be sure to consider your costs as well; you incur costs in the time you spend to contact them, and also in the time it takes to deliver their answer to your users. Everything in a business situation, in short, has a cost.

## SUMMARY

Spending wisely means knowing all the costs of the project, both the obvious ones, like equipment and installation, and the not-so-obvious ones, like training and maintenance. With the points in this chapter you will be much better equipped to make sensible, practical choices in planning and shopping for your network.

# RULES FOR MAGNIFICENT MAINTENANCE

# 29

Most systems are subject to what's called a *life-cycle*, which refers to the progression of any system from design to development or installation into maintenance and eventually obsolescence. It's kind of a shame that the front end pieces, design and installation, typically get all the glamour, because most system experts agree that 90% of the time and 70–90% of the resources devoted to any particular system will be expended during the maintenance period. An irreverent way of stating this relationship is to say, "You'll build a system only once or twice, but you'll live with it forever!"

Anything that has to be done forever—or at least for a long time, anyway—is worth doing well. That's why we've included so much information about maintenance and management of networks in this book on network design. Designing and installing a workable network requires an understanding of what comes after the network's installed and running, namely, a lifetime of maintenance, upgrades, and replacements, and very likely growth and expansion as well.

In this chapter we'll recap the rules you'll want to keep in mind as you live through the longest segment of your network's life-cycle. Remember, maintenance is more than just a set of activities, it's a way of life!

## USE THAT BASELINE!

The most important aspect of maintenance is to keep a vigilant eye on your system, ever-watchful for changes in usage or behavior. These changes can often signal that trouble is imminent, but if trouble is quelled before it becomes acute, nobody else need ever know.

In order to understand what incipient trouble looks like, you first need to know what's normal for your network. That's where the concept of a *baseline* come in: A baseline is essentially a profile of your network's vital statistics, and it should give you a snapshot of what your network typically looks and acts like. The reason it's called a baseline is because it establishes a frame of reference from which you can evaluate any particular set of statistics about the network, and look for differences. A baseline, therefore, is something of an abstraction, because it's a statistical summary of usage and behavior, as much as a real collection of numbers. Abstract or otherwise, though, a baseline is your first line of defense when it comes to dealing with difficulties on your network.

Building a baseline is sometimes called "network characterization," because it involves gathering lots of information about what's happening on your network, and with the shared resources and equipment that provide services to your network users. Here's a checklist of the kind of information you'll want to assemble to build your own baseline, broken down into several categories to tell you where to look for this information.

## Network Usage

- ✔ network utilization, for each cable segment, charted over an "average" 24-hour period, and for peak usage, over a monthly period (plotting this as a graph provides excellent visual cues as to usage levels and patterns over time)
- ✔ error rates, for all applicable error types (trends in error rates can be symptomatic of cabling bottlenecks or miswiring, network growth, or possible component failures)
- ✔ traffic rates, in packets per second, for each cable segment (this provides a different view of utilization, because it focuses on the number of active conversations, rather than the overall consumption of bandwidth, on the cabling)
- ✔ server activity levels, as measured by system utilization levels (this helps you keep track of where the action is on your network and will alert you to the need to redistribute and balance processing loads across servers, if applicable, or the need to add more servers)

## Server Usage

- ✔ disk consumption statistics, by drive and by user (monitoring the percentage of available free space alerts you to clean-up needs, to keep drives from filling up, and tells you when it's time to buy more storage; monitoring disk consumption by users lets you know who the big consumers are, and can also signal clean-ups or lead to larger disk allocations, if their needs are legitimate)

✔ application usage tells you which applications are popular, and can alert you to the need to purchase additional licenses when necessary

✔ login levels tell you how many users typically make use of a server, and can alert you to the need to add resources to a server (more memory, disk, or network interfaces) or even to when it's time to extend a network operating system license (since many of them can handle only a fixed number of connections), or to start thinking about dividing your user base for a given server across multiple servers to better balance the load

## Peripheral Usage

✔ check the usage of peripherals regularly, to see if the device is being used beyond its rated duty cycle (printers, copiers, and fax machines are rated by their manufacturers in terms of recommended maximum number of output pages per month, and over the life of the machine; if your usage rates exceed either one, it's time to think about trading it in for a heavier-duty model)

✔ check actual consumables used: For devices that can't give you usage statistics, this may be your only way to monitor use; another powerful clue can be statistics provided by the server's input or output queues for this device

✔ inspect all peripherals at least once a month to assess their general condition, to clean up moving parts, and to perform whatever regular maintenance is needed (do this more often, if recommended in the manufacturer's service manual for the device)

## Hubs, Routers, Concentrators, and Other Network Equipment

✔ check utilization rates for the device, on a per-port basis (This will tell you where the traffic's coming from and often, where it's going. This can be an important factor in assessing how your wiring layout is performing, and in identifying potential bottlenecks, which may require adding segments or redistributing nodes from overused segments across less-used segments.)

✔ check error rates and forwarding rates (Both of these will indicate trends toward overutilization of particular segments, or even improper forwarding of traffic from a local segment onto a feeder trunk or the network backbone.)

It's important to use averages to compile a baseline because spot-checks could occur either when the network is in a temporary condition of over- or underuse.

Working with averages smoothes out this effect, and helps to establish a normal level that incorporates both kinds of effects, without being unduly influenced by either one.

When it comes to examining a baseline, we've learned to favor graphical displays, either in the form of line graphs or bar charts, simply because the human eye is an excellent trend-analysis tool. Extending a trend line into the future is often nothing more than tracing a line, or trending a bar chart, to its next logical step. This will give you an excellent idea of where your network is going.

Once you've built a baseline, you can use it for comparison with any current set of performance or utilization figures. This will tell you which side of normal the current figures are on, and whether or not there's cause for concern. That's why we strongly recommend that you build one and use it regularly.

## WHAT'S NOT WORKING? WHY?

From time to time, things will go wrong on the network. A regular maintenance routine should keep this from happening frequently, but some things will still quit every now and then. Your first priority will be to restore whatever isn't working to working condition, but the job's not over when it's fixed.

The most important post-mortem after any failure is to diagnose its cause if at all possible. That's the only way you'll be able to take steps to prevent a recurrence, if it makes sense to do so. For instance, preventing power failures is out of your hands, but instructing a user to leave his or her computer running all the time because it has a remote printer attached to it is not. Only if you know why something happened can you decide if it's worth pursuing a more permanent solution to prevent the problem from happening again.

## ASK THEM HOW YOU'RE DOING

Starting in Chapter 18, we've consistently advocated a technique called Management by Walking Around (MBWA). This technique could just as easily be called Maintenance BWA, and it would capture the essence of this particular maintenance tip: Your users will always be a sensitive barometer for network performance and, even better, for how well the network is doing for them. Unless you use MBWA as a regular technique to make contact with users to ask them how the network is doing, you may not get the benefit of the feedback they can give you. Our advice is: Use the MBWA technique regularly, and don't let this opportunity slip by!

# Make a Plan and Stick to It!

As our life-cycle argument was meant to illustrate, maintenance of a system will be the overriding activity devoted to it, both in terms of time and expense. Why not, therefore, make a habit out of it?

The key to successful maintenance is not just to identify what needs to be done and how often, but then to follow through and actually do it. The best way to build a habit is to start with a plan, and then to make sure it gets executed as needed. Of course, you'll have to vary your activities over time, to accommodate changes and to take cognizance of the little emergencies that may force you to vary your routine from time to time.

Although your own maintenance plan will grow out of the requirements of your particular network, here are some elements that should find a place in it:

- ✔ regular backups (see Chapters 18 and 30 for more information)
- ✔ visual inspection of network cabling and connectors, networking equipment, and servers
- ✔ visual inspection of shared peripherals and related supplies; toss out old print-outs, faxes, etc.
- ✔ running network monitoring software to take a snapshot of the network's condition
- ✔ regular inspection of server file systems to delete old stuff, and clear out unnecessary junk
- ✔ cleaning tape or optical drives, as per manufacturer's recommendations

You'll build up a repertoire of maintenance activities for yourself that should include all of these, and probably others as well.

# Always Be Ready for Murphy

The watchword for networks is: "If you don't look for trouble, it'll come looking for you." The whole point of maintenance is to pay attention to the network, and to look for and deal with impending signs of trouble before it actually becomes acute. Once that happens, you'll have all kinds of help identifying what's wrong, but you'll get all kinds of unwelcome attention in the process!

Even so, Murphy will still occasionally drop in for a visit. When that happens, you'll be much better able to persuade him to leave if you're ready to deal with trouble. A disaster recovery plan can help to fend off the most troublesome events, when it looks like Murphy might be around for the duration. But by and large, practicing for network recovery makes sure you're ready to respond appropriately when something fails. If you've thought about what can go wrong, and have a good idea about what to do when it happens, you'll be able to react quickly and professionally, and move on from there.

## SUMMARY

In this chapter we've reviewed checklists and techniques for maintaining a smoothly running network. The basic idea is to pay close attention to your network, and to take preemptive steps to head off trouble as soon as it starts to make itself known. If you make regular, proactive maintenance a part of your daily networking routine, trouble should never linger too long at your door!

## FURTHER READING

Network characterization is an interesting, but somewhat undercovered, aspect of network maintenance. If this subject interests you, please consult Laura Chappell's book listed below. In addition to its value for that subject, it's also an excellent general primer on LAN protocols and a great tool for working with NetWare networks.

Laura Chappell, *NetWare LAN Analysis*, Novell Press/Sybex Books, 1993. ($29.95), San Jose, CA.

This book is focused specifically at analyzing NetWare networks, but it includes a terrific general primer on protocols and the best exposition of baseline construction and network characterization we've ever found anywhere.

# 30

# BACKUPS AND BEYOND

Any organization's ability to recover from a disaster hinges entirely on the availability of a current backup of the systems that have suddenly been rendered inaccessible. Put more baldly, it goes like this: No backup, no business! If you think you can skip the whole backup thing, go right ahead. Our experience has been that there are two kinds of people in this world when it comes to backups: Those who have been burned and now take backing up very seriously indeed, and those who haven't been burned yet, but will be someday. Bertrand Russell is rumored to have said, "Experience is a dear teacher, but fools will have no other." Don't be so foolish as to think you'll never get bitten—remember, Murphy's never so far away that he can't come around any time—and learn from our experience that backing up may be hard to do, but getting back on line without a backup is even harder.

Maybe we're optimists, though; statistics on networks in the United States illustrate that only 40 percent of the networks out there get backed up regularly. Talk about a disaster just waiting to happen. When it does, try not to be part of it!

## DAILY INCREMENTALS, WEEKLY COMPLETES

As we mentioned in Chapter 18, the frequency at which you should back up is constrained by two factors: first, by how much work you can afford to lose; and second, by the need to keep maintenance tasks like backup from unduly impacting your users, who are only trying to get their jobs done. In practice, this means that most backups happen at night and on the weekends, when the number of users is typically far lower than during prime-time working hours.

Ideally, you'd back up the whole network every night. That way you'd be able to restore last night's backup if anything every happened to the network, and proceed from there, having lost only one day's work at most. This requires that your backup system be able to accommodate the entire contents of the network without human intervention, which is quite possible, providing you're willing to spend the money on the right software and equipment with which to back up. Unfortunately, many networks have so much information stored on them that the laws of physics get in the way of realizing this goal, that is, there just aren't enough hours in the night to get a full or complete backup finished during that time. If your network isn't subject to that limitation (and this will be a boon for many smaller organizations), go ahead and do a full backup every night!

The rest of us will have to settle for a slightly more complicated backup strategy. For most systems, except some really gargantuan ones that have had to adopt more exotic and expensive backup strategies, the 48 hours of the weekend more than suffices to completely back up everything on the network. This establishes a checkpoint for the week, from which any restoration for the following week would have to begin. Then, each night of the week thereafter, an incremental backup gets performed on the network. An incremental backup captures only those files that have changed since the last backup and therefore consists of far less information. This poses no challenges to the time limits between one work day and the next and works quite well.

The only negative side effect of incremental backups is that any restore that occurs must begin with the most recent full backup and be followed by all the incrementals since that backup, in the order in which they were recorded. This essentially replays all of the changes to the network since the full backup, and leaves you only one day behind the point at which the crash occurred. It's more time-consuming than restoring only a single full backup, but it's something that many organizations have learned to live with nonetheless.

## ROTATION SCHEMES

Unless you're using write-once media for an optical-disk–based backup system, you'll want to put a rotation scheme for your backup media into effect. What this does is regulate how much backup information gets stored and how often tapes or disks get reused for subsequent backups. Since most backup media isn't exactly cheap, this lets you milk your media money more effectively, but since recording media do wear out over time, you need to count on cycling out the old, while cycling in new replacement media. Rotation schemes take cognizance of this, and are designed to maximize reuse without risking an unusable backup because of worn-out media.

In the following subsections, we'll examine the two most popular media rotation schemes. The first, known as Grandfather, Father, Son, is by far the most popular; your main exposure to the second, the Tower of Hanoi, probably comes from the puzzle of the same name. Neither may be entirely adequate for your needs, though, so don't be afraid to experiment with either one, and vary the number of sets of copies, the frequency of backup, or the rotation method. Just make sure you vary things on the safe side, not the unsafe one: That is, don't use a lower number of sets, a lower frequency of backup or try to keep your backup media in use forever. Taking chances with backups is like taking chances with your future!

## Grandfather, Father, Son (GFS)

Here's how GFS works:

- Backups occur every day of the week, and each backup is stored on a separate tape. If the backup cycle follows a five-day work week, you'll need four daily tapes, which can be full or incremental backups, as your network circumstances dictate.
- On the final day of the work week, a weekly tape is used. You'll need three of these, assuming a four-week monthly cycle.
- On the fourth week of the monthly cycle, you'll use a monthly tape instead. Because there are 13 four-week periods in a calendar year, you'll need 13 monthly tapes altogether.

In this scheme the dailies are the son, the weeklies the father, and the monthlies the grandfather. We recommend that you use daily tapes only five or six times, then promote them to weeklies, use them another five or six times, and promote them to monthlies, to use them one more time. For this approach, you'd need to start with 20 sets of backup media, and you'd go through 30 additional sets of media a year. If you need to archive copies off-site—and we recommend this very strongly—add whatever number of copies this would involve to your yearly total, and budget accordingly. Our advice is to store no less than a weekly backup tape off-site, for disaster recovery, so this would add another four sets of media to your annual costs, assuming you rotate your off-site copies on a monthly basis.

## Tower of Hanoi

This rotation method uses each tape set a different number of times. The basic concept is that each time a new set is introduced to the rotation schedule, it gets used every other rotation. The third set will be used every fourth time, the fourth every eighth time, and so on, in ascending powers of two. Six or seven backup sets would be more than sufficient for most needs. Here again, keep track of how many times an individual set gets used, and plan on discarding them after 10 to 12 uses (or less, if that's what the manufacturer recommends). Under this kind of scheme, the number of media sets will typically be somewhat lower than the GFS requirements, but the record keeping requirements will be more complex.

## Tally Up!

Whatever rotation scheme you use, make sure you keep a tally on each tape, disk, or cartridge, to add up the total number of uses so far. Remember, a worn-out backup medium may not be readable, and if that's the case, it's as bad as no backup at all. Keeping track of use and discarding or archiving as the limit approaches will keep you from winding up with a no-backup backup.

## KEEPING UP WITH CAPACITY

As a rule of thumb, your backup system should have at least 20 percent more capacity than the sum of the storage on your network systems that needs to be backed up. This will keep you from having to be around to switch tapes or cartridges in the middle of the night or on weekends, when you'd probably rather be doing something else anyway.

Since storage requirements creep up over time on most systems, make sure you keep tabs on the overall consumption. That way, you can plan to add capacity to your backup system, or swap it for a more commodious one, as you begin to break inside that 20 percent barrier.

For large networks, tape, cartridge, or disk changers are available for backup use. These will automatically change media for you as a particular item becomes filled. Because they're larger, more capable, and more complex than single-item backup units, they will cost more, but for larger networks they may be the only feasible solution for regular backups. There are quite a lot of them in use today, so somebody must think they're worth the extra expense!

# BACKING UP WORKSTATIONS:
# SHOULD YOU OR SHOULDN'T YOU?

It's commonplace for backups to include all of the data, applications, and other information stored on network servers, or from shared computing resources of any kind. It's less common that networked backups include the data from individual users' workstations, but the loss of a workstation can be just as much of a tragedy as the loss of a server or other shared computer, providing that there's something important stored on that machine.

Basically, there are two ways to proceed here: First, you can let your users know that they're responsible for their own machine and that you're not going to back them up. You can considerably soften this blow by informing them, in the same breath, that if they will just copy their important files to the server, they'll automatically get backed up every night. This will satisfy those people who are organized well enough to remember to follow those instructions.

However, there's always a hold-out who either can't or won't take that one little step that could guarantee a backup for his or her important work. For this type of individual, you'll have to make a decision about whether or not to back up the workstation yourself. It's possible to put backup agent software on just about every kind of PC available today so that the backup program can instruct that machine to send either a full or incremental backup late at night, without requiring human intervention, and do the job automatically. The trade-off, obviously, is protection and security against additional expense. If your budget permits workstation backup, or the work stored only on workstations is vital to your organization, this bears further investigation.

Only a handful of organizations we surveyed take this backup step. Most of them inform users about server backups, and leave it to the users as to whether they use that as their backup technique or take responsibility for backing up their own workstations.

## OFF-SITE STORAGE

If you're serious about backup, it's because you know you need to be able to restore your network if a problem makes that necessary. It's just a small step from there to realize that keeping your backups in the same room as the system they duplicate incurs the same risks to the backup as to the system, should anything happen to the place in which both are stored. Our advice is to store a copy of your weekly backup off-site, so that if a major disaster should occur, you'll lose only a week's work. If that level of loss is unpalatable or unaffordable, store copies of the dailies off-site as well.

This is the only precaution that makes disaster recovery possible. You can easily arrange for a service to pick up the off-site copies from you or, at least, take a set home daily or weekly. Personally, we like the idea that our off-site backups are stored in a fireproof underground bunker on the other side of town—it helps us get to sleep at night, knowing those backup copies are safe!

## Practice versus Panic

One final word of backup advice: Because of the regular frequency of backing up, you'll get very good at it quickly. Be sure to develop some proficiency at the flip side, too. If you don't practice restoring backups every now and then, you'll be forced to climb the learning curve if you should ever need to restore your system. Since restoration occurs under what can only be called stressful conditions, we recommend that you practice occasionally under experimental conditions, where a mistake won't be an even worse disaster. If you're in shape for restoration, you'll be much better able to do one when the time comes.

We recommend quarterly restoration drills, at a minimum. If you have a disaster recovery plan in place, don't forget to practice a full network restoration at least once or twice a year as well.

## Summary

The only good backup is a fresh backup. Make sure that your backup procedures are well oiled, and that you can get to a backup even if your building becomes inaccessible. If you get in the backup habit, there's very little that can happen that can keep your network down for long. If you're in the other 60 percent who doesn't do the backup thing, please try rethinking your position—the majority isn't always right!

# BREAKING IN YOUR USERS

If your users ever give you a case of heartburn, remember that they're the reason you're experimenting with the network in the first place. If you're able to be objective about it, you might even be able to look past the complaints to see that the users are only trying to do their jobs, and that against some unlikely odds. Chances are if they only knew more about what they were doing, they'd have less reason to complain and more ways to solve problems that you wouldn't even have to know about.

The key to good user relationships is information: lots of high-quality, hands-on, useful information about how to get the best bang for their networking activities. As a network administrator, you can be a powerful pipeline for progress, if you arm your users with the information they need to do their jobs.

## TELL THEM WHAT'S COMING

In many ways, we're all creatures of habit, slaves to what might seem to be a mindless routine. As a network administrator, you'll have occasion to alter the routine every now and then. Woe betide you if your efforts to maintain the network make it uncomfortable for users, or if it takes their network away during prime-time work hours. The element of surprise may be essential for combat, but it's anathema to maintaining a good relationship with your users.

We recommend that you warn them in advance of anything that could impact network use, even if it's scheduled to happen at midnight. You might think that no one will be the wiser, but we guarantee you that anybody who feels like they have to be using the network at that hour will be mighty irked if it slows to a crawl or disappears altogether at that time!

That's why we recommend the "tell 'em three times" approach to spreading the word about potential network impacts:

- Send out a message to users at least three days in advance of the event, preferably a week ahead.
- Re-send the message the day of the event, early in the morning, so that everybody gets reminded that day.
- Send notice again 15 to 30 minutes before the event, just to give your users fair warning that it's just about to happen.

It's also recommended that you follow up with a message immediately after the event to inform your users about what's happened, and to notify them about what has changed, particularly if they have to do things differently as a consequence of whatever changes you've made. If major changes result, let them know that they're coming in your pre-event messages, and plan a training class to review those changes as soon as possible (at the very least, pass around a handout explaining what's changed, how it impacts them, and why the change occurred).

## GIVE THEM THE DETAILS

Change can be scary, but mostly it's the fear of the unknown or unexpected that provokes user anxiety. When you install upgrades or replacements on your network, or add new capacity or capability, it's time to fill in your users about exactly what this means to them.

The best time to inform them about changes is before they actually occur. If you can hold a training class ahead of the installation of new features and functions, or replacement of a familiar program or version, you'll earn your users' gratitude for arming them before they're faced with something new and different. If you can't beat the changes to the starting gate, you don't want to lag behind by too much, because you'll be inundated with questions and complaints unless you can tell your users what they need to know.

Make sure you provide materials that capture the essential details of what they need to know, and that your training or handout doesn't go into the kinds of information that they're not interested in. Even if you have no choice but to hand out user manuals as your only form of training and documentation, you can earn a lot of kudos by taking the time to go through the materials and compiling a list of the things they should pay attention to the most. A simple road map like this will save them from wasting time on things they would rather not have to skim.

## Offer Constant Training

When it comes to first-time networkers, nothing helps to ease the technology transition as access to information about what they're going to face and how this mysterious stuff really works. As a network administrator, you should be armed with materials to welcome the uninitiated to the wonderful world of networking. A classroom encounter is nice, but not necessary, as long as you can provide some gentle guidance into a new kind of information environment for your neophytes.

Even the technologically savvy can benefit from training though. It's a good idea to keep an ongoing series of brown bag seminars on the network going to review new or changed applications for the folks who have been around for a while. It's also a good idea to occasionally provide subject overviews for new or inexperienced users—things like "Basics of Electronic Mail," "Introduction to Word Processing," and "Using the Order-Entry System" are always bound to attract an audience, especially if your organization has a regular influx of new employees.

The basic value of on-going training is that it sends a message to your users that you want them to know what's going on, and that you care enough about their skills to want them to continue developing them. As you perform upgrades and replacements, don't forget to ask your vendors if they can't help organize a class—many of them are thrilled at the opportunity to get in front of their customers—and try to work with everybody concerned to find a suitable place and time to continue your training efforts.

Don't forget that your job is a challenging one, too. Network administrators have to work with more technologies, equipment, and software than most people know about. You should plan on getting some training yourself, just to keep your skills sharp, and to keep learning more about how to use and run the network yourself.

## Ask for Feedback

It's important to provide your users with information, but even more important to tell them what they need to know. The only way to find out if you're hitting or missing this all-important target is to ask them how well equipped to deal with the network they feel that they are. This could be in the form of a training questionnaire, a suggestion box, or a question-and-answer period, and it should be part of your repertoire of questions during your MBWA rounds.

The best ways to assess your users' comfort level with the network is to gauge their questions and complaints, to see if they point at missing information; to ask them how they're doing point-blank; and to provide as many opportunities for continuing network education, to see who's biting!

## SUMMARY

Informed users are the best kind to have, from the standpoint of lightening your workload and from the standpoint of arming them to do their best with the network for your organization. Make sure you stay in touch with their needs and their feelings about the network, and try to offer them training that gives them the biggest return for the least amount of effort. If you can stay ahead of them, you'll be able to tell your users everything they need to know!

# NETWORKS IN THE REAL WORLD

# IV

## OVERVIEW

In the first three sections of the book we've given you all the background you need to understand, design, and install your own network. But they say experience is the best teacher, and we believe it, having learned from some experiences of our own! In this section we'll give you the opportunity to learn from other people's experience, to help augment your own.

Here we look at three different networks of very different sizes, and discuss what the installation was like for each one, what kinds of problems they had (and sometimes still have) with the network up and running, and what they plan for their networking futures. We look at what worked and what didn't, and what they're doing about it. These examples should illuminate some pitfalls for you to avoid, and may also suggest some interesting new ways of handling network details that you might be able to apply to your own network.

# A Smallish Network

RJL Graphics, of Austin, Texas, is a small graphics design firm with a fairly small network. It has fewer than 50 PCs networked together, with a combination of Apple Macintoshes (the favorite machine of graphic designers) and IBM-PC clones.

# The Mid-Sized Model

The second network we'll look at belongs to Vtel Corporation, a manufacturer of video conferencing systems, also based in Austin, Texas. Vtel has about 250 employees and its network has about the same number of PCs. In addition to IBM-PC clones, it has a group of UNIX workstations and some Apple Macintoshes, plus several types of remote connections.

# An Industrial-strength Network

For an example of a large network, we turn to MD Anderson Cancer Center, in Houston, Texas. The center is part of a hospital and medical school complex and is linked to the statewide University of Texas system. Their network has more than 5,500 PCs and representatives of just about every possible network technology, PC type, and networking format, along with many different types of medical equipment.

# Case Study: Smallish Co., Inc.

# 32

## About the Corporation

Our first case study is of a fairly small network, one that links together about 35 workstations and other computers. It belongs to a graphics imaging company called RJL Graphics, based in Austin, Texas.

RJL Graphics, 5900 Balcones Drive, Suite 150, Austin, TX, 78731, can be reached at 512-453-8989. RJL is a full-service type and image production firm, with a pronounced emphasis on digital imaging and PostScript-based phototypesetting services.

In a manner of speaking, RJL Graphics is a company the Macintosh made possible, because the introduction of Macintosh-based page layout software and PostScript-based printers made its business technically feasible. The company's origins in 1984 nearly coincide with the introduction of the Macintosh, and to a large extent Macintoshes are still the workstations of choice at RJL Graphics. This is true even though its network server is an IBM-PC clone. This combination is only possible because its network operating system, NetWare for Macintosh, supports award-winning Macintosh file and print services.

One of the major innovations in the Macintosh was its built-in LocalTalk networking. Every Macintosh came network-ready, which meant that users didn't have to install drivers or NICs into their new Macs; all they had to do was plug the Macs into the network. The same ease of use applied to attaching peripherals to the network, because any device that had an Apple LaserWriter-compatible driver could be attached to a LocalTalk network as if it were an Apple LaserWriter. A great number of the many output devices that RJL uses, from low-resolution proof-print laser printers to high-resolution color and monochrome imagesetters, have such drivers, so this feature of the Macintosh remains attractive to RJL Graphics.

Thus, the company's business is completely built around networking. Even though RJL Graphics has largely superseded its initial use of Apple's 230 kilobit-per-second LocalTalk twisted-pair network, there are still pockets of it in use there. Today, the bulk of its network runs over thinwire Ethernet, and it is planning to expand into 10BaseT Ethernet as well, with a more long-range view toward fast switched Ethernet (100 MBps).

Of the 26 employees currently employed at RJL Graphics, over half regularly use the network, and almost everyone uses a PC or a Macintosh at least occasionally in the course of their jobs. The network server acts as the principal repository for all incoming production jobs and is fed in one of several ways. Customers might bring jobs in on floppy disks or removable SyQuest cartridges. If the job is small enough to make modem transfer feasible, customers can dial into RJL's bulletin board service and upload the job file to the server through the bulletin board.

RJL also offers in-house type design, graphics, layout, and color pre-press services, and has a broad statewide clientele that ranges from agencies for the State of Texas to a mix of high- and low-tech companies with print and media needs.

Christian Jensen is the Network Manager for RJL Graphics and has been employed there for nearly four years. He has been instrumental in introducing the current network server, and in managing the conversion from LocalTalk to Ethernet, which has significantly increased the company's job-handling capacity. As you might expect, a narrow profit-margin business like RJL makes adding more networking or computing capacity difficult. Chris confesses to being a bit frustrated at the sometimes slow pace of technology adoption and upgrade, but immediately adds that he has no trouble understanding why the limitations exist.

## THE NETWORK LAYOUT

Figure 32.1 shows a diagram of the RJL Graphics network. Note that the network has three segments. The segment on the right in the diagram contains the bulletin board server, Macintosh IIci systems, and Linotype imagesetters. In the middle of the diagram is the segment that connects the systems for self-service customers and management; this segment has relatively low traffic. The segment on the left is the production segment, with the older Macintoshes and imagesetters linked via LocalTalk, and scanners and other production equipment. The Novell server acts as a router between the three network segments and also restricts traffic between the self-service machines and the rest of the network.

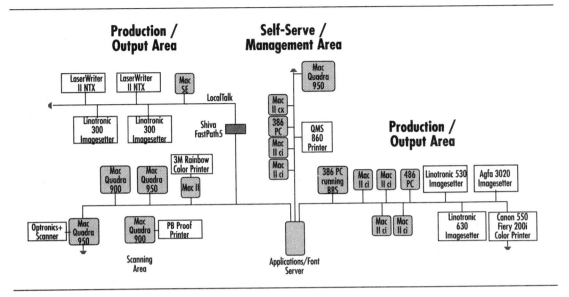

**Figure 32.1** *The RJL Graphics network.*

The only remote connection in the network is the single dial-up line to the bulletin board system. Here they have a modem so that customers can dial in and upload graphics jobs; something under 20 percent of RJL's customers deliver work this way. The low volume is as much a function of the size of the files that most customers submit to RJL—the most common media from customers are 44- and 88-megabyte removable SyQuest drive platters—as a lack of sophistication on the part of the users, says Chris.

When RJL was considering the move from LocalTalk to some other networking technology, it chose Ethernet over token ring or FDDI because it's used widely and because the company management was familiar enough with it to be comfortable making the change. It didn't want to risk installing something that might not have all the bugs out yet, or that would be hard to support.

## THE EQUIPMENT

Some of the older image setters can run only over the LocalTalk network, so RJL is retaining that portion of the network so that it can still network those machines. LocalTalk is slower than Ethernet, but this is not much of an issue for low-traffic users. Therefore, the self-service machines and those used by management, none of which generates large volumes of network traffic, are also linked via LocalTalk. The Ethernet segment and the LocalTalk segment are linked together by a Shiva FastPath 5 interlink.

The network links five IBM-clone PCs and 28 Macintoshes. The IBM clones are running DOS 3.31 or 5.0, while the Macintoshes are almost all running System 7.1. The exceptions are the self-service Macintoshes and some of the older Mac SE's, which are running System 6.0.8.

The network server is an Everex 486/50 with 65 megabytes of RAM and 6.5 gigabytes of hard disk space. It's running NetWare 3.11 with NetWare for Macintosh 3.011.

## The Wiring

The four systems that are linked via LocalTalk are connected using twisted-pair copper wiring. The remaining 30 or so systems on the network are on the newer Ethernet portion, which is wired with 10BaseT coaxial cable. RJL Graphics chose 10BaseT because it's flexible, easy to use, and affordable.

The cables run along the baseboards in offices and are carefully placed to prevent anyone contacting them. The cables attach to machines with standard 10Base2 T-connectors and terminators, and room-to-room links run above the acoustical tile ceiling.

## The Problems

As in any living network environment, RJL Graphics has its share of problems and network issues. It encountered some issues during the upgrade from the old AppleTalk network to the new Ethernet technology, and it has a lot of maintenance issues with the huge volume of data generated by the graphics production process. The combination of network types leads to some incompatibilities, as well.

### The Upgrade

The biggest problem encountered during the network upgrade was getting funding and management support for the necessary expenditures. "While the network is critical to RJL's activity and success," Christian Jensen says, "the need for imaging, typesetting, and computing equipment often overshadows the need for network equipment and materials. The other equipment is bigger, more obvious, and more glamorous, while the networking stuff is in the background and less likely to be considered when funds are available." To improve the process for next time, he'd like to see the budgeting and planning more formal and organized. While doing so might not necessarily speed the process of conversion, it would certainly streamline it and make it more straightforward and easier for everyone involved.

## The Maintenance

At RJL Graphics, the data for every job lives on the server. Graphics files can take up astonishing amounts of space, so a big part of the network administrator's job is to make sure the server doesn't get filled up with data. RJL's staff has an innovative way of handling this problem; as soon as they finish with a job, they move all the related files to a Macintosh folder that has a high-order character as the first character of the folder name. Their backup software then scans the entire disk every night, and when it encounters a folder with this special naming convention, it archives the files in that folder and deletes the folder from the server disk. Thus, within 24 hours of the time a job is finished, the related files are removed from the server, preventing clutter and wasted disk capacity. Best of all, this cleanup happens automatically.

## Compatibility Issues

Another problem RJL Graphics has had with its network is that NetWare and LocalTalk don't always interoperate as smoothly as they might. Generally any such software problems can be solved by rebooting the network server, but this is not really a satisfactory solution. Naturally, they would prefer perfect communication between the two network types, but currently this does not appear to be possible. Another incompatibility is that Macintosh printing is not fully supported by RJL's version of NetWare, particularly in the feature that should notify a user that his or her print job has finished printing or that there is a problem with the print job. RJL Graphics would like to see all of these features as Mac-like as possible, but currently no fixes are available.

# THE PLAN

In future expansions, RJL Graphics plans to increase the network size in both bandwidth and capacity, to add 10BaseT interfaces and functionality throughout the operation, and to improve network organization and performance. "In a very literal sense," Jensen says, "the network has to remain the backbone of RJL's business." Besides network expansions, they are constantly adding new image equipment to the existing network, such as a Silicon Graphics machine that they will use to transfer PC graphics onto film. The network at RJL Graphics is anything but static.

# CASE STUDY: THE MEDIUM CORPORATION

# 33

## THE CORPORATION

In this chapter we'll look at a medium-sized network, having fewer than 300 nodes, spread across two sites in the same city.

Vtel Corporation (formerly VideoTelecom Corp.), at 108 Wild Basin Road, Austin, Texas, 78746, can be reached at 512-314-2700. It makes video conferencing equipment, and designs, develops, and manufactures the video conferencing systems out of its two sites in Austin. The development and administrative branches of the company are housed at the Wild Basin address, while the manufacturing division is in a separate building on Technicenter Drive, also in Austin. In addition, the company has a sales and support office just outside of London, and several sales offices throughout the United States. Company employees, vendors, and other contacts all use the network regularly.

Vtel uses its network for three major purposes: to share files, especially engineering plans and software source code files; to provide messaging between employees and groups via e-mail; and to save money by using networked copies of software, by buying licenses for only the number of users who use a particular software package at any time rather than buying a copy for everyone who might ever use it. (They enforce this with SiteLock, as described in Chapter 3.) They also use it to share printers, modems, and Internet access, and possible future uses include shared CD-ROM drives and interactive video over the network.

The network management group at Vtel has grown dramatically in the last year, from one to six people. Sal Lozano is the director of the group, and has over two decades of experience in group computing management, primarily in the mainframe world. Sal's staff members' responsibilities include server administration, PC support, video network maintenance, and general troubleshooting, and they have between two and five years of experience each.

## THE NETWORK LAYOUT

As you can see in Figure 33.1, the Vtel network extends between the two Austin sites via a high-bandwidth, high-speed T1 link. Half of the bandwidth of the link is used for video transmissions, the other half for network data. It has one server at the Technicenter site and three more at the Wild Basin site. A pair of Cisco routers provide the main link between the two sites, and the Cisco router at Wild Basin also links the other segments of the network. One of these segments is the T1 connection to the Technicenter site, another attaches to the Internet link, a third connects the group of UNIX workstations, and the other segment connects to the three servers and workstations which comprise the bulk of the network.

The network operating system is NetWare 3.11. As Vtel brings new servers onto the network, it is currently installing them with the latest 3.X version of NetWare. Because it will have six servers on the network by the end of 1994, Vtel would like

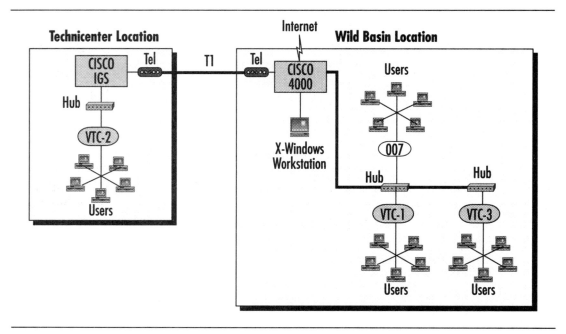

**Figure 33.1** *Vtel's present network layout.*

to upgrade to NetWare 4.x so it can take advantage of its centralized management capabilities. But its wary of moving to version 4.0; Vtel would prefer to wait until it's had a chance to stabilize, and the move to 4.0 will also be very time-consuming. Taken together, these factors mean that Vtel will probably not move to NetWare 4.x until the end of 1994 at the earliest.

## THE EQUIPMENT

### The Hubs and Routers

Originally all the hubs were Gateway EtherHubs, but that model has been discontinued, so now Vtel is moving to SynOptics hubs. The two routers that link the two sites are both Cisco brands.

### The PCs

All NetWare servers are 80486-based PCs, varying in speed from 33 to 60 megahertz. The Technicenter site has about 40 users attached to its server, while the Wild Basin servers have a total of about 200 users.

The UNIX systems are Sun SPARC 10 stations, all running Solaris UNIX.

Vtel has several Macintosh systems for graphics applications and publishing. Some are running System 7.1, others System 6.0.8.

The IBM-PCs and clones all run either DOS 5.0 or DOS 6.2. They are primarily 80486 systems. Some are 80386-based, but all new systems purchased are 80486-based.

### The Peripherals

The Vtel network has three LAN modems for dialing in or out; users dialing in on these can access all server resources. Vtel also has more than a dozen printers and plotters on the network and plans to add a shared CD-ROM drive in the near future.

## THE WIRING

The local networks are all running Ethernet over twisted-pair wiring, the most cost-effective solution for its installation. Every connection is made via a dual wall plate;

each plate has a slot for the network jack and another for the user's telephone. The backbone is a fiber link between the floors of the buildings and they expect that it will support up to 100 Mb of data traffic per second, essential for an organization that sends a lot of high-bandwidth data such as video.

# THE PROBLEMS

One big problem in administering the Vtel network, Lozano says, is the headaches involved in trying to keep track of the wide variety of equipment. Vtel has seven different brands of IBM-PC clones alone, all running different operating system versions, with different amounts of RAM and disk space, and various different equipment attached to them. They are working to solve this by standardizing on a few known brands and configurations.

Another issue is one of shared data. People need to be disciplined, he says, and make sure they don't have local copies of things they think they are getting from the network. A number of his problems have stemmed from user errors of this variety.

He cites disk space as a recurring problem. No matter how much disk space there is on the network, it fills to capacity quickly. Vtel will be adding considerably more network disk space in the coming year.

In a network of this size, Lozano notes, it is possible to accumulate costs comparable to mainframe levels, when you consider the total network cost. He observes that a mainframe sufficient to the organization's needs would cost between $300,00 and $500,000, while a networked PC costs around $2500. When you multiply that PC cost by 200 users, he points out, a network of PCs is comparable in cost to a mainframe solution with similar capabilities. On the other hand, he observes, with networked PCs you have much more flexibility in choosing hardware and software solutions to suit your needs, and the initial investment is much smaller, an important factor for small companies. Another advantage of networking is the ability to restrict traffic if necessary by the use of smart routers.

# THE PLAN

Vtel has a very specific plan for adding the bandwidth and capacity that every network administrator always wants to add. See Figure 33.2 for a diagram of its planned expansion, and compare it to the diagram of its current network layout in Figure 33.1.

As this diagram shows, Vtel plans to add a high-speed Kalpana Ethernet switch; this will become the central switching point of the network. This switch has eight

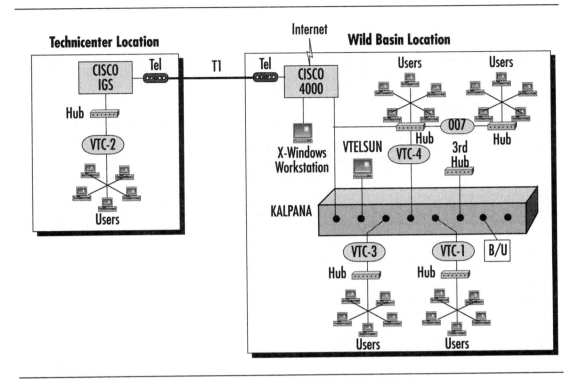

**Figure 33.2** *Vtel's planned network after expansion.*

ports; at the time it's installed, seven of them will be in use. One will link to the backup station, one to the Cisco router (which in turn links to the Technicenter site and the Internet), and the remaining ports attach to each of the Wild Basin servers. The addition of this switch, Lozano expects, will make the network faster and more reliable, and will increase his ability to segment the network, isolating groups of users from problems and changes to a greater extent.

# CASE STUDY: A LARGE INSTITUTION

## THE ORGANIZATION

Finally, let's look at an example of a large network. This one has thousands of nodes and users, and contains examples of just about every possible networking compatibility test you might imagine.

The University of Texas MD Anderson Cancer Center is located at 1515 Holcombe Boulevard, Houston, TX, 77030, and can be reached at 713-792-2121. MD Anderson is one of the preeminent cancer treatment centers in the world, and is located in the Houston Medical Center, a large medical campus near down town Houston that also includes the Baylor Medical Center, the University of Texas Medical School, and a variety of hospitals and other teaching and medical establishments.

MD Anderson typifies many larger organizations, in that its computing roots go back into the 1950s and it still boasts a major installation of IBM mainframes and related computing equipment. MD Anderson's network has been 12 years in the making, however, and currently supports over 5,500 individual PCs, of which 3,800 are IBM-PC clones, 1,500 are Macintoshes, and the remainder are high-end RISC- or SPARC-based workstations. Our contact at MD Anderson is Dan Kohner, Manager of the Network Services department, whose group oversees networking technologies.

Most of the major commercial networking technologies are in use at MD Anderson, including a dwindling arrangement of ARCnet and some LocalTalk, with the bulk of the networked nodes attached via Ethernet, which can be found in 10BaseT, 10Base2, 10Base5, and 10BaseF formats. MD Anderson is also connected to a campus-wide FDDI ring that encompasses the entire Houston Medical Center.

Because of the large number of laboratories, clinics, and operations at MD Anderson, networking is a crucial element in many aspects of the organization, from processing and forwarding patient records, to providing campus- and system-wide communications for networked employees. This organization's size also helps explain why three separate organizations plus all of the functional MD Anderson departments, taken together, share responsibilities for various aspects of the network. These organizations and entities are as follows:

- The MIS department, manages the mainframes and all organizational information assets and owns the campus internetwork and infrastructure.
- Each operational unit at MD Anderson that has a network has a designated network administrator to manage the network locally, and each unit also has its own backup administrator.
- The Network Services department provides overall network management and design, and works to define networking hardware, equipment, and software standards. This group also provides a second layer of support and expertise for networking configuration, software, and system issues.
- The cabling department manages all wiring installations and handles the purchase and installation of routers and hubs.

The network services group is currently comprised of seven individuals, each of whom is an expert in one or more areas of networking. The average number of years of industry experience in this group is over 10, and most of the individuals have advanced computer training and/or degrees in a computer-related field. Dan Kohner has been in the group for 12 years and has been responsible for most of the networking deployed at MD Anderson. He is a widely sought speaker for industry events and participates in several committees that oversee networking standards and events.

## THE NETWORK LAYOUT

It's helpful to look at the MD Anderson network as a three-level hierarchy, consisting of an intracampus backbone, a set of intrabuilding feeder trunks, and the distribution networks that bring connectivity to users' desktops.

Each NetWare server acts as a router among its local cable segments. The feeder trunks are served by Cisco routers that provide segmentation of intrabuilding networks, and Cisco routers also manage access to the intracampus FDDI backbone.

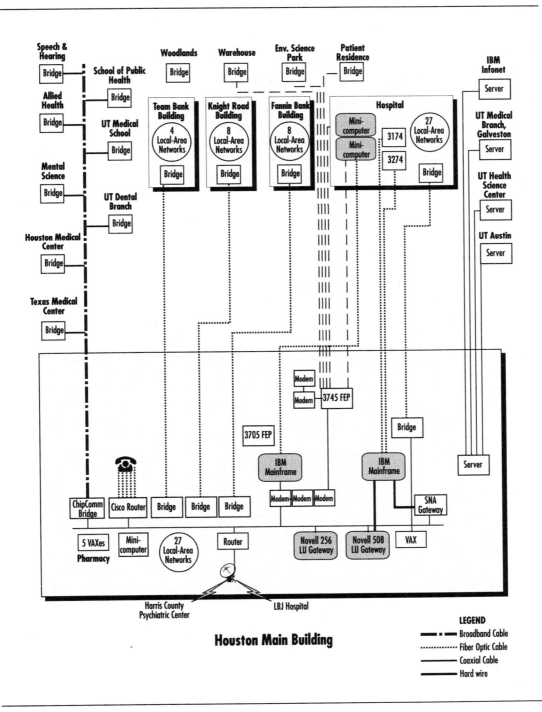

**Figure 34.1** *MD Anderson's enterprise-wide network layout.*

# THE EQUIPMENT

## The Servers

Across the campus, MD Anderson has about 80 NetWare servers, about half of which are running NetWare 4.01. The rest are still running NetWare 3.11, but the company expects to upgrade all of them by the end of 1994. It also has 20 or 30 UNIX servers, whose users typically access TCP/IP protocols and applications. And of course, it still has a significant cache of mainframes, which the users access via terminal emulation programs and NetWare for SAA, or through Telnet-based emulation.

## The Network Hardware

At the time of our interview the MD Anderson network was using five Cisco routers to tie the entire internetwork together, and planned to add four more during the course of 1994. In addition, it has a number of Cabletron and SynOptics hubs for the twisted-pair wiring, with a preference for the SynOptics hubs because of their superior manageability, with SynOptics Optivity management software.

## The PCs

On the PC side of things, the numbers are equally impressive. To start with, MD Anderson has 3,800 IBM-PC clones of various types as desktop machines, with about 300 portables or laptops. About 65 percent of these are running Windows 3.1 as the primary operating environment, 25 percent use some flavor of DOS, version 3.31 or higher, with the remaining systems split between UNIX and OS/2 operating systems.

MD Anderson also has about 1,500 Macintoshes of varying ages and capabilities, from old Mac SEs to newer Quadra 950 models. The older ones run version System 6.0.8, while the newer ones are running System 7.0.1 and 7.1. Besides these machines, it has about 300 portable or laptop Macintoshes (PowerBooks of various makes and models).

Finally, it has around 100 RISC- or SPARC-based workstations, typically running some variant of the UNIX operating system.

In addition to the PCs and workstations, the MD Anderson network links a wide variety of specialized equipment, from MRI to ultrasound.

## The Wiring

As you might expect in a network of this size and history, the MD Anderson network uses many different types and ages of wiring.

Like RJL Graphics, MD Anderson has some older Macintoshes, which it links together via LocalTalk. Also on the LocalTalk portions of the network are some LocalTalk based medical and printing devices, which could not be networked any other way.

In older areas of the campus, devices and workstations are networked over ARCnet, where the wiring uses recycled coaxial cable from their old 3270 terminal installations. (IBM's SNA terminals use the same type of coaxial cable that the ARCnet network requires.) This coaxial cable is of the RG-62 variety and is also the coax cable used to link the remaining 3270 terminals to the mainframes.

All the remaining wiring is some flavor of Ethernet cabling, including 10Base2, 10Base5, 10BaseT, and 10BaseF. As the company expands and replaces old wiring, it would like to move toward an installation that is entirely wired in 10BaseT or 10BaseF wiring.

The backbone linking all these networks is a two-way fiber-optic FDDI link, the same one that links the entire Houston Medical Center together. Currently this backbone provides high-speed interbuilding links, but other uses are being investigated for it.

The connectors throughout the network are fairly standard, and depend on the type of technology they are linking. Where they have coaxial cables, the connectors are standard BNC or T connectors; the twisted-pair connections are made using standard RJ-45 jacks with Amphenol wall plates; and the fiber links use ST-style connectors.

## The Problems

The primary difficulty, Kohner tells us, has been with political issues. There are two kinds of problems.

First, the network services group has had to overcome the desire for control and self-sufficiency perceived in the many autonomous departments at MD Anderson. While most people have accepted the need and understand the value of a campus-wide network, they're now grappling with the idea that enterprise-wide networking means that they have to share their data resources and information with the entire organization.

Second, MIS has maintained a consistently pro-mainframe attitude toward computing and has been slow in accepting the value of network computing. Despite considerable pressure to downsize, they believe the mainframe and its infrastructure should continue to take the front seat in the MD Anderson computing plans, even though usage patterns indicate that the network is a preferred tool for most users.

Another problem has been in integrating different types of equipment. Too often, someone purchases a new device without fully exploring what will be involved in getting the equipment working on the network. "Medical staffers work miracles every day," Kohner comments, "and expect network administrators to routinely do the same."

Managing multiple platforms, operating systems, and networking protocols is a challenging task, and Kohner would like to minimize the number of different platforms, software, and protocols he and his group have to support. With this in mind, he comments that he'd like to have completely phased out the ARCnet portions of the network sooner, and standardized on 10BaseT Ethernet sooner as well. This is mostly for convenience and simplicity, he tells us, adding that things are actually still working quite well with these various environments still in place.


## THE PLAN

The Network Services group has plenty to do. When we asked them what they'd like to do in the future, the list included:

- Develop or acquire more client-server based technology.
- Better shield users from the mainframes.
- Get the best value out of our mixed mainframe-LAN environment.
- Increase bandwidth and capability.
- Move all the wiring to 10BaseT or 10BaseF.
- Improve network organization and performance.
- Increase use of advanced services such as imaging, telephony, and multimedia.
- Expand the roles that networking can play at MD Anderson.

With an agenda like this, the company will have no trouble staying busy until well into the twenty-first century. Obviously, these plans are ambitious, but that's entirely in keeping with the character and reputation of the institution of which Network Services at MD Anderson is a part.

# VENDOR LIST

Here are the names and contact information for virtually all of the vendors mentioned in this book. If the vendor's contact information includes an 800 toll-free number, this will probably only work inside the United States, and possibly Canada, so we tried to include a toll-call number as well for those of you elsewhere in the world.

AG Group, Inc.: Macintosh-based network management software
2540 Camino Diablo, Suite 202
Walnut Creek, CA 94530
510-937-7900; Fax: 510-937-2479

American Research Group, Inc.: network training services
P.O. Box 1039
Cary, NC 27512
919-467-8797; Fax: 919-380-0097

AMP: cable testers, cables and connectors, hubs, concentrators, MAUs, multiplexers, transceivers, etc.
P.O. Box 3608
Harrisburg, PA 17105-3608
800-522-6752 or 714-564-0100; Fax: 717-986-7575

Amphenol (a division of Allied Signal): cables, connectors, tools
1925 A Ohio Street
Lisle, IL 60565
708-819-5640

Artisoft: networking software and hardware, including
network starter kits, LANtastic network OS
691 East River Road
Tucson, AZ 85704
800-846-9726 or 602-670-7000; Fax: 602-293-8065

Azure Technology: protocol analyzers
63 South Street
Hopkinton, MA 01148
800-233-3800 or 508-435-3800; Fax: 508-435-0448

Belden Wire & Cable, a division of Cooper Industries:
networking cable of all kinds
P.O. Box 1980-T
Richmond, IN 47375
800-235-3364 or 317-983-5200; Fax: 317-983-5294

Black Box Corporation: tools, cables, connectors, test equipment,
software, network consulting
P.O. Box 12800
Pittsburgh, PA, 15241
412-746-5500 (voice & fax); BBS: 412-746-7120

Blue Sky Software Corporation: software development tools & training aids
7586 LaJolla Boulevard, Suite 3
La Jolla, CA 92037
619-459-6365; Fax: 619-459-6366

Brightwork Development: network audit, license management, network
management software
766 Shrewsbury Avenue
Jerral Center West
Tinton Falls, NJ 07724
800-552-9876 or 908-530-0440; Fax: 908-530-0622

Cabletron Systems, Inc.: network hubs, interfaces, network management software
35 Industrial Way
P.O. Box 5005
Rochester, NH 03867-0505
603-332-9400; Fax: 603-337-2211

Cisco Systems: routers, communications servers
1525 O'Brien Drive
Menlo Park, CA 94026-1435
800-553-6387 or 415-326-1941; Fax: 415-326-1989

CompuServe Information Services: on-line information and research services, electronic mail
Attn: Customer Service
P.O. Box 20212
5000 Arlington Centre Boulevard
Columbus, OH 43220
800-848-8199 or 614-457-8650

Concord Electronics Corporation: manufacturer of connectors and other electronic components
30 Great Jones Street
New York, NY 10012
212-777-6571

Dolphin Networks: network management, protocol analyzers
4405 International Boulevard, Suite B-108
Norcross, GA 30093
404-279-7050; Fax: 404-279-1615

dtech, Inc.: network inventory and management software
15 West Sixth Street, Suite 1500
Tulsa, OK 74119-5455
800-800-4278 or 918-583-7446; Fax: 918-583-0560

Frye Computer Systems, Inc.: network management tools
19 Temple Place
Boston, MA 02111
800-234-3793 or 617-451-5400; Fax: 617-451-6711

FTP Software, Inc.: protocol analysis, TCP/IP software
2 High Street
North Andover, MA 01845
800-282-4387 or 508-685-4000; Fax: 508-794-4488

General Software: protocol analyzers
15600 NE 8th Street, Suite A-3
Bellevue, WA 98008
206-391-4285; Fax: 206-557-0736

Hewlett-Packard, Network Test Division: cable-testing equipment, network management software, protocol analyzers
5070 Centennial Boulevard
Colorado Springs, CO 80919
800-452-4844 or 303-229-3800; Fax: 408-345-8626

Horizons Technology
3900 Ruffin Road
San Diego, CA 92123
619-292-8320; Fax: 619-292-7321

Intel (Network Division): network monitoring, management,
interfaces, backup, security
5200 NE Elam Young Parkway
Hillsboro, OR 97124
800-538-3373 or 503-629-7000; Fax: 800-525-3019 or 503-629-7580

Internet: world-wide research and information access
Dial services to the Internet are available from a number of vendors, including:
Performance Systems International, Inc.: world-dial Internet access service
510 Huntmar Park Drive
Herndon, VA 22070
800-827-7482 or 703-620-6651

Jensen Tools
7815 South 46th Street
Phoenix, AZ 85044-5399
602-968-6231 (inside US) or 602-968-6241, ext. 316 or 347 (outside US)
Fax: 800-366-9662 (inside US) or 602-438-1690 (outside US)

Microsoft Corporation: network operating systems and software
1 Microsoft Way
Redmond, WA 98052
206-882-8080; Fax: 206-936-7329

Novell, Inc.: networking software, including network operating systems,
management, and protocol analysis
122 East 1700 South
Provo, UT 84606
800-638-6683 or 801-429-7000; Fax: 801-429-5155

Shattuck Industries, a subsidiary of Ideal, Inc.: cable tools
117 Fern Street
Santa Cruz, CA 95060
408-427-3122; Fax: 408-427-3134

Sun Microsystems, Sunselect Division: network management software
2 Elizabeth Drive
Chelmsford, MA 01824
800-247-3532 or 508-442-2300; Fax: 508-250-2300

Shiva Corporation: network interfaces, bridges, routers,
communications servers, remote bridges
Northwest Park
63 Third Avenue
Burlington, MA 01803
800-458-3550 or 617-270-8300; Fax: 617-270-8852

SynOptics: bridges, hubs, protocol analyzers, routers, WAN switches
4401 Great America Parkway
Santa Clara, CA 95052-8185
800-776-6895 or 408-988-2400

Xtree, a division of Symantec Corporation: network file management software
4115 Broad Street, Building 1
San Luis Obispo, CA 93401
800-395-8733 or 805-541-0604; Fax: 805-541-4762

# PUBLICATION LIST

There are a great many more networking- and computer-focused magazines available than those listed here. If we've overlooked one that you particularly like, forgive us (and drop us a line to let us know). These are the ones we read regularly and that seem to provide the most balanced network-related news and information. Most of them are free to qualified subscribers, so nothing should stop you from getting them. Just be sure to indicate that you have technical and budget responsibility for a network on the qualification forms, and you'll get what you deserve from these publications!

*Computer Shopper* is published 12 times a year by Coastal Associates, a division of Ziff Communications Company. The address is One Park Avenue, New York, NY, 10016, and its subscription department can be reached at 800-274-6384 (inside US) or at 303-447-9330 (outside US). The magazine costs $29.97 inside the United States, and an additional $39 for postage outside the United States. *Computer Shopper* is primarily a PC-focused advertising supplement—a normal issue looks like an over-sized phone book—but it includes ads and contact information for hundreds of mail-order dealers who carry networking equipment and software. It's a great place to shop around and to establish the floor for pricing on any items you might need to purchase.

*Computerworld* is published 53 times a year by IDG Publications, P.O. Box 9171, 375 Cochituate Road, Framingham, MA, 01701-9171, and can be reached at 800-669-1002 for subscriptions, 508-879-0700 for editorial information. The magazine costs

$48 inside the United States, and between $95 and $295 outside the country, depending on exact location. *Computerworld* covers the computer industry in general, but gives networking issues good coverage as well. It's a good counterpoint to the Ziff-Davis *PC Week*, in that its focus includes coverage of non-PC systems as well.

*Infoworld* is published 51 times a year by InfoWorld Publishing Company, a subsidiary of IDG, at 155 Bovet Road, San Mateo, CA, 94402, and can be reached at 415-572-7341. The magazine is free to qualified subscribers, but otherwise costs $130 inside the United States, and $145 in Canada (other subscription costs available upon request). *InfoWorld* covers the computer industry in general, but gives networking issues good coverage as well. It also publishes Rich Tennant's cartoons in every issue (our personal favorite nerdy form of entertainment).

*LAN: The Network Solutions Magazine* is published monthly by Miller Freeman, 600 Harrison Street, San Francisco, CA, 94107, who can be reached at 415-905-2200. An annual subscription costs $19.97. This magazine provides coverage on a broad range of networking topics, including technology overviews, user tutorials, and product reviews. For an excellent source of network product and vendor information, be sure to check out its annual *Buyers Guide* (published in September of each year).

*LAN Times* is published 25 times a year by McGraw-Hill, Inc., 1221 Avenue of the Americas, New York, NY, 10020, who can be reached at 415-513-6800. The magazine is free to qualified subscribers. *LAN Times* also provides coverage on a broad range of networking topics, including technology overviews, network industry news, product reviews, and includes editorials from networking industry leaders and personalities. For an excellent source of network product and vendor information, be sure to check out its annual *Buyers Directory* (published in August of each year).

*Networking Management* is published 12 times a year by PenWell Publishing Company, 1421 South Sheridan, Tulsa, OK, 74112, who can be reached at 918-831-9424 (subscriptions) or 508-692-0700 (editorial inquiries). The magazine is free to qualified subscribers, and costs $42 inside the United States, and $65 outside the country, for nonqualified subscribers. *Networking Management* provides coverage on a broad range of network management topics, including technology overviews, network industry news, and standards information.

*Network World* is published 51 times a year by IDG Publications, 161 Worcester Road, Framingham, MA, 01701-9172, and can be reached at 508-875-6400. The magazine is free to qualified subscribers, and costs $95 inside the United States, and between $95 and $245 outside the country, depending on exact location, for nonqualified subscribers. *Network World* provides weekly coverage on a broad range of network management topics, including technology overviews, network industry news, and offers special departments for enterprise internets, local networks, global services, and client-server applications.

*Open Systems Today* is published 28 times a year by CMP Publications, Inc., 600 Community Drive, Manhasset, NY, 11030-3875, 708-647-6834 (subscription). The magazine is free to qualified subscribers, and costs $79 inside the United States and Canada, and between $179 and $200 outside the country, depending on exact location, for non-qualified subscribers, per year. *OST* provides semi-monthly coverage on a broad range of computer industry topics, including technology overviews, and industry news, and offers special departments on networking, that is primarily focused at the open systems side of the computer industry, with a strong emphasis on UNIX. It offers a valuable complement to most of the other magazines mentioned here, which devote most of their networking coverage to PC-related topics.

*PC Week* is published 51 times a year by Ziff-Davis Publishing Company, a division of Ziff Communications Company, One Park Avenue, New York, NY, 10016, 609-786-8230 (subscriptions). The magazine is free to qualified subscribers, and costs $160 inside the United States, and between $200 and $350 outside the country, depending on exact location, for nonqualified subscribers, per year. *PC Week* provides weekly coverage on a broad range of computer industry topics, including technology overviews and industry news, and offers special departments on networking. It also publishes a weekly network-focused supplement, called *PCWeek Netweek*, that will be shipped to readers who express interest in networking.

# GLOSSARY OF NETWORK TERMS

**10Base2:** also known as *Thin Ethernet* or, fondly, *Cheapernet*. A cabling specification for running Ethernet over thin coax cable. If you have a choice, eschew this in favor of 10BaseT, unless you're trying to set up a small network of less than 8 nodes.

**10Base5:** the old way of running Ethernet, over thick coax cable. Also called *Thick Ethernet*.

**10BaseF:** Ethernet over fiber-optic cable.

**10BaseT:** Ethernet over twisted-pair cable. By far the most prevalent, and probably the one of the four you'll pick, if you have a choice.

**3270:** a particular model number of IBM mainframe, one of the most common of mainframes.

**80286, 80386, 80486:** "Nerd terms" for IBM-PC clones. This number is the number Intel prints on the CPU chip, which is the heart of these machines, and it tells a lot about the capabilities of the PC. The higher the number, the greater the capability.

**AC:** alternating current, the usual way electrical power is delivered.

**acronym:** an abbreviation formed by taking the first letter of each word of the phrase you want to abbreviate. Since networking terminology is loaded with long wordy phrases, it's also loaded with acronyms. Some networkers talk about TLAs, which stands for Three-Letter Acronyms, as being essential for legitimacy among nerds!

**address:** see *network address.*

**application:** any piece of software that you use for your computing tasks, such as a spreadsheet program, electronic mail program, or game.

**archival systems:** backup systems that automatically create copies of data every time something changes.

**ARCnet:** a token-passing type of network technology; inexpensive but rather slow by current standards.

**AUTOEXEC.BAT:** a file which contains instructions for a DOS-based computer to configure itself when you turn it on.

**backbone:** a link, typically of some high-speed medium, between the segments of a network.

**backup:** a copy of data preserved for purposes of disaster recovery. You can make a backup of a single data file, the contents of your hard drive, or the entire server hard drive (and you should).

**bandwidth:** the amount of data that can pass through a connection at any given time.

**baseline:** the level of network performance against which you judge any changes. You should measure your baseline when you first install your network.

**bend radius specification:** a measurement of how far you can bend a cable before you risk breaking it.

**bit:** a single unit of information. A bit has the value 1 or 0.

**blue-line plans:** architectural drawings of a building. They usually really are blue, which means a standard photocopier won't work on them. Take them to a drafting supply house to copy them.

**BNC connector:** the type of connector that attaches to coax cable.

**bridge:** a network device that allows you to connect different types of network media.

**brown-bag seminars:** lunch meetings during which you reveal the glory and wonder of the new network or changes thereto, without disrupting the flow of any body's workday. Best for imparting an hour or less of information.

**building codes**: the collection of rules and regulations that apply to buildings. These ordinances usually vary by locale; know the ones in your area before you start adding wiring.

**bulletin board**: in computer talk, a place where users can dial in, post messages, and read other messages.

**bus topology**: a network wiring layout in which each computer is connected to the two computers on either side of it, except for the ones on the ends.

**byte**: a collection of eight bits. This is, interestingly, about the amount of data it takes to store a single letter (in the Roman alphabet, that is).

**cable connectors**: the hardware gadgets that attach to the ends of your cables, which in turn will let you attach those cables to NICs or wall plates.

**cable plant**: the collection of cables that make up your network connections.

**cable stripper**: a tool that helps you remove some of the insulation from a cable, quickly and easily. You'll become very familiar with one of these if you decide to do your own wiring.

**cable tie**: plastic strip with a notched opening in one end, designed to cinch together a bundle of wires or cables. Essential for tidy cable installations.

**cabling**: also called wiring, this is just the whole collection of cables, connectors, and hubs that make up your network.

**CAD**: computer-aided design. Usually refers to high-powered graphics software that lets a user draw technical diagrams faster and more easily than with drafting.

**campus**: any collection of buildings that house an organization. Does not necessarily refer to an institute of higher learning.

**capital assets**: those expensive things that your accounting department probably wants to keep track of, such as buildings, trucks, and PCs.

**carrier sense**: a feature of Ethernet that indicates that every system on the network is always listening to what's traveling over the wire.

**CATV**: cable access television.

**CDDI**: copper distributed data interface, a variant of FDDI that runs over copper wire instead of fiber-optic cable.

**CD-ROM**: a computer storage medium that works with disks much like the CDs you use on your home stereo, but which stores computer data instead of music.

**cellular telephones**: telephones that work by transmitting a conversation over radio frequencies instead of wires.

**changers**: devices that automatically remove one disk, tape, or other storage mediums, from the drive, and replace it with another. See also *unattended operation*.

**cladding**: the insulation layer for fiber-optic cable, which is typically made of fiberglass or plastic.

**client**: a PC when it is in the position of requesting a service from a network server.

**clone**: shorthand for IBM-PC clone. This term refers to any machine which works the same way as an IBM-PC, including running the same software. A clone can do this because it has the same CPU as the IBM; see *80286*.

**coating**: the outer layer of a cable, typically made of PVC (polyvinyl chloride, a type of plastic), which is the most common type of coating for keyboard, modem, and other types of computer system cables, or Teflon, for use in ceilings and in walls for network cables (as required by most building codes).

**coax**: nickname for coaxial cable.

**coaxial cable**: a type of cable that has one "strand" inside, the other surrounding it, separated by an insulating layer. They both have the same axis, so they are coaxial. You'll recognize this as similar to the stuff that attaches your TV to your VCR.

**collapsed backbone**: a backbone that is a special hub or some other piece of network equipment, rather than a collection of cables.

**collision**: when two machines send out packets over the network at the same time, you get a collision. A fancy word for error, it might mean your network is getting taxed.

**collision detect**: a feature of Ethernet. It detects collisions, and if it sees that one has happened, everybody has to wait before re-sending.

**communications**: the language of a network. The protocol and networking software form the communications portion of a network.

**CompuServe**: a very large bulletin board. This is a great source of information about your network; nearly all computer equipment vendors maintain forums here. See the Reference Guide for more information.

**computer-aided design**: see *CAD*.

**concentrator**: see *hub*.

**conduit**: a kind of pipe designed to hold wires. You usually need it for electrical wires, and sometimes you see it used to carry telephone or network wiring as well.

**CONFIG.SYS**: a file that configures system software in a DOS-based computer. DOS reads this configuration when you first turn on the computer.

**connections**: the media over which the network messages are passed. Typically wiring, but could also be fiber-optic cable or radio transmissions.

**connector covers**: plastic "wrappers" that go over connectors and the wires going into the connectors, to protect them from damage.

**console**: usually refers to the main administrative station of a system, such as the screen and keyboard attached to your network server.

**consumables**: those items that get used up. For printers, for instance, consumables are paper, toner, and staples.

**CPU**: central processing unit. The brain of the computer. Everything else, including memory and disk drives, is just gravy.

**crash**: disaster. A crash is some catastrophic problem, such as a disk drive that the server can't read, or a server that won't boot up.

**crimp connector**: a cable connector that you attach by crimping, or squeezing, a metal mold around the end of a cable in a precise way. You need a special tool to do this right.

**crimping tool**: a tool that lets you attach a crimp connector to a cable.

**CSMA/CD**: carrier-sense, multiple-access/collision detect; an acronym for the way Ethernet works.

**DAT**: digital audio tape, a special format of tape often used as a computer backup medium.

**data-intensive application**: any application that sends or requests large amounts of data over the network.

**data packet**: see *packet*.

**dedicated server**: a PC that is used strictly as a server and is not available as a workstation.

**desktop, desktop system**: see *workstation*.

**dial-in connection**: also, dial-up connection. A method of accessing a network by calling into the network via a modem.

**die-based crimper**: the best kind of crimping tool to get, this one works by using a die to determine the precise size and shape of the cable and connector that you are joining together.

**directory**:    collection of data files in DOS and UNIX systems. In Macintosh language, they're folders.

**disaster recovery**:  the process of bringing a network or a network device back from the dead. This also means the large amount of preparation to make such recovery possible.

**disk consumption**:  the amount of space being used up on a disk drive. Usually this is space the network users are using to store things on the file server, and when it gets over about 80% of the total space available, you need to start looking for other places to store things.

**disk mirroring**:  a feature of some network operating systems that ensures that you will never lose file server data due to a disk failure, because your file server has two identical disk drives, and the network software writes every file change to both drives at the same time.

**display adapter**: a card that fits into a PC so that you can attach a particular display device to that PC.

**distributed application**:  any application that runs partly on one machine and partly on another (often a server) over the network, rather than keeping quietly to itself on a single PC.

**distributed computing**:  a concept of networking that views your PC as a tool that you use to access the network as one computing environment, rather than as a collection of unrelated resources.

**distribution medium**:  medium used primarily to send data out to many systems over relatively short distances.

**DOS**:        the most common operating system on IBM-clone PCs.

**driver**:     the piece of software that runs on a PC and provides translation between the network interface card in that PC and the network software running on that PC.

**drop cable**: AKA transceiver cable.

**dumb terminal**: a monitor and keyboard that are attached to a system that does all the work. If that system is not running, the terminal does nothing. Different from your networked PC, which can still do useful work if the network's not running.

**electrical interference**: noise generated by large electrical devices such as motors. You can't hear this kind of noise, but your TP network cables can.

**electromagnetic interference** (EMI): same as electrical interference.

**electronic data interchange** (EDI): a standard mechanism that allows companies to transfer funds and purchase orders electronically between themselves; many large vendors (like Ford Motor Company) won't do business any other way.

**electronic mail**: see *e-mail*.

**electronics supply house**: a store where you can buy anything from T-connectors to memory chips to PCs.

**e-mail**: messaging application that runs over a network.

**emergency kit**: collection of keys, passwords, and other information someone might need if trouble crops up on the network when you're not around. Store it in a safe place.

**EMI**: electromagnetic interference. Caused by large electrical devices, it can ruin the network signals traveling over your wires. You want to avoid EMI at all costs.

**error counts**: usually a group of measurements of packets that didn't go through, collisions, or other problems. Networks are designed to recover from these types of errors, but you want to keep an eye on the changes in the numbers.

**Ethernet**: a very common network technology; inexpensive to install but its age is showing, primarily in its speed limitations. Faster than ARCnet, though.

**evening classes**: alternative to brown-bag seminars. They let you get the message out about the network without interfering with the normal work of the company. Ideal for training that will take a couple of hours.

**fault-tolerant systems**: computers that are designed to keep running even if they encounter an error. Usually they do this by having multiple CPUs or disks.

**FDDI:**     Fiber Distributed Data Interface, the fastest of the four major network technologies (the others are ARCnet, Ethernet, and token ring), and also the most expensive.

**fiber-optic cable**: a type of cable that contains strands of plastic or glass which transmit information in the form of light pulses (instead of old-fashioned electrical pulses over metal wire).

**file server**: a server that is used primarily for data storage.

**file transfer**: the action of sending a file from one PC on the network to another, over the network.

**finish-out**: the stage of building construction when the wallboard, ceiling, carpets, and decorations get installed (after the walls go up but before the people move in).

**full backup**: a complete copy of everything, usually on a server. See also *incremental backup*.

**full-motion video**: video that moves quickly enough to seem like natural motion. This requires lots of data and is distinguished from stop-motion video, which is choppy, and stills, which don't move at all.

**graceful shutdown**: the act of turning off a system by first making sure all users are logged off, all files are closed, and the system software has been halted. This is what doesn't happen if the power goes out.

**groupware**: software designed to help people work together on projects. E-mail falls into this category, as do shared document editors and network scheduling software.

**hardware supplier**: a vendor who sells you computer equipment, including wires, connectors, and PCs.

**hierarchical**: a structure where each level is subordinate to the one above it. An essay outline is hierarchical; so is the Army.

**host:**     another word for server. The host is the computer that responds to a request from a client.

**hub:**      a device that consolidates and maintains signals in twisted-pair networks.

**hub topology**: topology where all systems are connected to a central point, rather than to each other.

**HVAC:**     heating, vacuum, air conditioning. The collection of building features that often appear together on building plans.

**impedance**: measured in ohms, this has to do with how the cable transmits electricity.

**incremental backup**: a partial copy of the data on a system, usually contains just the data that has changed since the last backup.

**incremental installation**: an installation that proceeds in slow, careful, well-thought-out steps, after thoroughly testing each previous step.

**industry standards**: sets of rules that assure you that all items which follow the rules will be able to work with each other. See also *proprietary*.

**initiator**:    the participant in a network conversation who made the request, that is, who initiated the conversation.

**insertion loss**: each device that gets attached to a cable imposes some impedance on the line; the insertion loss is the amount of cable you lose when you add a new device that corresponds to maintaining overall impedance. For thinwire Ethernet, each device lowers the 180-meter limit by approximately 2 meters.

**interactive application**: any application that allows two or more users to interact with each other live; this might mean a video application where the participants can see and hear each other, or a text-sharing application where each user can type and see the others' keystrokes at the same time.

**interrupt level**: in a PC, an interrupt is a signal that the computer sends to a card. Every card must use a different interrupt; which one it uses is called its interrupt level.

**I/O**:    input/output, or how the computer gets information (input) and arranges for it to be displayed, printed, plotted, etc. (output).

**I/O address**: every card in a PC has an I/O address. This address tells the computer where to look to get input from the card, or send output to it.

**IS**:    information services. The department that is, in many organizations, responsible for the organization's data and computing needs.

**LAN**:    local area network. This is a network that is connected within a relatively small area, typically a single building.

**LANtastic**: network software from Artisoft, which runs best on fairly small networks.

**life-cycle**:    the length of time during which a device or system, including your network, is useful.

**line printer**: a printer that prints a single line of text at a time. Different from a laser printer, which prints in terms of points on the page, not letters.

**local**:          refers to anything that happens on the machine sitting in front of you.

**magnetic resonance imaging** (MRI): a high-tech medical diagnostic procedure.

**mainframe**:     a large computer that allows many users to work on it at once.

**map**:            in the context of networks, this is the collection of data about your network, including a picture of the building and network layout, a database that contains information about every item in the network.

**MBWA**:          management by walking around. The practice of keeping tabs on things by asking people how things are, rather than waiting for memos or reports.

**media**:          the copper wires, fiber-optic cable, or radio transmissions that permit you to send information over the network.

**megabyte**:      a collection of 1024 bytes.

**megahertz**:     Hertz is a unit of cycles per second, so megahertz means a thousand cycles per second. This is the unit of speed in which modern CPUs are measured.

**memory management software**: software that lets your PC take advantage of more memory than DOS ever expected it to have.

**message**:       a piece of information sent between two entities. They might be users or computers on the network.

**messaging services**: network services that send messages between computers, as opposed to file information or printing information.

**MIS**:           Management Information Services. See *IS*.

**mobile computing**: the emerging trend of doing your computer work from wherever you are, and taking your computer everywhere you go.

**modem**:         stands for Modulator/Demodulator; a device that translates the digital signals of a computer into analog signals that can run over telephone lines.

**modular connectors**: connectors that allow you to plug and unplug them into any jack they fit; you can move network equipment around easily with these.

**monitor**:       also known as tube, screen, video display. The device on which your computer's interactive output is displayed.

**MRI**: See *magnetic resonance imaging*.

**multimedia application**: an application that presents information using sound, moving video, pictures, text, and other types of data together.

**multiple access**: a feature of Ethernet, which indicates that more than one client can try to send data on the network at the same time.

**NetWare**: the network operating system software developed by Novell, Inc. NetWare comes in several different flavors targeted at different sizes of installations.

**network**: a collection of computers linked together in order to share resources, including devices and information.

**network address**: a unique name by which a particular networked computer is distinguished from all other computers on the same network. The network address is usually a string of numbers, letters, or some combination of numbers and letters.

**network administrator**: a person whose responsibility it is to see that a network runs smoothly and efficiently and to maintain it and solve problems if they occur.

**network analysis tools**: hardware and software that can help you track down problems on your network.

**network driver**: see *driver*.

**network hub**: see *hub*.

**network interface card**: the piece of hardware that attaches somehow to your PC so that you can attach your PC to the network. The type of network interface card you use depends on the wiring in your network.

**network map**: see *map*.

**network operating system**: the software that runs on your network server and moderates the clients' access to the server resources.

**network performance**: how well the network is doing its job. Usually used to refer to speed of response (after you press return, does the request happen immediately or do you have to go get coffee while waiting for it?).

**network-ready**: a term that refers to computers that come with everything you need to attach them to the network, so you can put them on the network right out of the box, without adding NICs or drivers.

**NIC**: *see network interface card*.

**NOS:** see *network operating system*.

**off-site storage:** very important concept in backups. Once you have that copy of all your precious data, take it somewhere away from the building, so that if a fire or other disaster strikes, you don't lose your equipment *and* your backup.

**operating system:** the software that runs in your PC, whether you're on a network or not, and manages access to such resources in the PC as your PC's diskettes, hard drive, and memory.

**optical disk:** data storage device that writes to something that looks like a CD.

**packet:** the name for a chunk of data when it's getting sent over a network. The size and format of the packet depend on the network protocol over which it's being sent.

**Parkinson's Law:** that principle of world wisdom which states that everything always expands to fill available space.

**password:** a means of preventing unauthorized actions. Many network systems will request your password when you try to perform certain operations (like logging in); if you don't have one, you don't perform that operation.

**patch panel:** a collection of modular jacks that let you connect different network devices to each other easily, using a short cable called a patch cable rather than rewiring the network.

**PC:** see *personal computer*.

**peripheral:** any device attached to a PC, or to the network, that is not a PC. Peripherals include printers, scanners, modems, fax machines, and more.

**personal computer:** any computer that is typically used by one person at a time. Might refer to Amiga, Macintosh, IBM-PC or clone, or any other small computer.

**plenum airspace:** the area in many buildings between the acoustic ceiling tiles and the roof. Often used for air conditioning ventilation and to run network cables, among other things.

**phone closet:** often a place where all the phone wiring collects. If your network wiring has a lot in common with the phone system, you'll get to know this room.

**print server**: a PC whose main job is to handle print jobs, making sure they don't all print at the same time and notifying users when they are complete.

**printer sharing buffer**: a gadget that collects print jobs and doles them out to the printer one at a time, so that if several people send jobs to the printer at once they don't all print on top of each other. Not necessary if you have a full network, because the network software takes care of this for you.

**proprietary**: refers to anything developed by a particular company, and which works only with that company's other offerings.

**protocol**: a set of networking rules. Unless they share a protocol, two computers cannot talk to one another.

**protocol analysis software**: software that tells you about your network performance. Also called network monitoring software.

**protocol stack**: see *protocol*.

**pull strain**: specification for how much tension you can put on a cable before you risk breaking it. It's a lot more for TP than it is for fiber.

**punchdown block**: usually in the phone closet, this is where all the twisted-pair wiring converges in a TP network, or in a phone system.

**purchasing plan**: collection of all the things you need to buy for your network installation, and how much they will all cost.

**radio frequency interference** (RFI): high-frequency noise interference. Same problem as EMI.

**RAM**: random access memory. High-speed data storage in a computer. Usually anything stored in here vanishes when you turn off the computer.

**random access memory**: see *RAM*.

**redirector**: piece of software that runs in a workstation computer to determine whether a command should be handled locally or sent to the network. If it's a network command, the redirector also passes the command on to the network software.

**remote-control software**: software that lets you control one PC from another, over the network.

**repeater**: a network device that takes in signals and re-transmits them. Used to make sure that network signals don't get too weak as they travel over long distances.

**repertoire**:  the set of functions someone knows. In network users, it represents the things they do on the network; you want to make it a broad and useful one.

**replacement**:  pulling out the old network device and installing a completely new one.

**request for proposal** (RFP):  document that describes everything you need for your network installation or expansion, so that a vendor can give you an estimate on how much it will all cost (that's the proposal).

**revision level**:  every time a company releases software, it gives it a new revision number. Therefore, this number tells what features, and sometimes bugs, you can expect in that software.

**RFI**:  see *radio frequency interference.*

**RFP**:  see *request for proposal.*

**ring topology**:  a network layout in which each PC is connected to the one next to it. Much like a bus topology, except that the ends are connected together to form a circle.

**RJ-45**:  a type of connector that looks a bit like a modular phone connector.

**router**:  device that links two networks of the same type together, passing packets from one network to the other network, but ignoring any that it doesn't recognize.

**sag**:  a drop in the level of AC power.

**screen capture**:  a picture of everything on your display screen, printed on paper.

**screw-on connector**:  a connector that attaches by simply screwing rather than crimping. Not recommended.

**segment**:  a section of a network. Multiple segments are connected by the network's backbone.

**server**:  a PC whose function is to provide access to network resources.

**services**:  what networked computers request, or provide. The services available depend on the network software and the applications available on a particular network.

**shielded twisted-pair** (STP):  a type of copper-wire cable with an insulating layer around it, to shield it from EMI or RFI.

**shielding**:  the insulation around STP cable that prevents the cable from being susceptible to interference.

**short packets**: in Ethernet, the minimum size of a well-formed packet is 64 bytes; thus, a short packet is one whose length is 63 bytes or less. Also called "runts."

**shutdown**: the act of turning off a machine.

**Simple Network Management Protocol**: see *SNMP*.

**SNMP**: a set of rules describing how TCP/IP networks do basic maintenance and system management operations.

**Software Publishing Association (SPA)**: an agency that enforces software copyright laws. They have been known to level hefty fines at violators.

**solder-on connector**: a connector that you attach to a cable by getting out your soldering iron and fusing the two together. Not convenient.

**SPA**: see *Software Publishing Association*.

**specifications**: the collection of data about a piece of equipment that tells how you can expect it to behave. Specifications tell you how far you can run cable, how many ports you can have on a server, etc.

**specs**: nickname for specifications.

**spike**: a sudden increase in AC power.

**spread spectrum technology**: a type of transmission that works by sending signals via multiple frequencies, rather than the single frequencies of radio and TV.

**stack**: see *protocol stack*.

**star topology**: a network layout where every computer is connected to a central hub. See also *ring* and *bus topologies*.

**STP**: see *shielded twisted pair*.

**surge**: a sudden increase in AC power, but not as sharp as a spike.

**switch box**: a box that lets you connect two (or more) peripherals to it, and switch between them by turning a knob.

**TDR**: see *time domain reflectometer*.

**telephone support**: a type of help where you call the support person on the phone, and he or she answers your question over the phone. Nobody comes out to your installation or looks at your equipment; everything happens on the phone. Fine if you're the do-it-yourself type.

**template file**: a blank document that resides on the network in electronic form, so that everyone can use it to generate their own filled-out forms.

**terminator**: in certain types of network, this is required at each end of the bus to keep the network signals clear and detectable.

**test network**: a small but representative version of your network where you try out changes before loosing them on the world.

**third-party carriers**: anyone who's not you or who you're talking to. In a wireless network, for instance, you need a third party to provide the transmission between the nodes of the network.

**time-domain reflectometer** (TDR): a device that you can use to measure the cables in your network.

**token**:       a piece of data passed around in certain types of networks. It gives whoever holds it the ability to send data.

**token mechanism**:  a feature of some types of networks that determines when data gets sent and who can send it.

**Token Ring**: another networking technology, like ARCnet, that works by token passing. Can run much faster than either Ethernet or ARCnet.

**toner**:       powder that produces the writing on paper in a laser printer.

**toner cartridge**:  the convenient package that toner comes in, in new laser printers.

**topology**:    the pattern in which you lay out your network wiring. Common topologies are ring, bus, and star.

**torque level**:  amount of twisting force being applied to something. Too much will cause many things (like cables) to break.

**to-scale plans**:  drawings of your building, made in such a way that if your office is twice as wide as your hallway, the two have the same ratio on your drawing. More trouble, but worth it.

**TP**:          twisted-pair. A type of wiring that contains even numbers of copper wires, twisted together by twos.

**tractor feed**:  refers to a method of moving paper through printers. The feeders have little nubs that fit into holes on the sides of the paper; as the nubs advance like the tread on a tractor, the paper advances as well.

**traffic levels**:  amount of data that travels across your network.

**transceiver cable**:  see *drop cable*.

**trend line:** your baseline is your initial measure of all sorts of performance data about your network; the trend line tracks how those measures are changing as network usage's change.

**troubleshooting:** the art of detecting a problem, diagnosing its cause, and fixing it.

**twisted-pair:** see *TP*.

**UHF:** ultra-high frequency. Refers to the types of signals that can travel over coax cable.

**unattended operation:** when something works automatically, without you having to be there to baby-sit it.

**uninterruptable power supply (UPS):** device that sits between the AC power jack in the wall and your expensive network equipment, and protects the latter from spikes or sags in the former.

**unshielded twisted-pair (UTP):** twisted-pair wiring without the shielding. Vulnerable to EMI.

**upgrade:** adding new software or hardware to an existing network device, so you don't have to replace it.

**UPS:** see *uninterruptable power supply*.

**utilization rate:** how much of a medium is being used. You need network monitoring software and hardware to help you figure this out.

**UTP:** see *unshielded twisted pair*.

**vendor:** the seller of your networking supplies.

**VHF:** very high frequency. Refers to the types of signals that can travel over coax cable.

**voltohmmeter:** see *VOM*.

**VOM:** device for measuring voltage and ohms. In networking, you'll use one to test cables before you start using them in the network or when you suspect a problem with a cable.

**wall plates:** network connector plates that attach to the walls and provide a tidy way to plug in your computer to the network.

**WAN:** a network that extends over a relatively large area, certainly outside of a single building. Could extend across a city, a continent, or the entire globe.

**wireless network:** one that works, as you might imagine, without wires. Instead, the data signals are transmitted over broadcast frequencies.

**wiring:**     same as cabling; the wires or other media that connect the computers in your network.

**wiring center:**  see *hub*.

**work group:**  a name for a group of people who work together, whether on a project, in a department, or what have you.

**workstation:**  a PC that sits on somebody's desk, and which is used for that person's computing activities.

# INDEX

004.65     Tittel, Ed.
TIT
          Network design
          essentials.

$24.95 PB

| DATE | | | |
|---|---|---|---|
| | | | |
| | | | |
| | | | |
| | | | |
| | | | |
| | | | |
| | | | |
| | | | |
| | | | |
| | | | |
| | | | |
| | | | |